Queen of the 'B's
Ida Lupino Behind the Camera

Queen of the 'B's

Ida Lupino Behind the Camera

Edited by
Annette Kuhn

PRAEGER

Westport, Connecticut

Published in the United States and Canada by
Praeger Publishers, 88 Post Road West, Westport, CT 06881
An imprint of Greenwood Publishing Group, Inc.

English language editions, except the United States and Canada,
published by Flicks Books, England

First published 1995

The Library of Congress has cataloged the hardcover edition as follows:

Queen of the 'B's: Ida Lupino behind the camera / edited by Annette
    Kuhn.
        p.   cm. -- (Contributions to the study of popular culture.
    ISSN 0198-9871: no. 49)
        Includes bibliographical references and index.
        ISBN 0-313-29732-0 (alk. paper)
        1. Lupino, Ida, 1918- --Criticism and interpretation. I. Kuhn,
    Annette. II. Series.
    PN1998.3.L89Q44   1995
    791.43'028'092--dc20   95-12532

A hardcover edition of *Queen of the 'B's* is available from the Greenwood
Press imprint of Greenwood Publishing Group, Inc. (Contributions to the
Study of Popular Culture, Number 49; ISBN 0-313-29732-0).

Library of Congress Catalog Card Number: 95-12532

ISBN: 0-275-95332-7

Printed in Great Britain.

Contents

Acknowledgements

The editor gratefully acknowledges the assistance of the staffs of the Motion Picture, Broadcasting, and Recorded Sound Division of the Library of Congress, the Film Study Center at the Museum of Modern Art, and the National Film Archive for arranging screenings of films and television programmes; and the British Film Institute's Library and Information Service for making available published material on Ida Lupino and her work.

Illustrations are supplied courtesy of the Academy of Motion Picture Arts and Sciences, BFI Stills, Posters and Designs, the Museum of Modern Art, and the Wisconsin Center for Film and Theater Research.

Annette Kuhn
London
June 1995

Introduction: Intestinal fortitude

Annette Kuhn

> I never wrote just straight women's roles. I liked the strong characters. I don't mean women who have masculine qualities about them, but something that has some intestinal fortitude, some guts to it.[1]

Ida Lupino was born in London on 4 February 1918[2] into a theatrical dynasty tracing its roots to 17th century Italy. Ida's father, Stanley Lupino, was a well-known film and revue comedian; her mother, Connie Emerald, was a musical-comedy actress. Although later insisting that acting had never been her true métier (she started scriptwriting at age 7), Ida, with her younger sister, Rita, was brought up firmly within the family tradition: while still very young, the sisters practised adult dramatic roles in a hundred-seat theatre built by their father in the garden of the family home. At the age of 13, Ida underwent a year of formal training at stage school and started appearing in films as an extra.

Lupino's decisive film debut was soon to follow. As the (possibly apocryphal) story goes, she landed her first starring role when Connie Emerald, accompanied by the 14-year-old Ida, auditioned for the part of a young woman infatuated by an older man in a romantic comedy to be directed by Allan Dwan. Mother was passed over in favour of mature-looking daughter, who was offered, and took, the part of Anne in *Her First Affaire* (1933). This was to be the first of many similar roles for the young actress, who for some years continued playing women much older than herself.[3] Lupino starred in five more films in Britain before signing up with Paramount and moving to Hollywood: the intention was that she would take the title role in *Alice in Wonderland* (Norman Z McLeod, 1933). However, it was obvious to Paramount executives that this young woman was not for "little-girl" parts; she was offered instead an ingénue role in *Search for Beauty* (Erle C Kenton, 1934). Lupino remained at Paramount for another four years, appearing in a dozen or so mostly forgettable comedy dramas.

After a short break in her career – she left Paramount in 1937 and in 1938 married fellow-actor Louis Hayward – Lupino finally achieved her acting breakthrough with *The Light That Failed* (William Wellman, 1939), in which she played a cockney streetwalker opposite an initially reluctant Ronald Colman (the English-born star had wanted Vivien Leigh for the part). It was this film which established the screen persona by which Lupino is best known: the brittle, alone-in-the-world moll, outwardly tough and cynical, but "marshmallow on the inside".

While under contract with Warner Bros. between 1940 and 1947, Lupino was (in her own phrase) the poor man's Bette Davis: show business lore has it that Lupino's place in the studio pecking order was several rungs below Davis, with whom she and several others were in competition for the choice female roles. Nevertheless, she did pick up some challenging assignments: it was her work at Warners, in films such as *They Drive By Night* (Raoul Walsh, 1940), *High Sierra* (Raoul Walsh, 1941), *The Hard Way* (Vincent Sherman, 1943) – for which she received the New York Film Critics' Circle Award for best actress – and *Deep Valley* (Jean Negulesco, 1947), that consolidated the still youthful Lupino's reputation as a dramatic actress of considerable weight.

In the late 1940s Lupino's life took a new direction. In 1948 she assumed US citizenship and married her second husband, Collier Young, who was at this time executive assistant to Harry Cohn at Columbia. In the same year, with Young and Anson Bond, and while continuing her acting career, she founded an independent production company named (after her mother) Emerald Productions: in 1950 the company's name was changed to The Filmakers. Lupino's stated objectives in turning to independent production were to make high-quality but low-cost films with unorthodox and provocative subject-matter – films which, if they delivered a message, did so without being "preachy" – and to provide opportunities for new acting and technical talent (actors Keefe Brasselle, Sally Forrest and Mala Powers were Filmakers' discoveries).[4]

Between 1949 and 1954 Emerald Productions and The Filmakers produced at least twelve feature films. Lupino directed or co-directed six of these, scripted or co-scripted at least five, produced or co-produced at least one, and acted in three.[5] In these five years Lupino also appeared in four non-Filmakers' films, among them Nicholas Ray's *On Dangerous Ground* (1952). The Filmakers ceased production in 1954 with *Mad at the World* (Harry Essex), the explanation usually given for the company's demise being that its venture into self-distribution with *The Bigamist* had proved commercially disastrous (The Filmakers' distribution had previously been handled by RKO). During this extremely active period of her life Lupino, still only in her early thirties, found time to divorce Collier Young and marry actor Howard Duff, while keeping up a cordial and productive business and creative partnership with her second husband. In 1952 Lupino and Duff's daughter Bridget was born.

After the mid-1950s Lupino's work, both before and behind the camera, confined itself almost entirely to television: she was to direct only one more cinema film, *The Trouble With Angels* (1966). In 1953 she joined forces with fellow-actors Dick Powell, Charles Boyer and David Niven in Four Star Productions, which was responsible for CBS Television's highly regarded drama series, *Four Star Playhouse* (1953-56). Lupino's numerous other television acting credits include the odd movie-star couple comedy series, *Mr Adams and Eve* (CBS, 1956-58), in which she co-starred with Howard Duff and for which she received two Emmy® nominations: Lupino and Duff formed their own company, Bridget Productions, to make the series.

Until the late 1970s she continued to appear, although with decreasing frequency, in television series episodes and made-for-television movies, making a comeback to the cinema screen in 1972 as Elvira Bonner in Sam Peckinpah's *Junior Bonner*. Since the mid-1950s, however, Lupino has been at least as active behind the camera as in front of it. She holds authenticated directorial credits for at least 50 US television programmes and prime time series episodes, most of them made between the late 1950s and the early 1970s. Specialising in westerns, and action and mystery dramas, she has directed episodes of *Alfred Hitchcock Presents* (CBS, 1955-62), *Have Gun, Will Travel* (CBS, 1957-62) and *Thriller* (NBC, 1960-62), among many others.[6]

Ida Lupino is a woman of many talents: her career has embraced acting, scriptwriting, directing, producing and even musical composition (her *Aladdin Suite* was performed by the Los Angeles Philharmonic Orchestra in the late 1930s). But aside perhaps from the Filmakers years, these talents have never found adequate outlet, and her achievements have been much underrated. As Lupino biographers Parish and Stanke observe:

> Ida Lupino is an extremely talented maverick – a situation which has frustrated stereotype-demanding Hollywood. In turn, the movie industry has subtly lashed back at the star.[7]

Seemingly regarded in the industry as a "difficult" actress (Collier Young is reported to have joked about "Mad Idesey" and her temperament that "Things aren't normal unless Ida resigns three times on every picture – once before it starts and twice during production";[8] as a director, however, she disciplined herself always to stay calm on set), Lupino has received neither awards nor even nominations in Hollywood for any of her film performances. Her work as a director, too, has met with mixed responses, ranging mainly from simple disregard via damnation with faint praise to outright dismissal. Thus could critic Andrew Sarris repudiate the entire Lupino œuvre (together with those of all but a few women film directors) as an "oddity". (Called to account some years later for this piece of sexism, Sarris compounded the insult by dubbing the films Lupino directed "weepy social consciousness and snarling paranoia".)[9]

That the output of The Filmakers emerges in retrospect as the high point of Lupino's long career behind the camera suggests that she was most successful when working in a small-scale collaborative setting in which her various talents could be exercised in an atmosphere of mutual supportiveness and organisational and creative freedom. As a filmmaker who, by her own admission, achieved her best when she could call upon the advice and support of the "right" people (although, as Mary Celeste Kearney and James M Moran rightly point out [pages 137-150], her downplaying of personal ambition must be regarded as strategic), Lupino neither slots comfortably into the rigid hierarchies of the studio system, nor readily assumes the mantle of lonely genius. This may well be why she is so seldom seriously treated as an auteur, certainly by Anglo-American critics (although, interestingly, retrospectives of her films have elicited auteurist commentaries from a number of French writers).[10] Furthermore, the helpers Lupino acknowledges are all men (she cites William Wellman, Charles Vidor, Raoul Walsh, Michael Curtiz and Robert Aldrich as directorial mentors). This, together with the apparently antifeminist stance she has adopted in a number of interviews ("any woman who wishes to smash into the world of men isn't very feminine ... Baby, we can't go smashing. I believe women should be struck regularly—like a gong"),[11] has not always endeared her to feminist film critics, who might in other circumstances have been more forthcoming in their praise of a woman who worked consistently over many years in a male-dominated and very macho profession.

Lupino's films were "rediscovered" in the early 1970s, at a time when feminist critics were making efforts to document women's hitherto largely overlooked historical contribution to filmmaking. They figured regularly in the programmes of women's film festivals of the 1970s, and are unfailingly listed in histories of women's work behind the screen. Yet, Lupino and her work were, and indeed continue to be, relatively little known and, to the extent that they are known, are considered somewhat problematic as far as feminism is concerned. The films, for instance, have been characterised as "conventional, even sexist", and as treating "feminist questions from an anti-feminist perspective".[12] Claire Johnston stood alone among early feminist critics in the view that Ida Lupino's films might repay a reading that delves below such surface appearances. But Johnston's tantalisingly brief ideological reading of *Not Wanted* was very much *en passant* and was never developed into a detailed treatment of the order of that accorded to Lupino's Hollywood predecessor, Dorothy Arzner.[13]

In truth there lurks a sense that Lupino is something of a disappointment for feminist film criticism: not only does the filmmaker quite unapologetically cast herself as a man's woman, her work has also appeared to many critics difficult to claim for feminism. Considered neither stylistically innovative nor as offering "acceptable" representations of women (her heroines have been accused of passivity, for example), Lupino's films have received scant serious critical attention from feminists. Sceptical about the very idea of authorship in the cinema, early feminist film criticism could clearly not admit to a wish for Lupino to be a Great Woman Artist, and was all too evidently dismayed by her failure to be an acceptably protofeminist one. And yet, such a judgment, in seizing Lupino's œuvre out of its historical context and subjecting it to the political standards of a different era, is surely a little unfair. Finding it wanting by these standards, feminist criticism has found it hard to look at Ida Lupino's work on its own terms.

With critical approaches to Lupino's œuvre governed less by the work itself than by the preoccupations brought to it by critics (Is Lupino an auteur? Is the work feminist?), critical commentary has confined itself largely to the six films Lupino directed at Emerald/The Filmakers, all but ignoring not only the other cinema film she directed, but also her work as a film scriptwriter and producer, and the whole of her huge television output. Recent Lupino retrospectives (such as that at the Museum of Modern Art in New York in 1991) have attempted in some measure to redress these oversights and open out critical discussion, by programming television material as well as films. But so far there has been very little by way of serious critical response to this venture.

Concerning themselves as they do with a medium in which the individual programme is swept along, and often submerged, by a "flow", histories of television tend be preoccupied with the medium's institutional side rather than with individual texts. If such a focus delimits television criticism, it also highlights an opposite tendency in much film criticism – an obsession with the film text to the virtual exclusion of institutional considerations. Spanning both film and television, Ida Lupino's career offers an instructive case study in the social history of the moving image industry, and an opportunity to bridge the divide between film and television criticism.

When Lupino's production companies were formed, Hollywood was on the brink of huge changes. After the US Supreme Court ruling in *United States vs Paramount Pictures, Inc, et al* (1948) had put an end to the monopoly on film distribution and exhibition exercised by the major studios, the studio system, which had for many years provided Lupino and countless others with secure employment, began to break down. This coincided with the early years of television in the United

States (while in 1950 only 9% of US households had television sets, five years later the figure had risen to nearly 65%) and with the start of a downward slide in cinema attendances. As a response partly to the challenge of television and partly to the extension of First Amendment protection to films in 1952, the Hollywood Production Code Administration's (PCA) regulation of film content began to relax, and it became possible to contemplate bringing to the cinema screen stories that would have been unacceptable in earlier times. At the same time, in the UK the introduction in 1951 of the British Board of Film Censors' X certificate opened the way for screening relatively "daring" films in public cinemas. In addition, while all these changes were under way, the House Un-American Activities Committee (HUAC) was in the process of busily, and very publicly, purging Hollywood of all traces of communism.

As the major studios cut the numbers of employees under contract, a move began towards what we would today call casualization: many workers in the industry found themselves unemployed or forced to go freelance. The increased mobility of film industry labour, together with the introduction of certain tax incentives, the breaking of the majors' monopoly on exhibition and the relaxation of censorship, favoured the growth of an independent production sector: between 1946 and 1956, the number of independent companies in Hollywood more than doubled, from 70 to 165.[14] At the same time, however, competition from television, the shrinking of the cinema audience, and the confidence-sapping activities of HUAC made "going independent" a risky venture, both financially and artistically. Nevertheless, even under these difficulties work in a small independent production company could offer a measure of creative freedom inconceivable within the strict hierarchies and detailed divisions of labour still prevailing in a declining studio system. This, as Lucy Stewart points out, "was the atmosphere that existed when the independent production companies for which Ida Lupino directed were established".[15]

If Emerald Productions and The Filmakers were in some respects very much products of their time, their success in bringing provocative topics to the screen sets them apart. For instance, as Diane Waldman shows (pages 13-39), a very careful path had to be negotiated in order for a film such as *Not Wanted* (1949), with its theme of unmarried motherhood, to get past the PCA; this was true also of *Outrage* (1950), if not of other productions with which Lupino was associated. The independently-minded and multi-talented Lupino evidently flourished in such challenging conditions.

The Emerald/Filmakers productions met with mixed success at the box office, although the little critical attention they did receive was on the whole favourable. However, it seems that The Filmakers came to grief when it took on the distribution of its own productions: lacking experience in this area, it simply failed to get them into the cinemas. But had the company survived into the second half of the 1950s, by which time television had firmly established itself as the dominant mass medium, the Filmakers' story might well have ended differently. For it was not until 1955 that television programming ceased to be predominantly live: the shift to recorded programming after that date led to changes in sponsorship patterns and modes of production, with the networks joining with the Hollywood studios as major suppliers of prime time programming. Opportunities in the field of television production mushroomed, but The Filmakers had been on the scene too early to take advantage of them: though, as Pam Cook notes (pages 57-72), their 'B' feature films are in many respects highly televisual, with their spare storylines and low production values, not to mention their embodiment, *avant la lettre*, of many of the features of what was to become a quintessentially televisual fiction genre, the social problem melodrama.[16]

The transformations that took place in Hollywood's film and television industries between the late 1940s and the mid-1950s acted themselves out against a backcloth of wider changes in postwar US society. Men returning from war service had to readjust to a civilian life that was not always welcoming, and renegotiate relations with the women they had left behind; women in their turn were "encouraged" to leave the workplace and retreat into domesticity. Definitions of femininity and masculinity were ripe for revision. Pam Cook discerns parallels – and differences – between some of Lupino's films and other films of the postwar era, most notably *The Best Years of Our Lives* (William Wyler, 1946), in their treatment of the difficulties faced by returning war veterans forced to adjust their maleness to the requirements of peacetime, regular employment, and family life. Ronnie Scheib (pages 40-56) and Lauren Rabinovitz (pages 90-102) also register the preoccupation with postwar alienated masculinity that surfaces in several of Lupino's Emerald/The Filmakers films.

Ida Lupino's career behind the camera also offers, as Diane Waldman suggests, an instructive case study in the history of women's contribution to the film and television industries as workers behind the camera. As the only woman in 1950s Hollywood to have produced any kind of body of directorial work in film and television, Lupino is the least invisible face in an entire hidden army of women working in various media production jobs in these years: scriptwriters, editors, continuity girls, and many more.[17] Looking at Lupino's achievement in this way permits it to be viewed as part of an ongoing current of women's work on the production side of the moving image industries, rather than as isolated or one-off – an "oddity" even in the most complimentary sense, with the inflated expectations such a label inevitably brings. Paradoxically, perhaps, it also helps us see more clearly what is distinctive about Lupino's life's work. For, in common with other women working in these male-dominated industries, especially at a time when to be properly feminine meant never competing (at least openly) with men and when other women could not be counted on as allies, Lupino surely had a rocky path to tread simply in order to stay in work. In this light, her pronouncements that she did not care to order men around, and that directing is no job for a woman – not to mention her avowed delight at being called "Mother" on set – should perhaps be understood simply as necessary tactics for professional survival.

Just as fresh light is cast on Ida Lupino's life's work when it is viewed as part of a history of Hollywood's moving image industries, so the films and television programmes she made throw down a gauntlet before some of the central tenets of film criticism. They certainly challenge that idea of authorship in cinema which advances the view that certain narrative themes, motifs or visual "signatures" are recurrent across the œuvres of some film directors, these being the authentic auteurs of cinema. It is true, as Ronnie Scheib argues, that the films Lupino directed at Emerald/The Filmakers have certain features in common: they can all be characterised as "small-scale rite-of-passage films – passage into womanhood, into nightmare, into lack of control".[18] The discussion of *The Trouble With Angels* (pages 118-136) suggests, however, that some of these qualities, most notably the preoccupation with young women's coming of age, also surface in a film which, on the rare occasions it is discussed at all, has usually been dismissed, implicitly or explicitly, as aberrant. But if a certain authorial signature is discernible also in some of Lupino's television work (Ronnie Scheib cites several instances, to which might be added, *inter alia*, an episode in the 1963-64 season of NBC's *Mr Novak* – "Day in the Year", in which a young woman collapses from a drugs overdose), the television œuvre is so varied as to genre and storylines – Lupino nearly always directed other writers' material – that it is impossible to trace any pervasively recurrent motifs. But even if certain authorial marks are traceable through all the films and some of the television material she directed, to what extent are these attributable solely to the director?

Emerald Productions and The Filmakers appear to have been small, close-knit, family-like organisations in which collaboration was the norm: in particular, it is difficult to distinguish between the signatures of Lupino and Collier Young. Moreover, some of the characteristics which have been identified as Lupino signatures can be observed in Emerald/The Filmakers productions to which she has no credited input (although it is not unlikely that she had some form of creative involvement in all of the two companies' productions).

Does this mean that recurrences of theme and style are in this case attributable as much to a studio or a production company as to any individual director, that qualities which have been identified as Lupino's authorial marks might equally well be read as signatures of the Emerald/The Filmakers text? Not entirely, perhaps. For Lupino's Emerald/The Filmakers films deliver a slant on masculinity and femininity that is quite distinctive. Not only can we observe the already noted preoccupation with female rites of passage – apparent in *The Trouble With Angels*, as well as in the Emerald/The Filmakers films – but there is also a noticeable tendency to "reduce the male to the same sort of dangerous, irrational force that woman represented in most male-dominated examples of Hollywood *film noir*".[19]

Even if a case can indeed be put forward for an auteurist reading of the films which Lupino directed, her work in television presents obvious difficulties in this area. There has to date been no attempt to look at the whole of Lupino's television output in authorial, or indeed in any other critical, terms. Given its volume and diversity – not to mention the difficulty of access to past television material – this, as Mary Celeste Kearney and James M Moran suggest, is hardly surprising. Does this mean that the quest for a quintessentially "Lupinian" text, cinematic *and* televisual, is a wild goose chase? And if it is, would that invalidate any claims for the feminist credentials of Lupino's directorial work and for its qualification for a place in the feminist canon?

Unlike previous assessments of Lupino, many of the essays in this volume demonstrate that her work repays informed and sensitive feminist readings, and that it certainly does not deserve to be dismissed in flip soundbites about feminist questions and antifeminist perspectives. Yet this reassessment exposes the snares that beset the very idea of a feminist canon. Whose work is to qualify for entry, and on what grounds? Is Ida Lupino now to be regarded as a candidate for canonization? This question in turn raises the spectres of those all-too-patently absent Great Woman Artists of the Cinema. Would including Ida Lupino in some feminist pantheon, some woman-friendly rewriting of cinema history, amount to a declaration of artistic greatness? Or should the entire notion of a feminist canon be held in the deepest suspicion for even hinting at such a thing as genius? Whatever the answer, the Great Artist label would in any case sit ill on Lupino, a self-proclaimed team player and wearer of many creative and technical hats.

Perhaps such questions in the end divert attention from more important matters. It is surely admissible, without becoming embroiled in debates about auteurism, canon formation and who is and is not a genius, to propose that Ida Lupino's life's work behind the camera is worthy of greater, and, more importantly, of a different type of attention than it has received until now. This is not just because Ida Lupino is a woman, although her achievements as a woman in a man's world, and the "intestinal fortitude" which powered them, are unquestionably formidable. As great a justice, perhaps a greater one, will be done if Lupino's work – *all* of her work – is looked at as a whole and assessed not as some kind of oddity or curiosity, but as part of the main stream of the moving image industry's history and of the history of its most culturally influential products, the popular fictions of film and television.

Notes

[1]   Debra Weiner, "Interview with Ida Lupino", in Karyn Kay and Gerald Peary (eds), *Women and the Cinema: A Critical Anthology* (New York: E P Dutton, 1977): 174.

[2]   While most sources give Lupino's year of birth as 1918, one or two indicate 1916 or 1917. In 1936, her father wrote in a British fan magazine: "When [Ida] started in pictures over here, she was only thirteen, though she put a couple of years on her age, for professional purposes". (Stanley Lupino, "Ida's Adventures in Hollywood", *Film Weekly* 5 September 1936: 8).

[3]   Lupino's biography and the films in which she acted are well documented in Jerry Vermilye, *Ida Lupino: A Pyramid Illustrated History of the Movies* (New York: Pyramid Publications, 1977); and in James Robert Parish and Don E Stanke, *The Forties Gals* (Westport, CT: Arlington House, 1980): 131-193. See also Stanley Lupino, "My $120 a Week Daughter", *Film Weekly* 24 November 1933: 7.

[4]   Ida Lupino, "New Faces in New Places: They Are Needed Behind the Camera, Too", *Films in Review* 1: 9 (1950): 17-19; Margaret Hinxman, "She's Demure, But She's Dynamite", *Picturegoer* 27 December 1952: 8-9.

[5]   Some of Lupino's film credits are more reliably authenticated than others: for details, see pages 151-158.

[6]   While the listing of Lupino's television directing credits in this volume is the most comprehensive and fully documented to date, it is almost certainly not exhaustive.

[7]   Parish and Stanke: 132.

[8]   Quoted in Gladwin Hill, "Hollywood's Beautiful Bulldozer", *Collier's* 12 May 1951: 77.

[9]   Sarris, "The Ladies' Auxiliary, 1976", in Kay and Peary: 386. The "oddity" verdict was first delivered in "The American Cinema", *Film Culture* 28 (1963): 46.

[10] See, for example, Guy Braucourt, "*Avant de t'aimer; Faire face*: l'apprentissage de la vie", *Cinéma 70* 151 (1970): 138-140; Louella Interim, "Ida Lupino derrière la caméra: une femme dangereuse", *Cahiers du Cinéma* 347 (May 1983): vi-vii; Gérard Legrand, "La corde sensible", *Positif* 125 (March 1971): 74-77; Jacqueline Nacache, "Sur six films d'Ida Lupino", *Cinéma* 298 (October 1983): 6-10; and especially Cécile Thibaud, "Un pathétique en creux: Ida Lupino cinéaste", *Positif* 301 (March 1986): 17-22. Carrie Rickey ("Lupino Noir", *Village Voice* 29 October-4 November 1980: 43-45) and Ronnie Scheib ("Ida Lupino: Auteuress", *Film Comment* 16: 1 [1980]: 54-64) are in this respect exceptional among anglophone critics. On the basis of four of The Filmakers films, Lucy Stewart argues that Lupino does emerge as an auteur: see *Ida Lupino as Film Director, 1949-1953: an 'Auteur' Approach* (New York: Arno Press, 1980).

[11] Quoted in Louise Heck-Rabi, *Women Filmmakers: a Critical Reception* (Metuchen, NJ: Scarecrow Press, 1984): 245. On Lupino's mentors and helpers, see Weiner: 172, 177; Ida Lupino, "Me, Mother Directress", *Action* 2: 3 (1967): 14-15.

[12] Molly Haskell, *From Reverence to Rape: the Treatment of Women in the Movies*, second edition (Chicago: University of Chicago Press, 1987): 201; Weiner: 170.

[13] In *Notes on Women's Cinema* (London: Society for Education in Film and Television, 1973): 30, Johnston argues that the heroine of Lupino's *Not Wanted* finds in the person of the crippled, symbolically castrated, hero a substitute for the child she has lost. For early feminist work on Dorothy Arzner, see Claire Johnston (ed), *The Work of Dorothy Arzner: Towards a Feminist Cinema* (London: British Film Institute, 1975).

[14] Michael Conant, "The Impact of the *Paramount* Decrees", in Tino Balio (ed), *The American Film Industry* (Madison: University of Wisconsin Press, 1976): 349. On the spread of television in the United States, see Lynn Spigel, *Make Room for TV: Television and the Family Ideal in Postwar America* (Chicago: University of Chicago Press, 1992).

[15] Stewart: 62.

[16] Some sources (the original one appears to be Jerry Vermilye: see his *Ida Lupino*: 97) suggest that Lupino was involved in making a film for television prior to the formation of Emerald Productions. Although this could conceivably be *The Judge* (1948; see page 152 for details), this story remains unsubstantiated. Given the history of modes of programme production in US television, it seems unlikely to be true, however.

[17] Ally Acker documents some writers and editors in *Reel Women: Pioneers of the Cinema, 1896 to the Present* (New York: Continuum, 1991). On scriptwriters, see Lizzie Francke, *Script Girls: Women Screenwriters in Hollywood* (London: British Film Institute, 1994) and Marsha McCreadie, *The Women Who Write the Movies: From Frances Marion to Nora Ephron* (Secaucus, NJ: Birch Press, 1994).

[18] On Lupino as auteur, see also Scheib (see note 10).

[19] Richard Koszarski (ed), *Hollywood Directors 1941-1976* (New York: Oxford University Press, 1977): 371.

Not Wanted (1949)

Diane Waldman

A young woman named Sally Kelton is arrested for attempting to kidnap a baby. As she awaits arraignment in a jail cell, she thinks back upon the series of incidents which has led to her arrest.

Sally, a waitress, lives with her parents and quarrels with them frequently over her friends and her emerging sexuality. One night she goes to the lounge adjoining the restaurant where she works to hear the new piano player, Steve. An infatuation leads to a love affair and it is implied that Sally sleeps with Steve the night before he is to leave for a job in another city. On the way home Sally is pulled over for speeding by a policeman who returns her to her parents. After this humiliation Sally packs her bags and decides to follow Steve to Capitol City.

On the bus Sally is befriended by Drew, who gives her his telephone number and suggestions for a place to stay. After a cool reception from Steve, Sally turns to Drew and he gives her a job in the petrol station which he manages. Steve continues to ignore her, and a final confrontation between them reveals that he is about to leave for South America. Sally, meanwhile, develops a friendship with the wounded war veteran Drew, who asks her to marry him. Shortly afterwards, however, Sally discovers that she is pregnant and runs away to another city.

After trying to work as a waitress, but feeling too sick to continue, Sally finds shelter at The Haven, a home for unwed mothers. Drew manages to follow Sally to the home but the director, Mrs Stone, respects Sally's wish for anonymity and Drew leaves without seeing her. Within the supportive atmosphere of the home Sally gives birth to a boy, and decides to place him for adoption. However, after leaving the home, Sally begins to regret her decision and tries to get the baby back. Mrs Stone comforts her and, after Sally has left her office, gets in touch with Drew. Meanwhile, the despondent Sally picks up a baby left in its carriage outside a store.

The film then returns to the present. A sympathetic district attorney, who has heard Sally's story from Mrs Stone, decides to leave Sally's fate to the child's mother. The mother drops the charges and Sally leaves the police station, only to be approached by Drew. Sally runs from him and he follows, limping painfully. Finally, Drew collapses, Sally runs to him, and they embrace.

* * *

The eight features she directed, produced, or scripted between 1949 and 1954 for her independent company, Filmakers, dealt with bold, candid themes – rape, bigamy, unwanted pregnancy....Yet, before feminists get too excited, it must be noted that the solutions to women's problems within the films are often conventional, even conservative, more reinforcing of 1950s ideology than undercutting it. A terse summation of Lupino might be to say that she dealt with feminist questions from an antifeminist perspective. (Not that this summation necessarily would bear up under close scrutiny.)[1]

Feminist subjects from an anti-feminist perspective? That's an epithet, not a description, of Lupino's considerable directorial skills. She's unique in Hollywood not because she's a woman, but because she treated delicate subjects unsensationally, with a restraint and intelligence requisite to showing rape, bigamy, unwed motherhood et al as social problems rather than personality disorders.[2]

* * *

The films of Ida Lupino bring to the fore one of the challenges of feminist historical and critical work: reconciling the sometimes contradictory projects of reclaiming women's contributions to the cinema with critical analysis and evaluation of the representations they helped to create. In a world where women's work is often ignored, trivialized or summarily dismissed with a sneer, it is obviously important to search out and validate texts produced by women. It is tempting to look to these texts for clear-cut alternatives to the overwhelmingly patriarchal representations which most cinematic productions provide. But how do we proceed when the gender of the filmmaker and the ideology of the films to which she has contributed are not so neatly aligned?

Although I cannot pretend to offer a definitive answer to this question, I am fairly certain that these challenges cannot be met through the strategy of textual analysis alone. This conviction will inform my approach to *Not Wanted* (1949), the first film Lupino co-produced, co-wrote, and probably also directed.[3] Rather than arguing for or against the film's representation of "unwed motherhood" as feminist through textual analysis, I wish to analyse the factors which both enabled and constrained such a representation in Hollywood in 1949, and simultaneously to look at Lupino's role in shaping that representation. In addition to tracing the process of negotiation and accommodation which admitted such a subject to the screen in the first place, and the ways in which these strategies of accommodation make their way into the finished film, I wish to situate it in the context of the dominant postwar discourse on unwed motherhood, a discourse which was both historically contingent and racially specific.

The passages from feminist film critics' writing cited above use different phrases to describe the subject-matter of *Not Wanted* – "unwanted pregnancy" vs "unwed motherhood". To my mind, these are not synonymous, and the terminology reflects different constructions of similar (but not identical) phenomena. "Unwanted pregnancy" is principally a problem for a woman – regardless of her marital status – who must decide what to do about the unintentional results of a heterosexual encounter. "Unwed motherhood" (and its corollary term, "illegitimacy") is principally a problem for a society that wants to confine sexuality and parenting to the patriarchal family. Although it might be argued that *Not Wanted*, in granting narrational agency to and evoking sympathy for a woman who unexpectedly discovers she is pregnant, deals with "unwanted pregnancy", the discursive field in which the film operated at the time of its release was that of "unwed motherhood".[4]

Although women who engage in sex and become pregnant outside the institution of marriage have historically been censured by patriarchal societies, the social construction and interpretation of "illegitimacy" and "unwed motherhood" have varied across time and place. As several historians have recently suggested,[5] the interpretation of unwed motherhood in the United States has undergone a marked transformation during the 20th century, beginning as early as 1910, but culminating in the post-Second World War era.

Drawing heavily on religious discourse, late 19th century sexually active women, especially white women, were described by evangelical benevolent societies as "fallen women" (fallen from God's grace), "ruined girls" (ruined in terms of both their non-virginal status and their decreased opportunities for future marriage) and "sexual sinners". Devoid of sexual desires themselves, they were victimized by predatory males, particularly in a context of increased industrialization and urbanization:

In the bustle and activity of the age the women are following hard after the men. Not satisfied with their quiet country homes, many of them press their way to cities. What shall be done to care for these women? Be they never so pure, they are liable to fall into disgrace and sin, and they must be tenderly watched over and cared for....They do not realize the snares and pitfalls that lie so thickly about them. They do not know that many men go about "like roaring lions seeking whom they devour".[6]

Consequently, the fallen woman could best be redeemed through an evangelical rescue or in a maternity home through conversion to Christ, through cultivation of skills which would prepare her for earning an honest living,[7] and increasingly through "redemptive maternity", the notion that motherhood itself was the best way to spiritual recovery:

> There is that God-implanted instinct of motherhood that needs only to be aroused to be one of the strongest incentives to right living.[8]

In practical terms, this meant that the unwed mother was encouraged to stay in a maternity home for at least six months after the birth of her child (the better to facilitate both spiritual conversion and cementing of the mother-child bond) and to keep the baby with her when she left, even if her chances of marrying the father were minimal or non-existent.

As early as 1910, such attitudes and practices were viewed as "backward" or "unimaginative and unprogressive",[9] as a new generation of female reformers became professional social workers and the maternity home and the construction of unwed motherhood was increasingly secularized. This process accelerated in the 1940s and especially in the postwar period as nonmarital sex and pregnancy became more common,[10] and, as Rickie Solinger has argued, "it became increasingly difficult to sequester, punish, and insist on the permanent ruination of ever-larger numbers of girls and women".[11]

Accordingly, by the mid-1940s, social workers had rejected earlier explanations of white unwed motherhood, and psychological explanations replaced spiritual or environmental ones. Solinger succinctly summarizes this ideological shift:

> [Medical and social work professionals] accused [the earlier explanation's] proponents of depending on the pessimistic view that the individual unwed mother, or potential unwed mother, was at the mercy of harmful environmental and other 'forces' that had the power to determine her fate. The postwar, modern alternative claimed that illegitimacy reflected a mental not environmental or biological disorder and was, in general, a symptom of individual, treatable neuroses. An episode of illegitimacy was contingent upon the mutable mind, rather than fixed, physical entities – the city or the girl's body.

The girl could undergo psychological treatment; she could change. She could escape being permanently defined by her error. With professional help, in a triumph of individualism, she could prevail over her past, her mistakes, her neuroses. This more positive and forward-looking postwar explanation suggested that the American environment was not culpable, nor was the female *innately* flawed. Reliance on the psychological explanation redeemed both.[12]

Thus, instead of redemption through spiritual conversion, hard work and maternity, white unmarried pregnant women were offered rehabilitation through relinquishment of their children for adoption and the promise of future marriage.

Although this new construction of unwed motherhood was on the surface more compassionate and progressive, from a feminist perspective there were obviously compromises. For example, whereas the unmarried pregnant woman in the pre-war dominant discourse was viewed as devoid of sexual desire and victimized by predatory males, it did occasionally criticise the double standard and hold men accountable for their sexual behaviour. In the newer postwar discourse the woman herself or her dysfunctional family (especially one with "parents who did not offer appropriate models of sex roles or gender characteristics")[13] were held responsible for her pregnancy. Additionally, whereas in the earlier scenario the unmarried pregnant woman was a permanent social outcast, that scenario at least allowed her to live a life and raise a child outside the confines of a patriarchal marriage. In the postwar discourse the unwed mother's deviant status was temporary, but at the price of relinquishing her child and assuming a dependent and subordinate position to a man.

The postwar construction of and solution to the "problem" of unwed motherhood was also racially specific. Throughout the period under discussion, most maternity homes had "whites only" policies: these and the failure to support even segregated facilities were defended by the assumption that "illegitimate pregnancy was more readily accepted by blacks than by whites and that black unwed mothers therefore were less in need of the sheltered setting of the maternity home".[14] The belief in redemptive maternity, however, assured a certain uniformity in the construction of and prescribed treatment for black and white unwed mothers. But as the illegitimacy rate for white girls and women began to rise in the 1940s and social workers turned to psychological explanations, a phenomenon that was perceived "as a symptom of individual pathology in white women" was "reconceptualized as evidence of cultural pathology"[15] for African-American single mothers, who were often denied services and/or discouraged from the option of relinquishment.

What should be clear from this description of the dominant constructions and prescribed treatments for unwed motherhood is that none offered single pregnant women anything other than an extremely limited range of options. None constructed white women as sexual beings (black women were constructed as overly sexual by nature or, later, by culture), nor offered the means – birth control – to allow them to engage in heterosexual activity without fear of pregnancy. Nor did they offer abortion as an alternative. The dominant discourse was frequently coercive in practice, as in cases in the pre-war era where pregnant women were forced to agree to keep their children, or in the postwar era to relinquish them for adoption in order to receive maternity home or other services.

Both Solinger and historian Regina Kunzel provide evidence that unmarried pregnant women themselves occasionally contested these representations by giving explanations for their pregnancies which suggested the "genuine economic and sexual vulnerability" of (especially) working-class women, or by asserting their right to sexual pleasure and desire.[16] But both also argue that such explanations did not manage successfully to dislodge dominant constructions. This is the discursive field in which any cinematic representation of "unwed motherhood" in the postwar era would be positioned.

In 1940 the representation of an "illicit love affair" and an "illegitimate child" were at issue in the production of *Kitty Foyle* (Sam Wood). According to Lea Jacobs, Joseph Breen of the Production Code Administration (PCA) warned the producers of the film that several elements of the novel on which it was to be based were unacceptable under the provisions of the Code, among them the fact that the central character and her lover have "frequent illicit sex affairs" and that she aborts her illegitimate child.[17] Breen reminded the producers that they had to observe a "formula" for the representation of illicit liaisons ("The illicit sex affair must be shown affirmatively to be 'wrong'. It must not be 'condoned or justified, nor made to appear right and acceptable,' and the sinners must be 'punished'"). As Jacobs argues, several events in the narrative of the finished film might be construed as punishment of the heroine according to this proscription. Similarly, after negotiations, the abortion was eliminated from the story and the characters marry when the child is conceived, so rendering the child "legitimate". This was also of great concern to Breen:

> It will also be necessary to indicate that Kitty's child, born in the hospital, is the offspring of her *legitimate marriage* to Wyn, even though it is indicated that this marriage has been

annulled. The point, here, is to make certain that there be no doubt as to the legitimacy of the child.[18]

So how can we explain the sympathetic rendering of the plight of an unwed mother and the representation of her illegitimate child in 1949 in *Not Wanted*? What was Lupino's role in shaping that representation? How did she work to bring to the screen a story originally deemed "utterly impossible under the Code", and how are the negotiations and compromises which this entailed realised in the finished film?

Firstly, it is important to recognise that between 1940 and 1949 Hollywood had changed. As Lucy Stewart has argued, several factors encouraged independent production in the late 1940s: the end to the practice of block booking in the wake of the consent decrees negotiated as a result of the Paramount decision, which enabled independently produced films to compete against studio products for bookings; the discharge of studio personnel in response to the decline in film industry profits, which left talented performers and technicians free to work for independent producers; and tax incentives for high-income producers, directors or actors to form their own production companies.[19] There is also some evidence that a number of independent companies were willing to take on serious and/or controversial subjects which the studios were ignoring or avoiding. For example, in 1950 Lupino told a reporter from *The New York Times* that Emerald Productions was formed when her husband Collier Young, then a producer at Columbia, "tried and failed to get Harry Cohn to let him produce an original screen story by Malvin Wald about illegitimacy".[20]

Independently produced or not, however, filmmakers wanting their work to receive mainstream distribution and/or to avoid a "condemned rating" from the Legion of Decency had still, even in 1949, to negotiate with the PCA. This was the case for *Not Wanted*.

The text which became *Not Wanted* began as a treatment by screenwriters Paul Jarrico and Malvin Wald[21] entitled *Bad Company*. *Bad Company* begins with the kidnapping of a baby and the arrest of the perpetrator, Betty Jane Kelton, in St Louis. While Betty awaits arraignment, a confessional flashback explains her route to this desperate action. Betty Jane, a young high school girl, lives with her parents in Oklahoma City. There she experiences a series of conflicts with them involving the company she keeps and her sexuality. When she rejects the advances of her boss at her after-school job, she is fired in retaliation, and leaves home when her parents disbelieve her version of events.

On a bus to St Louis she meets an older girl, Nancy, who helps her get a job as a waitress in a hotel. One night they meet a group of "good-looking college boys" from Cleveland who come into the restaurant, and Betty Jane becomes infatuated with one of them, George. She rejects his sexual advances, but "borrows" some clothes from a fashionable guest at the hotel in order to impress him. After another struggle, George calls her a tease and orders her to leave his hotel room. Betty Jane is arrested by the hotel detective for the theft of the clothes, and dismissed.

Betty Jane decides to go to Cleveland, where she has a well-off uncle who owns a used car business. On the bus she meets Joe, who offers to help her get a job in the department store where he works. After a brush-off from her uncle, Betty Jane goes to work in the department store with Joe. Still obsessed with George, she contrives to meet him again through her cousin, a college student. This time "the seduction is successful". Betty Jane becomes pregnant, but George "furiously disclaims responsibility". Betty Jane finds refuge in a Catholic institution for unwed mothers, and gives birth to a baby boy whom she decides to place for adoption. Later she regrets her decision and tries to get the baby back by kidnapping him. Feeling sorry for her, the adoptive mother drops charges, and "Joe comes for Betty Jane, tells her they will marry and have lots of kids – of their own".[22]

At least two independent companies had consulted the PCA before they would even consider accepting *Bad Company* for production. A cover letter from David Hopkins of Enterprise Productions for a treatment of *Bad Company* stated: "We are considering this property for a forthcoming production and would appreciate an early reaction from you".[23] The reaction was swift and unequivocal: "The theme, as it is treated in this present version, is utterly impossible under the Code".[24] J A Vizzard of the PCA gave at least three reasons why the treatment was unacceptable:

> For one thing it tends to dissipate blame on the girl by using the old time worn gag of making the parents incompetent ninnies. Secondly, it takes no proper cognizance of the culpability of the boy involved....Thirdly, the actual details of the girl's relationship with the boy, terminating in her pregnancy, are atrocious, having about them little more than the flavor of a main street sex problem drama.

However, PCA personnel did not entirely rule out the possibility of a film on this subject, and it cautiously left the door open for future development:

> Mr Hopkins said that he realized before submitting the story that this present treatment would not be acceptable, but that

he was interested only in ascertaining whether such a theme could be done on the screen under the provisions of the Code. He was assured that there were no intrinsic difficulties to such a theme, were it to be treated properly. We stated that we were not overanxious, however, to go on record with a letter which might seem to give a carte blanche to stories involving illegitimacy and unwed motherhood, since it was too easy to misconstrue the true nature of our attitude from a cold letter. We said that should he desire to develop this theme, we would be anxious to sit down with him and his writers to discuss the ways and means necessary to bring this story within the requirements of the Code, and that there was no doubt but that this could be done.

Apparently Hopkins did not think it was worth the effort.

The second attempt to gauge the PCA's reaction to *Bad Company* came from Milton Sperling, United States Pictures, Warner Bros. Studios. On the principle of less is more, Sperling's strategy was to send only a one-page synopsis of the treatment and to stress the manner in which the subject of unwed motherhood and illegitimacy would be handled:

> I agree with you that the treatment of the subject matter borders on bad taste, but I can assure you that should I go into the subject of illegitimacy, I will make every effort to treat the subject with care, delicacy and restraint.

While Sperling was stressing the tasteful treatment he would give to such a topic, he revealed more sensational motives for his interest in the story:

> Apart from the whole subject of illegitimacy, on which I think it is time we make a movie, the situation in the existing story in which I am most interested is that of the girl kidnapping her own baby. It is for that situation alone I would buy the yarn.

Apparently sensing no contradiction, he closed by repeating assurances of "good taste" and that the subject "will be presented in an honest and almost documentary fashion".[25]

Vizzard's response to Sperling's letter and the synopsis was milder than his earlier response to Hopkins. Rather than pronouncing the material "utterly impossible under the Code" he instead "told him what difficulties he would be up against in preparing this for the screen".[26] These difficulties revolved around four specific points. Firstly, Vizzard argued that "the youngsters involved should be raised above high school level". Secondly, "The parents should not be depicted as inept nincompoops; this to avoid throwing the sympathy with the sin as well as the sinner". Thirdly, "He should be sure that in the preparation of his screen story, the sin is shown to be *wrong*. We told him that this was the *most important* item of all". Fourthly, "He would have to watch very carefully the *details* of the illicit relationship". Again, Vizzard noted that he preferred not to return a written statement on this material to the producer as "we were not too anxious to go on record, which might be quoted, about seeming to give 'open sesame' on stories of unwed motherhood". Once again, Sperling declined to pursue the matter further.

The PCA's objections to *Bad Company* thus centred on two areas – the actual representation of a sexual relationship which results in pregnancy, and the attitude of the film as a whole towards unmarried characters who engage in such a relationship. The Jarrico-Wald treatment and screenplay stressed environmental and familial factors in explaining unwed motherhood; it was also extremely class-conscious and in this came close to suggesting the "genuine economic and sexual vulnerability" of working-class girls and women that Kunzel found in the narratives of unmarried pregnant women which challenged dominant explanations for their situation. Thus, the Jarrico-Wald screenplay explores the limited vocational options for working-class women (Nancy explains that she is going to St Louis to look for a waitressing job at a big hotel with "Who wants to work in a packing house, like her old dried up sister?")[27] and what would now be described as sexual harassment on the jobs they manage to get. (In addition to the incident with her boss described in the synopsis of the treatment, when Betty Jane finds work as a waitress a middle-aged businessman asks her out, an offer she describes as her "third proposition tonight".) There is also the suggestion that George makes sexual advances towards Betty Jane because she is working-class and he assumes she is easy ("I bet you wouldn't take a college girl out to a place like that, like we went to"), and that he "furiously disclaims responsibility" for the pregnancy because he assumes he is not her only sexual partner. In the light of this, it is surprising that the PCA found the treatment "takes no proper cognizance of the culpability of the boy involved", since the treatment can be read as very critical of him. Perhaps they were bothered by the fact that George simply drops out of the picture, rather than being properly remorseful and/or punished in the tradition of the "compensating moral values" formula favoured by the PCA. In addition, the happy ending of the treatment – Betty Jane's reunion with Joe and promise of marriage and children – follows the optimistic rehabilitative scenario of the newer postwar discourse on unwed motherhood. None of this was compatible with the Production Code's construction of nonmarital sex as "sin" and the unmarried pregnant woman as a "sinner".

This series of exchanges between the PCA and potential producers of *Bad Company* supports the position taken by Lea Jacobs on the *productive* as opposed to the merely reactive role of the PCA in shaping film narratives and bringing to the fore certain generic conventions. Rather than simply eliminating the representation of illegitimacy and unwed motherhood, it was instrumental in shaping those representations. This is a position Lupino herself was to take, although she would put a positive spin on her interactions with PCA personnel, at least in her public statements.

Lupino and her colleagues became involved with the *Bad Company* project sometime late in 1948 or early 1949, perhaps because Young, then at Columbia, was unable to get the studio to agree to produce the script. Although the newly formed Emerald Productions had three partners (Lupino, Young and Anson Bond), industry publications referred to *Not Wanted* as Lupino's film ("Ida Lupino's forthcoming indie on unwed mothers").[28] The article from which this quotation is taken also notes that Lupino selected *Not Wanted* as the film's final title. While the story does not discuss the reasons for the change, it might reflect Lupino's ongoing negotiations with the PCA and/or her different conception of what the film was to be about. In any case, the new title undoubtedly shifts the emphasis away from the class-conscious and environmental explanations for unwed motherhood of the Jarrico-Wald script and towards the subjective experience of the woman involved, while leaving a certain ambiguity about what exactly is "not wanted" – the pregnancy, the woman herself, or the child resulting from the pregnancy.[29]

Lupino's strategy for obtaining PCA approval for *Not Wanted* was to negotiate personally, stress her cordial relations with industry censors and their constructive role in shaping the film, and to incorporate this into the film's promotion. For example, at some time in late January or early February 1949, she held a press conference which generated some industry publicity. Typical was a radio broadcast entitled "The Story of the Week in Hollywood: A Movie Queen Battles the Movie Censors".[30] Here Lupino, "filmtown's newest lady producer", is described as doing the unprecedented – showing up in person "to settle the squabble of sex in her new movie. And she amazed reporters by stating that the movie censors aren't big ugly beasts, after all, but nice, broadminded human beings!".[31] After describing some of the negotiations, the broadcast concluded:

> The picture will get underway in a couple of weeks with the hearty approval of the so-called ogres of the censor board!

How did Ida Lupino accomplish the feat? By charm and tact and the good old Lupino line of persuasion. What a girl!

Occasionally this strategy could backfire. For example, in a story by United Press Hollywood correspondent Virginia MacPherson, a more cynical Lupino emerges, "chuckling" over the censors' objections (including to what is described as "the rape scene"), and giving them what they want in order to gain their approval. An irate editor from Ashland, Wisconsin ran this story under the headline "A Degenerate Article About A Degenerate Industry" and fired off an angry letter to Joseph Breen. Viewing the article as indicative of "Hollywood's undermining influence on the American way of life", and "the whole sordid, commercialized, degenerate point of view", he concluded:

> The Hollywood attack upon normal family life has been and is deadly, and the criminals consciously carrying it on as a money-making proposition are criminals against our society, and if I had my way would be eliminated from circulation as traitors by electrocution.[32]

Breen sent Lupino a copy of the article and the letter and asked her to respond. She replied that she was "shocked and incensed" by MacPherson's handling of the story and again reiterated her gratitude to the PCA for its help:

> Believe me the key note of my remarks was gratitude and appreciation for the constructive help of the Code administrators in trying to make my production *Not Wanted* a picture both of truth and good taste. For your information the interview was arranged by our organization for just that purpose....Hope you heard George Fisher over CBS last Sunday. Fisher got the facts straight and thus may have partially undone the damage. Because I am so deeply grateful for the aid of your office, in treating a delicate subject we shall leave nothing undone to give the reading and listening public the correct impression.[33]

This exchange again reveals what anyone attempting a film on the subject of unwed motherhood was confronted with, and serves as a further reminder of the PCA's role as a buffer between filmmakers and a potentially disapproving public.[34]

Although no written account exists of the negotiations between Lupino and the PCA at this stage of the process, it is possible to reconstruct the nature of what was at issue from the various journalistic accounts of the press conference. As with *Bad Company*, the PCA's objections still focused on two areas – the representation of the sexual relationship and the attitude of the film towards the unmarried characters who engage in it. For example, both Fisher and MacPherson refer to problems with the "seduction scene", and to warnings that the unwed mother should not be "glamorized". There is also an indication that the PCA found the script's representation of Joe too absolving: "Her regular boyfriend couldn't forgive her, either. He could take her back, but he had to be awfully upset about it."[35] In this way Code administrators attempted to bring the script's sympathetic representation of the unwed mother more in line with their own conception of her as a "sinner".

Some of the censors' objections may also have concerned the question of class. For example, according to MacPherson, Lupino reported that they objected to "having the boy [the seducer] a rich man's no-good son. I said we'd make him a piano player". Similarly, "[t]hey didn't like our slum background. I said okay, we'd change it to a crowded apartment".[36] Although Lupino objected to MacPherson's representation of the press conference, the finished film does render Jarrico and Wald's description of the heroine's block ("The houses on this street are small and ramshackle, balancing precariously on the thin line between working-class and lower middle-class") as a row of neat bungalows, and the "rich man's no-good son" is indeed replaced by a piano player. Although the reasons for the PCA personnel's objections along these lines are not specified, they probably felt that the disparity in class between the two characters engendered too much sympathy for the woman. Perhaps they were uncomfortable with the suggestion that some men sexually exploit women they feel to be socially "beneath" them.

The Jarrico-Lupino script (*Not Wanted*) which eventually received PCA approval bore many similarities with the earlier Jarrico-Wald *Bad Company*. For example, it retained the basic kidnapping/confessional flashback structure, and a plot in which a young woman (now Sally) becomes involved with a "heel" (now Steve), gets pregnant, goes to a home for unwed mothers, regrets her decision to place her child for adoption, attempts to kidnap a baby,[37] is exonerated by the law when the baby's mother drops charges, and is reunited with a nice guy (now Drew) who promises a brighter future.

However, there were apparently sufficient significant changes from the earlier version to make the Jarrico-Lupino script palatable to the censors. Many of them addressed the objections the censors continually raised about the attitude of the film as a whole towards what they perceived as the "sin" and the "sinners". One of the changes concerned the representation of Sally's parents, which is somewhat softened and her reasons for leaving home altered to place more responsibility for the pregnancy on Sally. It should be recalled that in the Jarrico-Wald script, Betty Jane leaves home after an incident in which she is sexually harassed by her boss and her parents do not believe her. She subsequently "gets in trouble", both legally and sexually, when she is out on her own. The implication is thus that she has been treated unjustly, by both the boss and her parents, who must thus bear some responsibility for the events which follow. The Jarrico-Lupino script eliminates the incident with the boss, and has Sally begin and consummate her relationship with Steve while still living at home. She leaves after an incident in which she stays out all night with Steve, is stopped for speeding, and is brought home by a policeman who lectures her and her parents. Sally breaks the stony silence which follows his departure ("Say it, just say it!"), and runs out of the room. Her father moves to run after her, but is stopped by Mrs Kelton's gentle admonition that further discussions between them can wait until morning.[38] Sally, meanwhile, stares into the mirror, and "[a]shamed and miserable at what she sees, she suddenly turns and runs to the closet, pulls out a suitcase, and opens it on the bed".[39] She then follows Steve to "Capitol City". These changes thus mitigate somewhat the depiction of the parents as "inept nincompoops" responsible for their daughter's departure, and also suggest Sally's shame over her sexual/legal misadventure.

The Jarrico-Lupino script also substantially changed the representation of the young woman's sexual partner. As has already been mentioned, the college student, George ("a rich man's no-good son"), was transformed into a piano player, Steve, thus deflecting any connections between class and sexual irresponsibility onto what was still considered a slightly disreputable occupation, with its requirements of moving from gig to gig and town to town. (The motivation for Sally's having sex with Steve, it is implied, is that he is leaving the next day for a new job in another city.) Furthermore, although Steve is certainly represented as a "heel", someone who cynically exploits Sally's interest in him and his music, he actually breaks off their relationship *before* Sally discovers she is pregnant, as opposed to "furiously disclaiming responsibility" for it as George does. This may have satisfied the PCA's objection that *Bad Company* "takes no proper cognizance of the culpability of the boy involved".

The Jarrico-Lupino script also initiated some changes in the representation of the "good man", Joe (now Drew), changes which made him even more sympathetic from the censors' point of view and probably more clearly a mouthpiece for the film's attitude towards the unwed mother. For example, Drew was represented as a war veteran (one scene makes reference to his returning from "overseas") and, instead of working in a department store, he manages a petrol station, that perfect emblem of postwar mobility and the promise of prosperity. (When he first proposes to Sally he tells her, "We could have lots of little Gaseterias...a whole chain of them...maybe after that a flock of kids".) He is also transformed from Sally's co-worker to her boss: rather than simply helping her to get a job in the place where he works, now he hires her after she is rejected by Steve.

Several lines of dialogue were inserted which more clearly articulate the view of nonmarital sex and pregnancy as "wrong", and/or function to position Sally as morally inferior to Drew. For example, in a scene in the maternity home, Sally's friend Joan describes an aunt who would not have understood her predicament: "She's the kind that thinks you ought to be married to have a baby... and you know something [sobs], so do I! You can certainly get a rotten deal, can't you?". Sally comforts her and replies, "I knew a good guy once...He was too good for me".

However, the dialogue in the final reunion scene in the Jarrico-Lupino script[40] clearly establishes Drew's role as spokesperson for the film's perspective, while probably also satisfying the PCA's requirement that he not forgive Sally too quickly or too easily:

DREW

Look – Somewhere along the line – You made a mistake – You got off on the wrong foot and you've paid for it right down the line. *Now* you've got to get *both* feet smack on the ground – and take a whack at giving life a chance. (looking down at her) That's why I'm here – I want to help you, Sally.

SALLY (her eyes unbelieving)

How can you say that, Drew – after what I've done?

DREW (huskily)

Oh – you gave me a bad time for a while, Sally. I didn't think I could make it (pausing for a while). But *knowing* you – what you did – must have been on the level. You got hurt badly, Sally, and well – that's where I come in. If I can – I want to help you forget a little...You see – I've always believed that people were put on this earth to kind of look out for each other – makes you feel you're doing a little work for – well I guess – God. For a while I forgot that...But that's all past – I'm right back to believing again – (pausing) I love you – I always have – I want you to marry me.

SALLY

Oh Drew – Do you *really* want me?

DREW

We're going to take the first bus back to your home town and

I'm going to ask your old man if I can marry you – because I happen to know they'd like it that way.

SALLY

Yes, Drew.

DREW

Well, come on ....

This dialogue is quoted in full in order to convey the flavour of the patriarchal nature of this ending, with the lofty Drew ("looking down at her", doing the work of God) absolving a penitent and self-abnegating Sally ("her eyes unbelieving", "Do you *really* want me?") from her mistake, and promising not only marriage but a marriage blessed by her father. I cite this dialogue in full also because this scene was to be radically altered in the finished film, with crucial consequences for the film's ideological positioning.

The revised script for *Not Wanted* was sent to the PCA on 9 February and received approval on 14 February. In a letter to Anson Bond, Breen indicated that he had read the script and that the "basic material seems acceptable under the provisions of the Production Code".[41] Apparently the censors' objections to the film's attitude towards the unwed mother and her sexual partner had been addressed; but several problematic areas remained, centring mainly on the representation of sexuality and pregnancy.[42] For example, they seemed nervous about the potential suggestiveness of the lyrics of any songs which Steve might sing during his performances, and were worried about the outfit Sally wears on her first date with him: "[w]e presume that the 'off-the-shoulder effect' of the dress does not mean that there is any exposure of Sally's breasts whatsoever". They were most concerned, however, with how the lovemaking which results in the pregnancy would be represented: "It was not good to indicate an actual precise 'point of contact' between Steve and Sally, a point at which the audience will have it brought home to them that here our two young people indulge in an illicit sex affair". The PCA thus appeared to be taking the somewhat bizarre position of promoting a film which was to be a cautionary tale about one of the dangers and consequences of extramarital sex – unwanted pregnancy – which would not allow the filmmakers to give even the vaguest notion of how such a pregnancy might occur. This only makes sense if we remember the PCA's intermediary position between on the one hand filmmakers wanting to push the bounds of representation of controversial subjects, and on the other political censorship boards and certain segments of the public who did not want those subjects represented at all.

Breen was similarly concerned with the representation of pregnancy and childbirth. For example, he warned that "[t]he actual use of the word 'pregnancy' may be deleted by some political censor boards. We suggest that you find a somewhat less pointed substitute". He was also worried about a notation in the script which stated that "the technical shots of the delivery would be inserted later by a doctor":

> We would have to go very carefully on the questions of labor and childbirth....Not only is this an extremely delicate subject from the point of view of the Code, but also it can prove a seriously embarrassing subject from the point of view of audience reception.

Again Breen was put in the somewhat paradoxical position of agreeing to allow the representation of labour and delivery in part in order to frighten young girls away from engaging in sex,[43] while at the same time preventing the filmmakers from presenting them sufficiently concretely to have that effect.

Lupino promised to make some of the requested changes and production began in late February. *Not Wanted* dealt with the "precise point of contact" that results in the pregnancy in the following manner in the finished film. On the night before Steve is to leave for Capitol City, he and Sally go to a park. Sally talks about how she will miss Steve when he goes, and he tells her to "Miss me over here". In response to Sally's query about whether he will miss her as well, Steve brushes her cheek and forehead, and replies, "Sure, I'll miss you". He kisses her on the lips, and the camera pans over to his hand, which drops the cigarette he is smoking. The film then cuts to the cigarette floating in a creek, dissolves to a clock which indicates that it is 4.40 am, cuts to Mrs Kelton lying awake, and then dissolves to the street where Sally is pulled over for speeding.

Lupino also made some changes in the references to and depiction of pregnancy and labour. For example, in a conversation between Sally and another young woman in the maternity home about another woman's labour and delivery, a reference to the number of hours of her labour is deleted in the film. Similarly, Sally's own labour and delivery are made less graphic: the film eliminates the script's description of Sally screaming and being given a hypodermic needle, and renders the labour and delivery through a subjective sequence (point of view shots, firstly from a stretcher, then from an operating table, which go in and out of focus; discordant music) which differs markedly in style from the rest of the film.

All these changes enabled the finished film to receive PCA approval without further deletions or modifications, although this, as I shall argue, was in part because censors were familiar with the script and projected some of what they had read there onto the film's much more ambiguous sounds and images. Breen was prescient, however, about the representation of the "precise point of contact" and the representation of pregnancy as problematic areas for state and national censorship boards: all the required deletions were of scenes involving these topics. For example, Ohio censors deleted everything in the "seduction scene" from the point where the camera pans over to Steve's hand flicking his cigarette into the water to the exterior scene of the street where Sally is pulled over for speeding, thus effectively eliminating even the allusive reference to the sexual act and the suggestion that Sally has stayed out all night. Other boards deleted in part or in entirety a scene in the home for unwed mothers where the women discuss "the sex of their unborn children" (Kansas especially gave instructions to eliminate "Irene thinks she will have a boy 'cause she's so short of wind"), and even the modified discussion of Irene's labour and parts of the delivery scene. One board eliminated lines of dialogue which one would think were inserted in order to make the moral perspective of the film even clearer: for example, "[s]he's the kind that thinks you ought to be married to have a baby" (said of the aunt who would not have understood the unmarried mother's predicament, but followed by "and you know something...so do I"), and "[h]e must never hear the word they call children like that" (Sally explaining her decision to place her child for adoption).[44] Again this demonstrates that the PCA's solutions for admitting the representation of controversial subjects were not always sufficiently strong to override prohibitions against representing those subjects at all.

One area of censorship in *Not Wanted* emanated from neither the PCA nor political censors, but from another source entirely. This was the issue of race and ethnicity. In 1950 Lupino told a reporter that she had visited a home for unwed mothers while scouting for locations, and saw "young Negro, Mexican and Chinese girls. To make the scene a faithful presentation of life, and to show the democracy of the home" she wanted to use actresses who would represent these "nationalities and races" but "was ordered not to". "We sneaked in one Chinese girl", Lupino said, "and we got a hot letter from this gentleman. But by then the picture was in release".[45] Although Lupino refused to name the source of this directive, Lucy Stewart assumes it was a backer, and indeed it is difficult to see who else could exert this kind of power over Jarrico and Lupino's liberal vision[46] – especially since the PCA had approved the script in which one of the nuns says of the maternity home, "[t]here's room here for all faiths, races, and creeds. Believing is the main thing". Lupino's description of this incident explains the elimination of this line of dialogue from the finished film, as it may an otherwise inexplicable substitution: "Queen Elizabeth" in the film for

"Harriet Beecher Stowe" (Drew's response: "You mean you played the old dame who freed the slaves?") in the script in a scene where Sally nostalgically describes a part she played in a school production. The only explicit reference to race which remains in the film is the assurance of the maternity home director that Sally's baby will be adopted by "people of your own race and your own religion".

I have focused at length on the negotiations between various filmmakers and the PCA, and on Lupino's role in those negotiations for several reasons. Firstly, I wished to demonstrate the difficulties faced by any filmmaker desiring mainstream distribution for a film on the subjects of "illegitimacy" and "unwed motherhood" in 1949. Secondly, I wished to emphasize Lupino's role as *negotiator*, enabling a film on these subjects to receive financing and PCA approval, but at the cost both of sacrificing some of the acute articulations of gender and class in the original script, and of bringing the film's construction of unwed motherhood more in line with those of the PCA and Lupino's backers, regardless of her own views on the subject.[47] This is a role somewhat at odds with the Ida Lupino of certain versions of feminist film history, a Lupino who was able to subvert the patriarchal institutions of Hollywood from within.

However, I would not wish to leave the impression that this was Lupino's only role in the production of *Not Wanted*. Firstly, there were changes in the script which she co-wrote and in the film she most likely directed which do present a more female-centred, if not a feminist, perspective. I have already mentioned the softening of the character of Mrs Kelton (see note 38), and the subjective childbirth sequence in the finished film which, while satisfying censors' desires for a less graphic representation, also quite literally places more emphasis on a woman's point of view. Additionally, I would argue that there is a shift from a focus on (a predatory) male sexuality in the original script to an active female sexuality and desire. For example, the Jarrico-Wald script describes a sexual encounter in a manner which invokes rather stereotypical notions and emphasizes the subjective experience of the male (George):

> She smilingly bats her eyes at him and runs off, leaving him
> tense. For a moment he glares after her, angry; then he grins
> a good sport who made a good try and may have better luck
> tomorrow.

The Jarrico-Lupino script, particularly as it is realised in the completed film, eliminates any such instances of sexual struggle or "teasing" and hints at an active female desire. The first and the subsequent meeting between Sally and Steve emphasize *her* gaze and her desire through camerawork and editing: the first line of dialogue between them is his "What are you looking at?". Several short sequences after these encounters emphasize her viewpoint: shots of Sally sitting pensively, as lines of dialogue from previous meetings are repeated; shots of Sally dreaming in bed followed by superimpositions of Steve's hands playing the piano accompanied by the sound of his music. Another sequence represents her desire to be desired, as she dresses for a date with Steve, putting perfume behind her ears and pulling down the shoulders of her blouse. All this is presented sympathetically, especially in the light of Mrs Kelton's puritanical tirades ("Pull that dress up...it's disgusting!"). This representation of an active female desire contrasts both with an earlier dominant discourse which would deny it altogether and with the contemporary version which rendered such desire pathological if pursued outside marriage.

I would also argue that there are aspects of the completed film which are much more ambiguous than the script which eventually received PCA approval, thus conveying much less clearly, if at all, moralistic constructions upon which approval was contingent. For example, in the scene in which Sally decides to leave home, the script describes her as "ashamed and miserable at what she sees" as she stares into the mirror; and, since they incorporated this phrase into their synopsis of it, this is clearly how the censors read the film. Having seen the film before reading the script, however, I interpreted the sequence as illustrating Sally's finally becoming fed up with what has by now become the literal policing of her sex life. This is, I believe, why the finished film was able to receive PCA approval: the censors were familiar with the script and projected some of what they read there onto the film's much more ambiguous sounds and images.

Nowhere is this truer than for the film's ending, which was radically changed from the approved script but still read by the PCA as if the "prospective marriage of Sally Forrest (Sally) and Keefe Brasselle (Drew) is indicated".[48] At some point between the approval of the Jarrico-Lupino script and the shooting of the film the decision was made to make the character of Drew a *wounded* veteran ("Drew lightly dismisses the fact that he wears a plastic leg as the result of a mortar shell"),[49] to jettison the lengthy dialogue sequence quoted above,[50] and to substitute a painfully protracted chase sequence which, according to Carrie Rickey, "makes the finales of Vidor's *La Boheme* and *Duel in the Sun* look like 'Romper Room'".[51] In this version Sally leaves the police station after the charges against her are dropped and is pursued by a limping Drew down busy streets and up and down several flights of stairs until he finally collapses. After an exchange of glances between them, Sally runs to him and they embrace, with not a line of dialogue spoken.

In light of this revised ending, it is difficult to perceive Drew as the patriarchal "father figure" some feminist critics have made of him,[52] a description more appropriate to the Drew of the Jarrico-Lupino screenplay approved by the PCA. Much more to the point, I think, is Claire Johnston's analysis of this character as a substitute for the child Sally has lost, "a crippled young man, who, through a process of symbolic castration – in which he is forced to chase her until he can no longer stand, whereupon she takes him up in her arms as he performs child-like gestures – provides the 'happy ending.'"[53]

There is some indication that Lupino intended the wounding/ castration of Drew and this revised ending to imply a more equitable and reciprocal relationship between Sally and Drew; for example, the revised treatment for the film concludes: "Sally and Drew *have found one another* and for keeps" (my emphasis). Additionally, an earlier sequence in the film establishes that she will be able to love him in spite of his injuries (Drew asks: "Could you learn to care for me...the way I am and everything?" [Glances down at his leg]; to which Sally replies indignantly: "How could you even ask such a thing?") as he will be able to love her despite her sexual transgressions. If such a change was intended to function in this manner, it reveals much about the ideological connections between masculinity and physical perfection and femininity and sexual purity that such an equation relies upon. In any case, this ending presents a much less preachy Drew and a much less penitent Sally, and is certainly less explicit than the script which received PCA approval about the rehabilitation of the unwed mother through marriage and reconciliation with the family.

The depiction of the unwed mother in *Not Wanted* thus represents a curious compromise between various forces, each vying for their own construction of her: a victim of class and sexual exploitation; a sinner; a woman who has made a "mistake" and deserves to be appreciated and "understood". Each of these constructions makes its way into the finished film, to coexist in an uneasy and somewhat contradictory alliance. The noirish kidnapping plot and confessional flashback structure, for example, grant narrational agency to the unwed mother, while at the same time linking nonmarital sexuality with criminality, a connection reinforced by the district attorney's arguments for dropping the charges against Sally: "There's a law that no one may be tried twice for the same wrong....In a way you've been tried once, Miss Kelton, and you sentenced yourself to a bitter memory that only time may erase". The trajectory of the film follows the optimistic scenario of the more progressive postwar discourse, in that the white unwed mother gives birth to her baby in the secluded but supportive atmosphere of the maternity home, places him for adoption, and is rehabilitated through the promise of marriage to a good man. Yet, in its emphasis on the difficulties of that decision and in its painful and ambiguous ending, it problematizes that scenario. Moralistic reasons for placing the child for adoption ("She's the kind that thinks you ought to be married to have a baby...and you know something, so do I"/"He must never hear the word they call children like that") compete with economic ones. For example, in a poignant scene after Sally gives birth she envisions the future for her son: "You and I in a cold-water flat...with no one to take care of you while I'm at work....Couldn't you take care of yourself? Wash your own diapers? Feed yourself?". This, as Carrie Rickey has similarly argued,[54] is as compelling an argument for day care as it is for placing a child for adoption.

To a generation of (hetero)sexually active women who came of age after *Roe vs Wade* – whose discursive framework is "unwanted pregnancy" and not "unwed motherhood", and whose options include birth control and abortion in addition to giving birth to and raising a child as a single mother or placing it for adoption – *Not Wanted* might seem like a period piece. However, the number of maternity homes actually rose in the 1980s; as part of the anti-abortion programme of the evangelical right, states attempt through legislation to chip away at the protections granted by *Roe vs Wade*; Dan Quayle excoriates the fictional television character Murphy Brown for her decision to raise her child as a single mother;[55] politicians threaten to deny welfare benefits to women who have children "out of wedlock" and/or to take their children from them; and, as I write, a long-overdue national health care plan in the United States is foundering over the issue of whether or not access to abortion will be included among its provisions. In a context such as this, the struggle over the representation of the "unwed mother" and her "illegitimate child" in a film of an earlier era takes on a new and chilling relevance.

Notes

[1] Debra Weiner, "Introduction" to "Interview with Ida Lupino", in Karyn Kay and Gerald Peary (eds), *Women and the Cinema: A Critical Anthology* (New York: E P Dutton, 1977): 169-170.

[2] Carrie Rickey, "Lupino Noir", *Village Voice* 29 October-4 November 1980: 44.

[3] As is well-known, Lupino did not receive directorial credit on the film (this goes to Elmer Clifton). However, in the 1960s she began to claim in interviews that she was forced to direct the film when Clifton suffered a heart attack three days into production: "We were much too poor to afford another director so I stepped in and took over" (Ida Lupino, "Me, Mother Directress", *Action* [May-June 1967]: 15; see also Weiner: 171.) Although the heart attack story is undoubtedly true (Clifton died later that year), there is also some indication that Lupino was both interested in directing and reluctant to say so

much earlier. Whatever the reason for her reluctance, the myth of "accidentally falling into directing" seems to have been an enabling one for Lupino, allowing her to move officially into that position in her next independent production, *Never Fear* (1950). Lupino would maintain, however, that the screen credit on *Not Wanted* was appropriate, since she received assistance from Clifton (and from William Ziegler, the editor) throughout the film's production.

4   For example, on a radio programme broadcast over KECA on 18 February 1949, Lupino is introduced by Anna Roosevelt as "a famous actress, who is deeply interested and active in the welfare of illegitimate children and unwed mothers". Lupino herself describes the problem at one point in terms of "girls becoming mothers outside of marriage". (Radio transcript, Production Code Administration file, *Not Wanted*, Margaret Herrick Library, Academy of Motion Picture Arts and Sciences.) Similarly, reviews at the time of the film's release refer to its subject as that of "unmarried mothers" or "unwed mothers".

5   See, for example, Rickie Solinger, *Wake Up Little Susie: Single Pregnancy and Race Before Roe v. Wade* (New York: Routledge, 1992); Marian J Morton, *And Sin No More: Social Policy and Unwed Mothers in Cleveland, 1855-1990* (Columbus: Ohio State University Press, 1993); and Regina Kunzel, *Fallen Women, Problem Girls: Unmarried Mothers and the Professionalization of Social Work, 1890-1945* (New Haven: Yale University Press, 1993). See also Sheri Broder, "Illegitimate mothers", *The Women's Review of Books* 11: 7 (April 1994): 25-27, a review of Morton, Kunzel and David I Kerzer, *Sacrificed for Honor: Infant Abandonment and the Politics of Reproductive Control*. The description that follows is based upon these accounts.

6   Newspaper clipping, 1869, Young Women's Christian Association, cited in Morton: 42.

7   Morton cites the annual report of one such home: "The instruction which is given in housework, in sewing, and in the care of children, is in most cases, very much needed and makes possible and probable a life of virtuous independence". (YMCA Annual Report, 1907: 22, cited in Morton: 45.)

8   Speech by Dr Kate Waller Barrett, National Florence Crittendon Mission, cited in Morton: 59.

9   Morton: 62.

10   In her discussion of *Not Wanted*, Marjorie Rosen cites the 1953 Kinsey Report statistic that one half of all married young women had premarital sexual experiences (*Popcorn Venus* [New York: Avon, 1974]: 303); Solinger argues that the illegitimacy rate (percentage of women of childbearing age who had babies out of wedlock) tripled between 1940 and 1957: 13.

11   Solinger: 15.

12   Ibid: 16.

[13] Ibid: 91.

[14] Morton: 96.

[15] Broder, paraphrasing Kunzel: 27.

[16] Broder, citing Kunzel: 27.

[17] Breen to Joseph Nolan, 27 March 1940, *Kitty Foyle*, MPPDA Case Files, cited in Lea Jacobs, *The Wages of Sin: Censorship and the Fallen Woman Film, 1928-1942* (Madison: University of Wisconsin Press, 1991): 139.

[18] Breen to Nolan, 15 July 1940, cited in Jacobs: 184. Emphasis in original.

[19] Lucy Stewart, *Ida Lupino as Film Director, 1949-1953: an 'Auteur' Approach* (New York: Arno Press, 1980): 51-54.

[20] Helen Colton, "Ida Lupino, Filmland's Lady of Distinction", *The New York Times* 30 April 1950: X5.

[21] Jarrico, a leftist screenwriter, was later fired from RKO after he invoked the Fifth Amendment before the House Un-American Activities Committee (HUAC). He later produced the independent classic *Salt of the Earth* (1954). Wald, nominated for an Academy Award® for his work on *The Naked City* (1948), later became the treasurer of Young and Lupino's second independent production company, The Filmakers. He also co-wrote *Outrage* (1950), The Filmakers' second production.

[22] I am basing this description on a one-page synopsis and a fragment of a script included in the PCA file for *Not Wanted*, Margaret Herrick Library. The material in quotation marks comes from the synopsis, which was submitted to Jack Vizzard of the PCA by Milton Sperling of United States Pictures, Inc., Warner Bros. Studios, on 6 December 1948. A 50-page treatment was submitted earlier by David Hopkins, Enterprise Productions (3 June 1948) and, since it is not available in the file, I have no way of determining whether it was substantially different from the 6 December version. The PCA's response to both of these items, however, would suggest that they were similar. In any case, this does not detract from my major point of comparison, which is between the *unproduced* Jarrico-Wald version(s) and the *eventually produced* Jarrico-Lupino version.

[23] Hopkins to Judge Stephen Jackson, 3 June 1948, PCA file, *Not Wanted*.

[24] J A Vizzard, "Memo for the files on *Bad Company*", 11 June 1948, PCA file, *Not Wanted*.

[25] Milton Sperling to Jack Vizzard, 6 December 1948, PCA file, *Not Wanted*.

[26] J A Vizzard, "Memo on *Bad Company*", 10 December 1948, PCA file, *Not Wanted*.

[27] This and subsequent quotations are from Paul Jarrico and Malvin Wald,

"*Bad Company*, An Original Continuity", PCA file, *Not Wanted*.

[28] *The Hollywood Reporter*® 24 January 1949, *Not Wanted* clippings file, Margaret Herrick Library.

[29] Jarrico and Wald use the term "bad company" somewhat pointedly. The first time it is introduced is when Betty Jane's mother is complaining about the motorcycle gang Betty Jane spends time with:

> They're bad company – Bad company! How do you ever expect to meet a man that can support you if you hang around with boys like that? You'll end up with a man like your father!

There is thus a certain irony to the fact that it is an upper-class boy who seduces, impregnates, and subsequently dumps Betty Jane.

[30] George Fisher, broadcast over Station KNX [sic], 6 February 1949, PCA file, *Not Wanted*.

[31] In a similar article Lupino is quoted as saying, "I found them amazingly helpful....We went over the script with them and they pointed out what it must do. They virtually wrote the story for us." (Bob Thomas, "Lupino Trying Low Budget 'Unwed Mother' Drama Film", *San Diego Tribune Sun* 9 February 1949, PCA file, *Not Wanted*.)

[32] John Chapple to Joseph Breen, 3 February 1949, PCA file, *Not Wanted*.

[33] Ida Lupino to Joseph Breen, PCA file, *Not Wanted*.

[34] On this latter point see also Jacobs, especially Chapter Two, "The Studio Relations Committee's Policies and Procedures".

[35] Fisher, 6 February 1949, PCA file, *Not Wanted*. An almost identical description appears in MacPherson.

[36] MacPherson, PCA file, *Not Wanted*.

[37] In the Jarrico-Lupino script Sally does not attempt to kidnap her biological child, which is in my opinion a move in a less sensational direction.

[38] The change in Mrs Kelton's behaviour is completely unmotivated in the Jarrico-Lupino script. In the Jarrico-Wald version, she is described as a "self-righteous puritanical nag" whose tirades reveal "revulsion and fear towards her daughter's maturing sexuality", and much harsher in attitude than her husband. Much of this characterisation is retained in the Jarrico-Lupino script, and there is nothing in the narrative to justify the shift in her behaviour in this scene. Ideologically, however, it takes some of the pressure off the mother, a frequent target in the postwar discourse on the causes of sexually delinquent behaviour in daughters.

[39] Paul Jarrico and Ida Lupino, screenplay, *Not Wanted*: 36, Margaret Herrick Library.

[40] Since only a fragment of the original Jarrico-Wald script is available (pages 1-25), I have no idea whether or not or how much of this dialogue was in the original. However, given the nature of that script and the PCA's objections to it, I would guess that little or none of it appeared there.

[41] Breen to Anson Bond, 14 February 1949, PCA file, *Not Wanted*.

[42] Other areas of contestation involved the age of the lead player, which the PCA argued should be raised "even a little more", and the representation of "Sister Theresa and of any other nuns who may appear in this story". (Breen warned that they should be filmed "with adequate and proper technical advice".) Lupino dealt with these problems by including some dialogue in which Steve asks Sally how old she is and she replies, "About twenty", and by transforming the Catholic home for unwed mothers into the non-denominational "The Haven".

[43] For example, in the Associated Press story by Bob Thomas, Lupino is quoted as saying in the context of her discussion of the helpfulness of the PCA that the story should be aimed in part at teenage girls, whose "emotions are immature" and whose "biggest fear is pain": "Therefore, we must show as much of Labor as we can". MacPherson similarly reports Lupino telling censors "she could scare 'teen-agers into behaving themselves by showing the labor room – in all its grim details'", and the PCA replying "Leave it in....Nobody's ever done it before – but maybe it's time they did". This particularly incensed the Wisconsin newspaper editor who wrote to Breen: "But the lowest thing of all is use of labor room scenes – normal for any mother – as a warning to teenage kids not to become pregnant". Thomas, MacPherson, Chapple, PCA file, *Not Wanted*.

[44] PCA file, *Not Wanted*.

[45] Colton.

[46] I describe this as a "liberal vision" since Lupino's description of the maternity home she visited is so at odds with the policies of exclusion and segregation described by historians such as Solinger, Morton and Kunzel. Although Lupino defends her vision of the home with an appeal to realism, the home she describes would have been an exception in any case, making the institution Lupino wanted to depict, multicultural as well as "democratic", decidedly utopian.

[47] In her radio interview with Anna Roosevelt, Lupino indicates some agreement with what had by then become the progressive view of the white unwed mother as someone deserving to be "understood". For example, her praise of the maternity homes she visited while conducting her research ("The only thought is to help the mother to recover from her mistake and to give her child a fair start in life") coincides with the optimistic rehabilitative scenario of postwar discourse. However, another of her statements hints at a much more radical perspective which cites confining institutions rather than those who deviate from their rules as the "social problem": "All human beings need to love and be loved. Life doesn't give us the means of finding love

within the bounds of our conventions and many of us will find it outside."

[48] *Content Analysis Chart*, PCA file, *Not Wanted*: 1.

[49] This is from an eight-page treatment which follows the approved script, PCA file, *Not Wanted*: 4.

[50] Francine Parker claims that the last eight pages of dialogue were thrown away on the day of shooting in "Discovering Ida Lupino", *Action* 8: 4 (1973): 21.

[51] Rickey.

[52] In particular, see Rosemary Kowalski, *A Vision of One's Own: Four Women Film Directors*, unpublished doctoral dissertation, Ann Arbor: University of Michigan-Ann Arbor, 1980: 77-83.

[53] Claire Johnston, "Women's Cinema as Counter-Cinema", in Bill Nichols (ed), *Movies and Methods: An Anthology* (Berkeley: University of California Press, 1976): 216. For other discussions of the prevalence of the motif of the crippled, mutilated or castrated male in women's fiction, see Tania Modleski, *Loving With a Vengeance: Mass-Produced Fantasies for Women* (New York: Methuen, 1984): 46-47, and Tony Bennett and Janet Woollacott, *Bond and Beyond: The Political Career of a Popular Hero* (New York: Methuen, 1987): 221-227.

[54] Rickey.

[55] During the 1991-92 television season, the fictional character newswoman Murphy Brown discovers that she is pregnant and makes the decision to give birth to and raise the child as a single mother. In a campaign speech in May 1992, then US Vice-President Dan Quayle accused the show of glamorizing single motherhood. In its 1992-93 season premiere, the show responded with a special hour-long episode in which the harried new mother Murphy hears Quayle's remarks on television and reacts, "I'm glamorizing single motherhood? What planet is he on? I agonized over that decision." For a description and analysis of this incident see, for example, Richard Zoglin, "Sitcom Politics", *Time* 21 September 1992: 44-47.

Never Fear (1950)

Ronnie Scheib

As Guy Richards and Carol Williams celebrate a Los Angeles booking for their dance act, Guy proposes marriage and together they dream of a happy and successful future. The next day during rehearsal, however, Carol collapses; the diagnosis is polio. When Guy and his father visit Carol in hospital, she tells Guy that the doctor has told her she will never dance again. When Guy insists that there are places which can put her back on her feet, all she wants is to be left alone. Carol becomes a patient at Santa Monica's Kabat-Kaiser Institute, where Dr Middleton outlines the therapy ahead for her. Carol is sceptical, even when the doctor reveals that, although polio robbed him of his ambition to become a surgeon, this did not defeat him. A fellow-patient, Len Randall, offers Carol friendship. She despairs of ever recovering, but gradually progresses from wheelchair to crutches. In the meantime, Guy has found a job as a salesman. Carol protests that staying near her means his giving up his dancing career. Later that night, alone in her room, Carol tries to walk but falls, defeated. In an attempt to cheer her up, Len invites her to a square dance. Guy appears and shows her a wedding ring, but she reacts with bitterness, insisting that he forget her because she is a cripple. When Guy loses his job, he becomes involved with Phyllis, a secretary at his former firm. Realising how he feels about Carol, Phyllis urges him to see it through and return to dancing. Through the courage of the other patients, Carol realises that she can rebuild her life, and begins to work at her therapy. She is dismayed when Guy visits to tell her that he took her advice and found another dancing partner. After Guy leaves, the hysterical Carol seeks out Len to ask for reassurance that she is a woman and not a failure. Len points out that loving and being in love are two different things, and that she is too young to settle for comfort. The day finally arrives when Carol is ready to leave the institute. As she walks out into the world, she finds Guy waiting for her.

* * *

A young girl, working overtime at a factory, locks up and starts for home. In the foreground, unseen by her, a man finishes closing up a coffee stand. In the lonely silence of the empty city streets, broken only by the passage of a huge municipal machine of uncertain function, both girl and man are caught up in the inexorable cross-cut logic of the chase. She is running now; darting into an alley, she pounds frantically on the metal sides of a barrack-shaped building. No one hears – except the man, drawn on by the sounds of her passage. In the high-angled distance she runs towards the protective-vulnerable circle of diffused light cast by a single street lamp where a taxi passes just beyond her reach.

But always, at each stopping place in her flight, the camera cuts back to an earlier stopping-place, now occupied by the man, the twice-told topography, as if through some dream-distorted memory-trace laid out with the irrevocable clarity of a Walshian flight from destiny. This destiny is neither of character nor of nightmare, but rather of a self-creating present, the time of trauma – a time that has linked up and will do so again – but not now, for the present moment is suddenly primal. No moral psychological or social determinism structures this experiential time and space, as closed as it has just been open – it happens to those that live it, suspended in its arbitrary logic. The rapist is no loathsome behaviouristic specimen of pathological violence (a maladjusted misfit let loose on an unsuspecting society), nor is he a lurking expressionistic menace (a shadow-casting incubus at one with the sexual darkness), but merely a background figure led by impulse and circumstance into a major role in an event which he as yet only half-wills or understands.

In the closed-off maze of a truck yard, however, the event takes on a new configuration, and the players a new relationship to their roles. The follow-the-leader chase, with its curious balance of active and passive (he precipitating the action by which she is impelled; she carving out the time and space through which he must pass), resolves itself into a cat-and-mouse waiting game. The predator roams free somewhere outside the fragile frame-lines, and the prey huddles against the large uncertain truck shapes until, breaking cover, she presses a horn in a drawn-out cry for help and then, hypnotized by fear, stumbles onto a loading platform. As he advances out of the shadows towards her, the camera pulls up and away from the two figures soon lost to sight, pausing on the other side of an adjacent building, where a man at an upstairs window peers out and, seeing nothing, closes the window on the rape scene of Ida Lupino's 1950 film *Outrage*.

In its riveting imagery, this sequence seems to crystallize a curious active/passive dialectic which informs all Lupino's work as a film director, but which up to this point had not found so straightforward or focused a form. Together with other scenes in *Outrage* – the flatly recorded police line-up with its unexpected eruption of intercutting and angles that constitute a free-floating accusation of male guilt, for example, or the girl's return to the office after the rape, where the paper-stamping of her co-workers reaches hellishly symphonic proportions amidst the dry functionalism of the accounting rooms – this scene represented a new, hard-fought balance in Lupino's work as a director, a balance between the dynamic stylistic impetus of drama and the open-ended "documentary" autonomy of real location space. Once achieved, this balance was soon integrated into Lupino's signature style, from the tennis sequences in *Hard, Fast and Beautiful* (the crosscut convergence of myriad conflicting expectations upon the serve-and-volley demands of the game), to the intersection of the psychotic and the bureaucratic in *The Hitch-Hiker* (the claustrophobic paranoid shiftings of the three men in their fixed positions in a hijacked car vs the matter-of-fact, entirely non-stereotypical, professional deployment of the Mexican police). It is this balance towards which Lupino's first two films, *Not Wanted* and, particularly, *Never Fear* are always groping, and rarely reaching – although a convincing argument could be made that the see-saw imbalance and confusions of the earlier films are not without their stylistic high points.

To a limited extent, the comparative sense of tentativeness and ambivalence that one experiences in her earlier two films, as opposed to her later work, can be partially ascribed to changes in casting. Ingénue Sally Forrest is called upon to carry both of Lupino's initial directorial efforts, and her physically expressive but rather shrill emotive style sometimes makes her appear crude and unformed in contrast with the more adroitly responsive Mala Powers in *Outrage*, or seasoned professionals such as Claire Trevor, Edmond O'Brien or Lupino herself in subsequent films. Of course, since the characters which Sally Forrest played were themselves unformed, her limitations were not necessarily a handicap, and even the strange feeling one sometimes has of seeing the ghost of Lupino's acted-out performance in Sally Forrest's stabs at interpretation works on its own subliminal level. Changes in casting, however, can hardly explain Lupino's clearly evolving grasp of camera direction; and certainly Lupino's struggle to come to terms with her own assertiveness as a director and the whole question of the "rightness" of the camera's control over what it films are issues that *Not Wanted* and *Never Fear* grapple with more viscerally than any of her other works. For Lupino directing was always problematic, and its problematic quality always involved sexual identity, the nature of film, and the politics of control. It was also on the other side of the camera from acting.

Today, when many prominent actors try their hand at least once at directing, it is difficult to imagine Ida Lupino's transition from actor to director as a blind leap into the void. Yet, during the heyday of the Hollywood studio system, relatively few established stars ventured behind the cameras. After the Second World War, things began to change: Robert Montgomery directed some interesting 'B' movies, and Dick Powell and Lupino's old Warners co-star Paul Henreid started directing independent films in the mid-1950s (curiously, Lupino would be reunited with Henreid when they alternated directing episodes of the television series *Mr Novak* in the 1960s), but such ventures were definitely risky. It is no secret that, until quite recently, women – with the exception of screenwriters and a few noted film editors – have never really been involved in the filmmaking process.

There were of course a few women directors, among them Lois Weber in the 1910s and 1920s, Dorothy Arzner in the 1930s and 1940s, and Ida Lupino in the 1950s and 1960s. The re-evaluation of women artists spearheaded by feminist critics in the 1960s and 1970s has tended to abandon the cinematically challenging subtleties of Weber and Lupino in favour of the more obvious pronouncements of Arzner. The irony is that the genuine struggle for control over studio conditions and story content that led both Weber and Lupino to found their own independent production companies has made prints of their films harder to track down than the big-studio efforts of Arzner.

As a result, and because of the difficulty for critics, male and female alike, in dealing with the peculiar generic conventions of melodrama, Lupino's pioneering role in the development of postwar location-shot small-scale independent filmmaking has never really been acknowledged in English-language criticism, nor have her unique contributions as a director. In *The American Cinema*, the pocket bible of the bygone glory days of US auteurism, Andrew Sarris consigned Ida Lupino to genteel oblivion in a single sentence: "Ida Lupino's directed films express much of the feeling if little of the skill which she has projected so admirably as an actress".[1] Not content with thus summarily dispatching Lupino's lifetime opus, Sarris – "while...on the subject" – cites Lillian Gish's one directorial attempt and allows her conclusion to speak for itself: "directing was no job for a lady" (women obviously lack the "skill", although they are apparently uniquely equipped to spill "feelings" all over the screen through some mysterious process of osmosis operating under, over and around the camera). It seems particularly perverse to link Lupino, a "rough-and-tumble" television director *par excellence* late in her career, with the Victorian delicacy of Gish.

If anything, Lupino compares more felicitously with the postwar modernist directors, Nicholas Ray, Samuel Fuller, Robert Aldrich *et al*, many of them, like Lupino, writer-directors making low-budget, highly personalized, strong "little" films in the margins of the studio system. Lupino's were of the socially conscious "problem movie" type and, like many of Ray's, are small-scale rite-of-passage films – passage into womanhood, nightmare and lack of control. Cast out from a familiar, protective environment, torn by conflicting desires or no desire at all, Lupino's characters do not know how to act. Their "problems" – rape, polio, unmarried motherhood, bigamy – have put them beyond the pale, beyond the patterned security of their foreseeable futures. The problem is not how to reintegrate them into the mainstream, but it is the shallowness of the mainstream and the void it projects around itself – the essential passivity of ready-made lives.

Some might argue that this is what makes Lupino's films antifeminist – the portrayal of women as passive – and certainly many of her films are about women and all about passivity. Lupino makes films about the inability to act in much the same way that Wellman and particularly Walsh (from whom she learned her craft) make films about action – not the narrative action ascribed to the character, but the energy deployed by her/him. This is in contrast to a Joan Crawford or Bette Davis vehicle, where the locked-in one-to-one confrontation scenes and the complete stasis of the camera in recording the true field of action – the emotion-swept face of the heroine – disguise and naturalize passivity, deny change, and record only the labour pains of action and the stillborn death which follows. Lupino's films denaturalize passivity; it is unwanted, restless, anxious, impotent. Her characters are sleepwalkers, their subjectivity condemned to incompleteness, their faces swept by emotions that happen to them but never belong to them, the image of what they see distorted by nightmare or manifesting a presence that resists assimilation. Between their subjectivity and the world there is nothing.

Lupino's heroines display none of the qualities that illuminate her own stand-out performances as an actress – from the vulnerable, tenderly probing love of one have-not for another (*High Sierra* [Raoul Walsh, 1941], *On Dangerous Ground* [Nicholas Ray, 1952], *Deep Valley* [Jean Negulesco, 1947]), to the cool vital self-assurance and on-line energy (*The Man I Love* [Raoul Walsh, 1947], *Road House* [Jean Negulesco, 1948], *While the City Sleeps* [Fritz Lang, 1956]), to the nervously alternating currents of neurotic drive (*Ladies in Retirement* [Charles Vidor, 1941], *They Drive By Night* [Raoul Walsh, 1940], *The Hard Way* [Vincent Sherman, 1943]). Instead, her characters walk around in a daze, mutilated, traumatized, displaced persons wandering aimlessly from halfway house to halfway house on the byways of small-city America. A capsule biography of a typical early heroine finds her working for a living since high school, not as a brisk, efficient secretary or a boss-struck little helper, but as a waitress, factory worker or bookkeeper, neither in glamour nor in drudgery, not for self-fulfilment nor for independence or upward mobility, but because her family needs the money. She has lived on girlish fantasies and half-formed expectations, she has dreamed of love in darkened bedrooms and brought her fiancé home for dinner. And then suddenly, brutally, she becomes a woman – and can relate to nothing and no one around her. If Lupino made films about adolescent coming-to-consciousness, the emphasis was less on the shock of discovery of a world which is different from expectations than on her sleepwalker-heroines' complete inability to read their place in the world – an inability compounded, one supposes, by the limitations imposed on them by both their gender and their class. Yet this reading fails to take into account the degree to which Lupino would later elaborate the same thematic concerns and apply them to figures played by indubitably masculine, middle-aged "character actors" such as Edmond O'Brien, Charles McGraw and Jack Klugman.

Although Lupino's peculiar vision of passivity was doubtless shaped by her own femininity and her experiences as a woman, and most "naturally" finds expression in stories about women, it in no way proved to be exclusive to a feminine point of view, and was easily extended to include men, although the genre trappings of "men's pictures" tended to disguise it. *The Hitch-Hiker* (1953), in which two friends on a fishing trip are held hostage by a gun-toting psychopath who forces them to drive him across Mexico, provides a case study in contrasting, somewhat class-based, reactions to enforced passivity. It is a man's thoughtful indecision which dominates *The Bigamist* (1953), as he vacillates between two complementary spouses. The self-reflective heroine is a device which novelists, at least, have used for centuries to trace the process of consciousness. It is far less common to find Hollywood films structured around a self-reflective hero. What is extraordinary in *The Bigamist*, as in all Lupino's work, is the depiction of passivity not as a state but as a process of consciousness. The husband's position, one of total clarity in terms of his understanding and feelings towards the two women, but one of complete befuddlement as to how to handle the psychological juggling act required to reconcile largely incompatible actions, gives him a peculiar relationship to his role. More than his reaction to the situation itself, the film traces the bigamist's deepening awareness of the complexities, values, ironies and contradictions inherent in his situation, the literal coexistence of so many possible, yet impossible, alternatives.

This is even clearer in "The Torpedo", a Lupino-directed episode of *The Untouchables* (ABC, 1963), in which Charles McGraw plays a gunman who comes to the realisation, after a six-month gangland truce, that he has lost his nerve. What Lupino chronicles is not the usual story of a man displaying his nervousness or revealing his impotence, but rather a man watching, as if from a great distance, his own dysfunctionality and breakup, as he tests and retests the process of disintegration as one might probe a rotten tooth. That same terrible wonderment pervades "The Threatening Eye", Lupino's hour-long *Kraft Suspense Theater* offering (NBC, 1964), in which an equally dazzled Jack Klugman finds himself at the centre of a web of sexuality, murder and blackmail without even performing the "unthinking" or "innocent" act generally necessary to such a descent: events happening so far outside his will or control that he can only desire, passionately but passively, to understand. Indeed, the narrative disjunction between the story's comparatively realistic treatment of Klugman's confusion and the leap of faith required to comprehend the inexplicable, almost supernatural Mabuse-like machinations of the woman responsible for his plunge into nightmare, the petite French *gamine fatale* who spies on his every movement, suggest how very "unnatural" the circumstances must be to reduce a man to passivity. It seems that some are born to passivity, while others have passivity thrust upon them.

But Lupino is an auteur in a very literal sense, having co-scripted many of her films, and it is not difficult to schematize the overall pattern of many of her narratives: a brief opening positing a continuing "normal" life; a sudden traumatic interruption of that flow; an overwhelming sense of alienation and disorientation; a brief respite at some sheltered communal refuge; a reversal of trauma by the active assumption of what was initially passively experienced; and a tentative start of a new life. Yet within this narrative unity and within the even greater unity of style, there is constant exploration and experimentation.

Never Fear (1950), the first film Lupino officially fully directed, is a case in point. Here Lupino very explicitly comes to terms with the ramifications of her new role as director and her greater control of the camera, as she tells the story of a woman who is herself in transition, trying to take control of her life. *Never Fear*, unlike *Not Wanted* (1949), is not about an unformed girl passing into womanhood; rather it is about an active, creative woman forced into a new, mutilated form of womanhood. Carol Williams is a dancer; Guy Richards, her partner/fiancé, is a choreographer. The opening scenes of *Never Fear* spotlight a series of professional and personal celebrations by the couple: the big dance routine glimpsed briefly as it is successfully performed in rehearsal, then played out fully in a sexy love/fencing duel, enacting both within the mime narrative of the dance and in its flawless execution the vibrant responsiveness of Carol's body, her shaping of space, her symbolic mastery of danger (the duelling épées) and willing post-victory surrender of her emblematic heart, body and sword to her partner/rival; the announcement of a booking promising them success; and the plighting of their troth on a sunset-lit beach. Poised on the threshold of stardom and marriage, the couple seems to have their future planned out.

46

A quick flare-up and equally rapid flare-down during rehearsal reveals the built-in working-out mechanisms within a relationship which seems remarkably well-balanced, both in reconciling the personal and professional duality of the couple and in setting up an equalized interdependence (Guy proposing to Carol: "I always knew you had talent as a dancer. I wanted to make sure I could keep up with you"). However, it is Guy who inaugurates, institutes and marks the celebrations by his proffered gifts – a star surreptitiously pasted on Carol's dressing-room door; an engagement ring prestidigitated at a beach – and, unfailingly, by the offering of a gardenia at every juncture of their relationship, a sign of his constancy and affection (a gardenia for all occasions, even if he has to steal one, the activity that opens the film). He is, if not the measure, at least the measurer of Carol's success (a function later assumed by her doctor).

The celebrations are short-lived, however: the camera dollies into and holds on Guy (up to this point the central focus of the camera and the one whose movements are followed; he is shown without her, she never without him) working on a new routine at the piano, offhandedly throwing enthusiastic remarks over his shoulder to Carol behind him on the stage. Then there is a surprise cut to the stage against which Carol reclines, struck, as we soon learn, with polio. There are few moments in any film that rival in intensity those brief minutes of Carol's slowly dawning awareness of her illness. She literally hangs on the ropes of the stage, exploring the silent disaster, the invisible process of change within her. The inwardness of that experience is intensified by a few out-of-focus, sound-warped point-of-view shots of Guy at the piano, supremely unaware of what is happening behind him; his implicit belief in the intimacy of a shared work time underscoring her newborn awareness of being apart and excluded.

Depictions of extreme emotional or physical stress, or moments of total obliviousness to the world, occur in Lupino's earlier work (as Sally Forrest in *Not Wanted* at a cash-register in a diner, unaware of the woman impatient to pay her bill, gives the wrong change; earlier on, sick with waiting to hear from her footloose piano-player boyfriend, she dazedly wipes windshields for long unconscious minutes), but not until the imagistically charged, poetically condensed scene in *Never Fear* in which Carol is stricken with polio is there such an overt directorial imposition of style, complete with visual and sound distortion, mismatched points of view and deliberately disjunctive editing.

There were to be many such compellingly "spacy" moments in Lupino's later films, moments that are never purely subjective, nor purely indicative of stress. Rather, they bear witness to the radical dysfunction that forms the spoken or unspeakable subject of so many modern women writers (Jean Rhys first among them). The specific problems of Lupino's characters are neither exemplary nor causal, and Lupino's oddly non-complicit camera captures neither the judgmental nor the emotional content of their thought, but the inwardness and intensity of a process of consciousness unrelated to ego, fixated on images of desire intuitively recognised as both primordial and banal, vibrating with emotion that has renounced belief in itself and exhausted its own possibilities. For passivity in Lupino's films is no comfortable sinking into despair, no well-fed suffering spiced with revolt or self-abnegation, but a stark, stock-still simultaneous inevitability and impossibility of consciousness. This consciousness is neither of nor outside the world: there is a constant interreaction between this insistent subjectivity and a world it can neither encompass nor assimilate – positively or negatively. Lupino's characters are always on the verge of breakdown, breakdown not of their ability to relate to others but of their ability to be congruent with the world. Their passivity is a force, an autistic integrity. Passivity poses a self as pure subjectivity, devoid of will and intentionality, hypnotically powerful in its absolute resistance to time and becoming.

For the next few scenes, Carol is never seen in close-up. She recedes from the camera, at a distance from all who would seek to be close to her. In the doctor's office, the hospital, the corridors of the rehabilitation centre, always accompanied by Guy and often by her father but unresponsive to them, she is merely a patient, an illness. It is only when she is finally alone in her room that the camera again takes a position of intimacy, a position it will not again lose, with Carol's voice-over cry ("I want to be alone, quite alone. Let me be!") reinforcing the impact of that regained subjectivity.

Space is often an emotional entity in Lupino's films; not that the space expressionistically reflects the character's emotional state, but that her/his way of inhabiting it, of sharing or defending it against intrusion, defines a relationship to the world. A desire to fortress or break down isolation, fear or yearning for spatial continuity, a need to protect or avoid enclosure, is felt in every gesture and movement. Thus, although Carol cannot always choose where she is or what she is doing in the somewhat regimented context of a physical therapy facility, her inclusion or exclusion of others in or from her personal space is something she does control.

Yet the subjectivity Carol regains is itself isolated and no longer shapes the world around her. A large part of *Never Fear* was shot on location at the Kabat-Kaiser Institute, an actual rehabilitation centre, whose staff and patients mingle indistinguishably with the remainder of the cast. Indeed, the "true story", upon which the film claims it is based, happened in this facility. *Never Fear* fully explores one of the most fascinating aspects of Lupino's films: the intersection of a claustrophobic "woman's picture" emotionalism with a full-frame documentary realism (complete with extensively-researched detail, location shooting, non-professional actors and, in many instances, true stories), creating a kind of two-level space of alternating, shifting focus, neither pole of which – uniquely – subsumes the other. Thus, at times – as in the ordered symmetry of group exercise – Carol is differentiated only, like the others, by the extent of her paralysis (some move arms, some move legs, some move one of each). At other times the very autonomous, fully-staffed functioning rehabilitation centre forms a mere backdrop to Carol's dramatic breakup with Guy. Between the two poles there can be coincidence, congruence, irony and interaction, but there is never any confusion of the subjective and the objective. The usual hierarchical imbalance between the inherently "special" star, destined, precisely because she is the star, to escape, accuse or validate any non-stellar surroundings, and the "ordinary" world of documented otherness (insane asylums, tenements, and so forth), peopled by divine casting with inherently "secondary" forms of consciousness, is short-circuited by Lupino's refusal to grant hegemony to one side or the other of the insistently dysfunctional subjective/objective split.

It is Lupino's decision not to grant transcendence (that quality she of all Hollywood stars possessed), privilege or heroism to the existential "otherness" of consciousness that makes her not only a modernist director, but also a feminist one. French critics in particular have been fascinated by the way Lupino's films confound the self-sufficiency of melodrama:

> She [Lupino] chooses restraint and ellipses, leaving in the void the obviously pathetic moments, such as the farewell to a child one is abandoning, the terror when the doctor names the disease, the discovery of bigamy by the wives. But she also gives free rein to the rage, the desire and the sadness of her heroines. This peculiar rhythmic alternation creates an incisive tone and introduces a certain distance, whereas the system of melodrama is... based on the immediacy of its impact. In other words, for Lupino, emotional overkill in itself does not automatically confer star status. (Cécile Thibaud)[2]

The intensity of the subjective experience in women carries with it no validation beyond that of a rather hysterical individuality whose very limitations are measured here. Even while following Carol, one always has the sense that there are other "stories" in *Never Fear*, true stories equally worthy of being centre-screen. And it is quite clear that, even if polio enters into each story, none is the story of the disease.

The physical space created in the scene where Carol is struck with polio – the space of convergence, of physical limitation – becomes in the rehabilitation centre strong montages of individual therapy sessions. Lupino manages (as few other filmmakers have) to capture a nonsexual but very physical sense of a woman's body, of the will that animates it, or fails to animate it. These therapy scenes, in their extreme fragmentation and matter-of-fact doggedness, both validate and place Carol's efforts and triumphs: sufficient energy, dedication and training to master fifty complex dance routines are now marshalled to raise one leg slightly. But Carol, more than any other early Lupino heroine, is a fighter. After the initial despair comes a desire to force her body to respond, to will herself back into the person she has been. Talismanically mantled in Guy's faith-restoring gift of a nightgown, caught up in a light-spilled epiphany, she wills herself to walk in a mixture of fervent hope and outspoken defiance, all in voice-over ("That's what I want – and I won't wait!"), only to pitch forward, pounding the floor with her fists. This is the same gesture of hopelessness and impotence as that of Keefe Brasselle as a one-legged cripple on a bridge after an exhausting, fruitless chase at the end of *Not Wanted*. There it got him the girl, here it brings Carol only bitterness.

Once convinced that she can no longer determine her own life, and deprived of her identity as a dancer, Carol begins to define herself passively and becomes her limitations – a cripple. Yet, paradoxically, becoming a cripple is not a completely negative experience. If, in successively acerbic unwilling tête-à-têtes with Guy, Carol becomes increasingly cold, hard and resistant ("I can't be a woman for you – not the kind I want to be"), she begins to feel for her fellow patients an empathic solidarity very reminiscent of that which united the women in the home for unwed mothers in *Not Wanted*, but deeper and more complete, since here all strive together and make progress in ways entirely valid only within the relative world of shared incapacity. In the alternation of individual therapy sessions and mutually encouraging group exercise, Carol's struggle has a meaning that is quickly lost in the world of perfect health. This is brought home strikingly in the film's finale, when Carol finally ventures out, walking now with the aid of a cane, shrinking, bewildered and overcome by the street full of unhampered, hurried locomotion which lies right outside the door, people jostling by (including two men carrying a large sofa), Carol hugging the wall, her tentative steps, hailed before as great milestones, here a snail's painful progress on the scale of functioning normality.

As the Carol/Guy couple begins to break up, each drifts into new ties. For Carol it is a thoroughly "together" patient, Len, whose inspirational drawings and stories for the children make him the unofficial "do-it-yourself sanity" principle of the rehabilitation centre. Len is the first to welcome her into the centre, and, unfazed by her hostility, he keeps trying. Guy's new attachment is Phyllis, a secretary in the real estate office where he gets a job selling "Happy Homes". They meet in typical Lupino absurdist fashion when Guy, nervously awaiting a job interview with Phyllis's boss, cools his heels in the outer office while his irate would-be employer chews out his prey on the telephone just beyond an open door ("I'll throw him out into the street!"). Guy and Phyllis half-start sentences, only to be checked by the barrage of abuse coming from the inner office, and achieve instant rapport in a dumb show of sympathy, apprehension and amusement.

Yet the "primal" couple of Carol and Guy symbolically overloads and overcharges both characters' attempted romantic flings. Carol's first response to Len's repeated attempts to break down her isolation comes in an art therapy session, immediately after she has savagely hacked away at the female half of a clay couple she has modelled, mutilating it beyond recognition. Their first "date", a wheelchair square dance, is an uneasy mirror-image of her past dance partnership with Guy. Unlike the paraplegic basketball game in *The Men* (Fred Zinnemann, 1950), which grandiosely trumpets bravery, effort and human drama, the hero's individual struggle magnified in its multiple reflection, the square dance, with its undoubtedly authentic local cowboy band and unstudied motley group of onlookers, is here characterised by a down-home, low-key matter-of-factness. In the precise coordination of the chrome-flashing wheelchairs, and the shifting patterned formations and reformations of couples, the hero-centred inserts (the flustered tangle of Carol's machine with Len's, her flushed, eager face) appear as colourful details in the long-shot fresco of the dance – until Carol looks up to see Guy, like some dream-doubled spectre of her past life, standing against a giant gardenia-papered wall holding a gardenia. Led unwillingly to a shadowy room laden with bric-à-brac, Carol becomes stiff and resistant, Guy's struggle to break through her defences played out in shadowscape against a large, somehow sinister, statue of Pan, god of the sexuality that has fled.

This heavy symbolic presence forms part of the claustrophobic stasis of *Never Fear*, attesting to a kind of dramatic overload within the shrunken parameters and repetitive gestures that define Carol's "rehabilitation". The film is strewn with objects charged with symbolic significance. Most pervasive are the ubiquitous cigarettes which mark every stage of any relationship: Len is first introduced bumming a cigarette from Carol's pack; and Guy and Phyllis accomplish some introductory acquaintanceship around a cigarette exchange. But most of the symbolic objects are consciously manipulated and exchanged – the swords and heart of the choreographed dance; the moulded and then mutilated clay couple; Guy's signature gardenias. Even when the objects around them link up in ways which the characters cannot control, the meaning never completely escapes their purview, whether or not they are willing to interpret it. Thus, we see the layered link between a crippled man's hand exercises in therapy and the image of Guy's "bandaged" fingers walking a drunken disillusioned path over his desk after he has been fired from his interim job selling "Happy Homes".

This is in marked contrast with the much sparser, subjectively loaded objects and figures of *Not Wanted* and *Outrage*, where the aimless perambulations of the far more passive heroines are haunted by unsolicited reminders of loss and absence in a life they never succeeded in making their own – the omnipresent children for the woman who has given up her out-of-wedlock baby in *Not Wanted*; a wedding dress in a shop window for the raped heroine of *Outrage*.

For the dramatis personae of *Never Fear* are mature characters with experiences they have understood sufficiently actively to give concrete expression. They are perfectly capable of creating their own symbols – Len's drawings of a "fleap", a hybrid of flea and fly whose adventures trace for the crippled children of the centre the onward progress of their mitigated state; the secretary's apartment dominated by her ex-husband's spoils-of-war Japanese sword, a memento of the confluence of his battle and hers. In the case of Guy and Carol, as we have seen, a constant symbolic investiture of meaning into objects and movements informs their praxis. At least this was true of Carol at the beginning of the film, when she was still able to make Guy's vision real. But now all her efforts are aimed towards a "normality" whose personal stamp seems all but invisible.

The failure of Carol and Guy's efforts to forge new relationships in this context represents the "positive" version of limitation, seen as emotional continuum surmounting trauma. On a denotative level, Guy is definitely "good" for Carol – he even has her doctor's seal of approval, as evinced by the latter helping Guy kidnap Carol against her will so that they may "work things out". When Carol bitterly rejects Guy after the square dance, throwing her being a cripple at him in hurt defiance, she earns the censure of another couple lurking unseen in the room. Yet Guy, unlike the other "healthy" halves of couples, is obviously very ill-at-ease in the institution; everything in his stance and body language denies that he – and, by extension, Carol – belong there. This is particularly true of the one apparently harmonious scene between Guy and Carol, early in her stay, at an impromptu alfresco gathering. While everyone listens to a wry, guitar-accompanied rendition of "Why Must We Go To Guaymas", sprawled around in relaxed groups, Guy, apparently unaware of his surroundings, except as a mild source of annoyance, is focused entirely on a future outside the centre's walls. And there is something strangely belligerent about his male bonding with Carol's father in the lift, on the first occasion they accompany Carol to the centre, in their head-shaking, bemused dismissal of Len and an attendant as they go into an obviously well-rehearsed "fleap" routine.

Although Len and Phyllis seem to represent romantic alternatives, they in fact function as "outside" consciousnesses who can "read" the rightness and inevitability of the couple, a reading given force by its negative consequences for them (both are half in love with half the couple). When, finally able to accept Guy's love at the very moment Guy accepts its loss, Carol turns to Len in her desperation ("Tell me I'm a woman. Tell me I'm not a failure... I feel like I'm breaking up inside. I don't know what I am or where I'm going. Len, please love me..."), he is able to calm and support Carol, deepening their friendship but passing on the rebound. Meanwhile, Phyllis tells Guy to return to Carol: "I played a scene like that once. Just got caught by words. Deep down it was the opposite."

Yet the emphases of the two renunciation scenes are very different. Carol's terror of dissolution dominates her confrontation with Len, and his rational, regretful rejection of shared dependency forces her to define her own life. During most of Guy's scene with Phyllis, on the other hand, he is asleep. In a series of arresting extreme close-ups, in that special deep thoughtfulness that comes with the heightened sense of being the only one awake, Phyllis's face expresses her full consciousness of the impossibility of love between them: her complete, almost bitter, knowledge of her situation, cruelly unknown and unshared by the sleeping (or waking) man beside her. At the same time, she experiences a kind of identification with Carol's loss, but also a sadness at her own unwilled, inevitable yet generous, sacrifice to reverse it. If, at the end of *Never Fear*, Carol finds Guy waiting for her, ending her struggle with loneliness, there is another woman who is less lucky.

The scene with Phyllis is one of those moments of direction-change, when the revelation of the subjectivity of a "secondary" character refocuses the context of the film, unexpectedly widening and layering its field of consciousness, calling into question the whole star/ other axis of consciousness. But, more importantly, it emphasizes the "feminine" cast of perception in the film – the peculiar, introspective connection with self and far-seeing yet momentaneous grasp of situation that seems almost the exclusive province of the women, as opposed to the more empirical, action-oriented, positivistic "understanding" of the men. Phyllis's time-arresting, other-dimensional face haunts the film beyond all story functionalism, and represents a consciousness doomed to transcend its own usefulness – to itself or to others. It measures a lost potential the film never quite admits to tracing. If the men are constantly supportive, "doctor" types – given authority either by the "objective" nature of their disinterested professionalism or by the overriding needs of their love – whose therapeutic demands "cure" Carol, the women are linked by a mute, compassionate solidarity condemned to immanence and incompleteness. The silent concern of a fellow patient, Josie (played by Lupino's sister, Rita), is confined to the frame-lines and borders of the main action for several scenes, to create a kind of tension and resistance of that which cannot come centre-screen, and promise more than the brief, if important, subsequent exchanges between them, as the touch of her hand on Carol's conveys more than her unwitting example-setting post-polio marriage. Women seem to help each other by accident or to their own detriment: not out of lack of generosity, but because, unlike the men, not possessing their own lives, they have no funds to cover their largesse.

There is an extraordinary scene in "The Closed Cabinet", an episode of *Thriller* directed by Lupino (NBC, 1961), which very dramatically underscores the strengths and limitations of female "bonding". In a storm-tossed room a woman confronts the ghost of the tragic abused wife and murderess who has haunted the family of the woman's would-be lover for three hundred years. They cannot quite communicate – the ghost condemned to muteness, the woman experiencing emotions she is too young and naïve either to name or to understand. Yet, for impossibly long, charged moments they stand and stare at each other, in the process solving a riddle whose words had been lost and lifting a curse from the last remaining male heirs, a curse that the men had either denied or despaired of.

In many ways *Never Fear* is about "being a woman" or, more precisely, about the difficulty of accepting a mutilated, dependent, intersubjective version of womanhood which quite disturbingly corresponds to the more traditional, limited definition generally ascribed to that state.[3] To a contemporary audience the film arouses very ambivalent feelings, which are not unrepresented within the film (the opening caption proclaiming that this is a true story arouses heroic expectations – Carol will become a great dancer, found a school for paraplegic dancers, or do something momentous – that are never met, nor, in fact, denied), yet are located more within an ambivalence in Lupino than within the admitted problematic axis of the film. On the one hand, Carol's adjustment is treated very much in the same way as a man's would be – in both emphasizing the difficulty of accepting dependency, a sense that "being a man" or "being a woman" is a question of guts through compromise with an unalterable situation. Yet, on the other hand, "being a man" and "being a woman" imply two quite dissimilar things, as is strongly shown by the fact that no future beyond Guy is sought or projected: Carol is able to salvage her personality, but not her life.

The final image of the film, Carol in Guy's arms throwing away her cane, unleashes conflicting implications – is it a rejection of dependence or of independence? Even more disorienting is the earlier scene in which Carol first "leaves the rail" and begins to walk unaided, regaining a certain autonomy. Afraid and uncertain of her ability to "go it alone", and distrustful now of her body and her will, her faltering rail-aided steps are presented with a mixed voice-over track of pep talks by her coaxing doctor and by memory-echoed reprises of her father, and then Guy, all crying out their need for her, until she lifts her hands and – lo! – she walks. The will of others succeeds where her own has failed (as opposed to the earlier scene in which an unsuccessful attempt to walk is activated by Carol's own voice-over desire). However, the schizophrenia implicit in the sound/image split underscores the alienation latent in her recreated "autonomy". For through her dancing Carol had realised a synthesis of self-for-self and self-for-others, of potential and realisation, quite unique in a Lupino film and quite unlike the constant need for male affirmation qua self-will which defines her "womanhood" by the end.

In many ways *Never Fear* is the most autobiographical of all Lupino's films (Lupino herself was apparently struck with polio early in her career, shortly after her arrival in Hollywood).[4] But, like all her films, it is a road-not-taken autobiography, a "reverse" autobiography, the story of a dancer who could not become a choreographer – read actress who could not become a director. (And this despite the fact that the actress Sally Forrest, who played Carol, was herself both a dancer and a choreographer.) Lupino has said that she wanted to make films about bewildered lost people – men and women – and she perfectly understands the experience of passivity and the social forces that maintain and exploit it.[5] Yet, as a woman who has gone very far beyond that stage in her own life, Lupino is of necessity in a privileged position in terms of situation, talent and class, which makes her own experience and destiny seem inapplicable to the situation of her character. Ultimately her films, like those of Nicholas Ray, are liberal films which, despite being critical of liberalism and aware of its limitations and contradictions, cannot see or move beyond it. Indeed, in both cases, the closer they come to their own class situation (Ray in *Bigger Than Life* [1956], Lupino in *Hard, Fast and Beautiful* [1951]), the stronger the social critique and the more grotesque and biting the contradictions; the farther they stray from their own class situations (Ray in *They Live By Night* [1948], Lupino in *Not Wanted* – both, interestingly, first films), the more lyrical, tragic and poetic their vision.

Lupino's attitude towards her characters is not without a kind of quietly understated, almost maternal, concern; a concern not unrelated to her own complicity and situation as creator of the film. To describe victims one must create their victimization and, ultimately, designate its source. In closing off to her characters the options she herself enjoys (and has fought for), Lupino finds herself in a very equivocal position, one it is both the strength and weakness of her early films never completely to avoid or resolve. *Never Fear*, in the decidedly gruesome form of paralysis by polio, traces among other things Lupino's struggle fully to accept herself as a director and to make the transition to the other side of the camera. Since the film is in itself a positive product of her decision, it should not be too surprising to see the negative side of the equation represented within the film as loss and mutilation.

* * *

The author extends her heartfelt thanks to Greg Ford, for his critical perception and structural expertise during the writing of this essay.

Notes

[1] Andrew Sarris, *The American Cinema: Directors and Directions 1929-1968* (New York: E P Dutton, 1968): 216.

[2] Translated from the French: "Elle [Lupino] choisit la retenue et l'ellipse, laissant en creux les instants aisément pathétiques, tels l'adieu à un enfant que l'on abandonne, l'effroi quand la maladie est nommée par le médecin, la découverte de la bigamie par les épouses. Mais elle laisse aussi cours à la rage, au désir ou à la tristesse de ses héroïnes. Cette rythmique particulière donne un ton tranchant et introduit une certaine distance, tandis que le système du mélodrame est...basé sur l'immédiateté de son impact." (Cécile Thibaud, "Un pathétique en creux: Ida Lupino cinéaste", *Positif* 301 [March 1986]: 19.)

[3] On this aspect of *Never Fear*, see Guy Braucourt, *Avant de t'aimer; Faire face:* l'apprentissage de la vie", *Cinéma 70* 151 (1970): 138-140.

[4] See, for instance, Margaret Hinxman, "She's Demure, But She's Dynamite", *Picturegoer* 27 December 1952: 8-9.

[5] Cited by Francine Parker in "Discovering Ida Lupino", *Action* July/August 1973: 22.

Outrage (1950)

Pam Cook

20-year-old Ann Walton works as a book-keeper at the Bradshaw Milling Company in a small midwest city. Her boyfriend Jim Owens is given a salary increase and they decide to get married. When they break the news to Ann's parents, her father, who has great plans for his daughter, is initially resistant, but comes round to the idea.

The following day, Ann agrees to cover for her friend Stella Carter by working late. As she leaves the office she is followed by a man who runs a nearby lunch counter and who has already tried to flirt with her. He pursues her through the dark, deserted city streets and the terrified Ann hides in a truck yard. She falls, hitting her head, and, while she is in a dazed condition, the man rapes her. She returns home confused and upset, where she is treated by the family doctor and questioned by police. To add to her distress, the incident becomes headline news, making Ann and her family the focus of gossip and curiosity. Ann's sense of guilt and shame increases when she is asked to attend an identification parade, and when Jim pressurises her to marry him immediately, she rejects him and runs away from home, getting on the bus to Los Angeles.

The bus stops at a Californian town, where Ann hears a radio broadcast describing her as a missing person. She panics and takes off down the highway. She twists her ankle and collapses by the side of the road, where she is found by a young minister, Dr Bruce Ferguson, who takes her to the home of his friends, the Harrisons, who own an orange ranch. Although still very withdrawn, Ann begins to recover, taking a job at the ranch and gradually responding to Bruce's attempts to draw her out. At his suggestion, she attends the local harvest party, where she is approached by ranch employee Frank Marini, who, despite her resistance, insists on kissing her. Ann recalls the rape and, confusing Marini with the rapist, hits him with a wrench, almost killing him.

Ann flees, and is eventually found by Bruce, who, after hearing her story, persuades her to go to the police. In court, Bruce argues for compassion towards Ann and the man who raped her, who has been arrested after confessing to the crime. Marini withdraws charges and Ann is released into Bruce's care on condition that she undergo a year's psychiatric treatment. Some time later, Bruce advises Ann to return to her parents and Jim, and pick up the threads of her life. Despite the fact that Ann says she would prefer to stay with him, Bruce puts Ann on the bus and sadly watches as she is driven away.

*　*　*

In 1949 Ida Lupino, an actress known for her powerful, memorable roles in many 'B' films noirs, together with her second husband, Collier Young, and Anson Bond, formed her own production company, Emerald Productions, and made *Not Wanted* (1949), a drama about unwanted pregnancy. Later that year, Lupino, Young and Malvin Wald started The Filmakers.[1] There followed a string of low-budget, black and white films about contemporary social issues, featuring lesser known actors and often based on real events. The Filmakers' second production was *Outrage* (1950), which deals with the controversial subject of rape. Lupino's role in the company appears to have been very "hands-on": she co-produced, co-scripted and directed and, according to one press release,[2] also designed sets and costumes. She clearly enjoyed a great deal of control over the company's projects. Lupino's venture into independent production was not that unusual; as Douglas Gomery points out,[3] in the late 1940s and 1950s many leading stars formed their own production companies. What is unusual is that Lupino succeeded in building a reputation as a director and managed to sustain it, subsequently working in television on popular series such as *The Untouchables* (ABC, 1959-62) and *The Fugitive* (ABC, 1963-66).

The success of The Filmakers' productions with audiences and critics seems to have resided in their uncompromising approach to "difficult" subject-matter: unmarried mothers, disability, rape, bigamy and so forth. Most of them were given an X rating for UK release.[4] These low-budget films had a gritty, tabloid quality and, although technically unsophisticated, were well received by the British press – generally suspicious of Hollywood "artificiality" – for their frank presentation of "the facts of life".[5] They were also praised by contemporary reviewers for their feminist stance on social issues directly relevant to women's everyday experience.[6]

On the surface, therefore, Lupino's productions for The Filmakers are prototypes of feminist work. Independently produced, adventurous in choice of subject and breaking with Hollywood studio aesthetics, they sowed the seeds for the feminist independent cinema that blossomed twenty years later. Yet, at least one feminist critic writing in the 1970s was less than enthusiastic. Molly Haskell assesses Lupino's films as a director as far inferior to her tough, gutsy roles as an actress, describing them as "conventional, even sexist".[7] An uncertainty as regards their feminist status hovers over The Filmakers' movies, even when Lupino's achievements are celebrated. Patricia White, writing in *Village Voice* in 1991 about the Lupino retrospective at New York's Museum of Modern Art (MOMA), extols the virtues of the actress while remaining ambivalent about the director's "conventional" treatment of her subject-matter.[8] While Lupino's acting is seen as transcending the limitations of classical Hollywood cinema, empowering the heroines she played, her directing is often seen as conforming to those narrative constraints.

It is possible to turn this judgment on its head, as Ronnie Scheib brilliantly does in a programme note on Lupino for the MOMA retrospective.[9] For Scheib, Lupino's characters in The Filmakers' movies are modern, postwar, post-classical cinema, alienated figures, victims of an uncomprehending society who struggle to find an identity, and who at best achieve an uneasy equilibrium. Scheib's analysis delves beneath the surface of the films to find a common structure: a "normal" way of life disrupted by trauma, leading to profound alienation, a brief respite, followed by a reversal of trauma and the tentative start of a new life. Certainly, this pattern applies to *Outrage*, in which a young woman's expectations of marriage, home and family are shattered when she is raped and then repeatedly victimized by society and the legal system. Helped by a compassionate young minister, she is able to face up to what happened to her and return to the normal life she had rejected. Such a reading enables us to move beyond the sanctimonious "message" aspect of *Outrage*, personified by minister Bruce Ferguson and his fondness for sermonising, to something more interesting: female impotence in a male-dominated world – the difficulty, precisely, of occupying the place allotted to women in patriarchal society.

It is worth pursuing Scheib's analysis further in relation to *Outrage*. At first sight, the film's narrative does not look promising. Traumatized rape victim Ann Walton flees to California where she is "rescued" by Dr Bruce Ferguson, who takes a compassionate interest in the withdrawn young woman. At this point, attention shifts away from Ann as rape victim towards Bruce as healer, a direction which is continued when Ann is traumatized once more by the unwelcome advances of another man, whom she attacks in self-defence and nearly kills before taking flight. Bruce comes to her aid yet again, pleading on her behalf – since she is too disturbed to speak for herself – to the court for therapeutic methods to be used in treating Ann and the man who raped her, himself a victim of psychological damage inflicted by war. Having been criminalised and pathologized, Ann is told by Bruce that her fiancé and family want her back home. Ann tells Bruce that she wants to stay with him – raising the question of his motives in taking care of her, and of her own desire. Bruce, however, misses his chance, insisting that he "has a job to do" and Ann "has a life to lead", so she must leave.

This ending, apparently shoring up traditional family values, is difficult for feminists to accept. The rites-of-passage scenario identified by Scheib as common to all Lupino's Emerald/The Filmakers' movies is particularly relentless in *Outrage*, and Ann's rehabilitation is apparently endorsed by the director. Bruce is presented as a "good" character – indeed, as Ann's saviour. Yet *Outrage* is melodrama, and in melodrama matters are not that simple. Feminist study of the genre has emphasized its creation of a "feminine", domesticated world in which women's experience and point of view are privileged, not least by the employment of *mise en scène* and sound to convey heightened affect. In *Outrage* the moralistic, punitive trajectory of the narrative is undercut and commented on by the visual and auditory codes, which are used expressionistically to convey Ann's state of mind and existential predicament.[10] This ensures that the shift of emphasis to Bruce as agent of truth and stability is never entirely secure. Indeed, Bruce's authority is most significantly undermined at the point at which it should have been clearly legitimized – in the sequence in which he refuses Ann's request to stay with him and insists that she should return to her former life. This is the first time since the rape that Ann has been able to articulate her own desire, to speak for herself. To Bruce as agent of narrative resolution, this means that she is "cured". In this painful scene Ann's desire is liberated only to be denied, and Bruce's "faith", which has been so important in the healing process, becomes the instrument of repression. The extent of the repression is emphasized in the film's final shot, which has Bruce gazing regretfully after Ann's departing bus.

The reality principle brought into play here substantiates Scheib's argument that the heroines of the films Lupino directed are not in control of their own destiny, that they are acted upon rather than active. Ann's rite of passage confirms that she must submit to the demands of society. Yet, a reading of *Outrage* as melodrama reveals that there is more to it than this. As Scheib rightly points out, *Outrage* is the product of a US postwar consciousness still in the throes of readjustment and reconstruction, dealing with the personal pain and devastation inflicted, and struggling to establish new identities and aspirations. Scheib refers to Nicholas Ray, Samuel Fuller and Robert Aldrich as Lupino's spiritual brothers in angst, but there is an influential precursor in William Wyler's *The Best Years of Our Lives* (1946).

Independently produced by Samuel Goldwyn for RKO, *The Best Years of Our Lives* is a key transitional postwar reconstruction film, bridging the gap between 1940s film noir and 1950s melodrama. It is centrally concerned with the war-damaged psyches of soldiers returning home to a materialistic and uncaring society, and with the pivotal role of women in providing a nurturing environment in which the men can pick up the pieces of their lives. Wyler's film is liberal in tone and aesthetics, with Gregg Toland's deep-focus black and white cinematography refusing to privilege any one protagonist over another and projecting a "democratic" field of vision in which the viewer is encouraged to understand and identify with multiple points of view. Despite this apparent democracy, there is clearly a hierarchy at work, in which the male characters' problems and desires take precedence and the female characters are expected to perform a supportive, therapeutic role. Emphasis is placed on the neurosis resulting from experience of battle and the consequent difficulty of forming and maintaining "normal" heterosexual relationships. The rites-of-passage element is strong, with all the major characters working through their problems to achieve happiness through reconciliation.

Outrage owes a great deal to *The Best Years of Our Lives*, which was hugely successful, both critically and commercially. *Outrage* was also independently produced for RKO, who would have been looking to repeat the success of Wyler's film, particularly since the studio's Golden Age had ended in 1946 with the death of Charles Koerner, after which it had entered a problematic era characterised by experiment and controversy rather than profitability.[11] The impact of the earlier film on *Outrage* can be detected in the latter's focus on postwar impaired masculinity and in the notion that this has a cumulative effect, so that Ann's traumatization by the rapist is seen as the outcome of his own prior psychological disturbance and victimization, rather than as a result of heterosexual power relations. The liberal thrust of this message, which appears to give everyone an equal hearing, is expressed in Bruce's heartfelt speech to the court for compassion rather than punishment to be meted out to society's victims, of which Ann is only one. The rapist is absolved of guilt, which is placed firmly at the door of society, with the consequence that the specificity of Ann's experience of rape is subsumed into the rapist's experience of war, and both are perceived as neurotics who need to be cured.

Outrage's liberal social message, clearly intended by the filmmakers to be read as such, provides what might be called its dominant layer of meaning. In the space it gives to the recognition of the psychological problems of the rapist and the raped, and to the need for therapeutic treatment, it can be seen as progressive, even by today's standards. It would be dangerous, even perverse, to ignore this level of meaning – yet there is more to the film than this. Despite the brutal way in which Ann is divested of her subjectivity, the filmmakers ensure that the process of disenfranchisement, and its consequences for Ann, remain visible. Most importantly, the narrative structure is based on flight. After the rape, Ann flees the hostile city for the pastoral idyll of California. The rape itself takes place after a prolonged chase in which Ann is stalked by the rapist through the deserted city streets, and the pursuit/flight motif dominates the remainder of the film. The pursuit is presented from the point of view of the fugitive, who is seen as the victim of incomprehension and authoritarianism. (It is interesting in this respect that Lupino directed three episodes of the 1960s US television series *The Fugitive*, starring David Janssen, which also took the perspective of the victim fleeing injustice.)

Male authoritarianism pervades *Outrage*, from the forbidding intransigence of Ann's father when faced with her impending marriage, to her fiancé Jim's attempt to bully her into marrying him immediately after the rape, the insistence of Frank Marini as he tries to kiss her at the harvest party, and the punitive response of the legal system to her desperate attempt to defend herself against his unwelcome advances. Thus, Ann's impulse to take flight, although motivated by trauma and neurosis, is entirely validated, and her journey can be seen in terms of a wish to discover forms of male identity more hospitable to female subjectivity. In this context, Bruce is a feminised man, given more to nurturing and enabling than to dominating and controlling – and, significantly, he is asexual. (The script playfully alludes to the character's emasculated status by having him suck on a pipe empty of tobacco, suggesting that he has "no lead in his pencil".) It is precisely Bruce's lack of sexuality that appeals to Ann, since her flight is as much from her destiny as wife and mother as from the site of her sexual trauma. This is marked visually and auditorily in the film through expressionist motifs which evoke childhood and the loss of innocence – poignantly in the playing of the song "Johnny's So Long At the Fair" over Ann and Jim's meeting in the park when they decide to get married, and dramatically when the rapist stalking Ann viciously slashes a circus poster bearing the image of a clown, or when Ann herself shatters her first communion photograph just before running away from home. Ann is repeatedly filmed as if she is in prison – the bars of her bedstead framing her distress when she is questioned by police about the rape are echoed in the hard lines of the farm machinery and the fence that ensnare her after Marini's assault – until, of course, she does end up behind bars. The loss of innocence theme shifts onto a national level with Bruce's declaration that the peaceful Californian valley where he refound his faith after his war experiences and illness is in fact the valley of his childhood. Ann's trauma and neurosis, and her flight from violent city to tranquil countryside, become symptomatic of the need for the United States to rediscover its own lost innocence.

It is entirely fitting, in the context of this crisis of national identity, that Ann should be perpetually on the run, and unable to find a place to call home. Even her refuge with Bruce is shortlived, since he decides that they should both defer to higher authority. The ending of *Outrage* is, as is usual in melodrama, strangely ambiguous. The final shot is not, as one might expect, of Ann on the bus taking her home, but of Bruce gazing ruefully out of frame at the departing vehicle, before turning away to return to his car. In this closing moment Bruce is the subject and Ann the lost object, her absence from the shot almost like a disappearance, marking her lack of subjectivity. This is an anxious ending, charged with loss. There is a sense that Ann may never reach her destination, that she is a permanently displaced person.

Unsatisfactory narrative closure is of course a feature not only of cinematic melodrama. The open-ended structure of serial forms of narrative may well have been an influence on *Outrage*, which ends with its heroine "on the road" once more, rather like the close of an episode in a television serial. In fact, although television was in its early stages at the time of *Outrage*'s production, there is considerable evidence of the film's anticipation of television aesthetics. As Lynn Spigel points out,[12] between 1948 and 1955 television became a dominant mass medium in the United States, to be greeted with a combination of hope and fear. The film industry responded with a similar ambivalence: on the one hand, television was its biggest competitor; on the other, it was its salvation, as the beleaguered studios attempted to move into television production. *Outrage* manifests many of the signs of this competitive relationship – for example, in its self-conscious use of depth of field, which early television was unable to achieve; in its employment of the travel motif identified by Spigel as central to television's early "space conquering" appeal;[13] and in its somewhat histrionic mixture of theatricality and realism. The "imaginary experiences of social integration"[14] projected by television programming during this period is of course undercut by *Outrage*'s focus on its heroine's sense of social isolation – but there is no doubt that Lupino's film bears a striking resemblance to what was to become television social issue melodrama. This is one of a number of ways in which *Outrage* bridges different genres and production contexts.

A reading of *Outrage* in terms of melodrama produces intriguing results. It reveals a text fraught with conflict and contradiction in which the manifest ideological project – the discourse of liberalism and rehabilitation enacted by the narrative – is overtly contested (and revealed as deeply flawed) by the drama of female subjectivity carried by the visual and auditory codes. It is this conflict which produces the sense of anomie, the failure, so acutely observed by Scheib, to produce a comfortable position from which to understand "the human condition". This reading also challenges the "antifeminist" view of Lupino's work as a director. Ann's flight and her search for subjectivity are a rejection of traditional femininity. Her victim status and "neurosis" are the direct result of social forces, yet they exceed that too-neat explanation. They are symptomatic of a culture that will not acknowledge its own affliction and prefers to remain in the grip of disease.

If the reading of *Outrage* as melodrama offers an interpretation which redresses the balance in favour of its heroine and her predicament, a reading of the film as rape drama seems to belong to the opposite camp. Carol J Clover, in her impressive study of low-budget horror movies, *Men, Women and Chain Saws*,[15] includes a chapter on rape-revenge films which not only usefully delineates the parameters of the rape genre, but also puts forward a cogent revisionist argument. Clover claims that the accusations of rampant misogyny levelled at low-budget rape-revenge are misplaced, and that the focus of these films on the perspective of the victim-turned-avenger, far from pandering to sadistic male fantasy, actually places viewers in a masochistic position – doubly so, in that they are invited to identify not only with the rape victim, but also with her male victims, as she goes about killing, maiming and castrating those who have harmed her. Furthermore, the male perpetrators are hardly presented as heroic: on the contrary, they are sexually, psychologically and often physically impaired. Clover detects a shift – which she puts down to the influence of 1970s feminism – from male-centred rape films of the early 1970s, such as *Straw Dogs* (Sam Peckinpah, 1971) and *Frenzy* (Alfred Hitchcock, 1972), to female-centred revenge narratives such as Abel Ferrara's *Ms .45* (aka *Angel of Vengeance*, 1980).

Clover's argument hinges on a comparison between Jonathan Kaplan's mainstream film *The Accused* (1988) and the ultra-violent, low-budget revenge drama *I Spit On Your Grave* (aka *Day of the Woman*, 1977), directed by Meir Zarchi. She sees the former's focus on the inadequacies of the legal system as wresting control from the rape victim and shifting narrative emphasis to the female lawyer who defends her. The refusal to allow the victim to speak for herself is doubly enforced by having one of the male witnesses to the rape finally speak the "truth" about what happened, which is the first time the rape is actually seen. This strategy, in which a male character complicit with the crime "changes sides" to support the rape victim, also enables masculinity to be redeemed to some extent, by demonstrating that not all men are rapists. *I Spit On Your Grave*, on the other hand, takes the legal system's impotence for granted, and puts its vengeful heroine at the story's centre, allowing her to solve her own problems – indeed, presenting her as the best person to do so. There is no redemption here, nor is it looked for. The only law is *lex talionis*, and both victims and perpetrators live by it. Implicit in Clover's position is the idea that the "rough justice" scenario of low-budget rape-revenge empowers the victim-hero, creating her as a victorious castrating figure who is deeply unsettling for male viewers. In contrast, the more liberal mainstream rape films repeatedly disenfranchise the victim, rendering her victory at the least ambiguous.

Linda Williams has already questioned the subversive potential of Clover's bisexual victim-heroes.[16] It could also be argued that this "masculinisation" of the rape-revenge heroines may have the comforting effect for male spectators of re-establishing the equation between masculinity and power in the face of the "feminisation" (disempowering) of the male perpetrators. At the end of the low-budget rape-revenge scenario, the woman has the phallus, and the phallus is secure as signifier of power, in effect confirming existing gender power relations. This point is important in relation to *Outrage*, where the rape victim is systematically prevented from taking control, and her victim status is continually reiterated.

Clover does not include *Outrage* in her discussion – perhaps because her focus on horror precludes it, or perhaps because Lupino's film remains "hidden from history", even to feminists. Certainly, as a low-budget rape film which appears to have more in common thematically with the up-market production *The Accused* than with the table-turning gender confusions of *I Spit On Your Grave*, it problematizes her high/low distinction. *Outrage* shares many of the features of the rape-revenge format as outlined by Clover, but it reverses some of them. The city/country axis, defined by Clover as crucial to the have/have not relationship between victims and perpetrators, is inflected differently in *Outrage*. Ann is raped in the city, which is seen as the locus of her disempowerment and represented as a dangerous, threatening place. She arrives in the country already a victim, looking for refuge. She finds it temporarily, but then, ironically, the country also turns hostile, and she is assaulted again. In other words, the city/country division dissolves in Lupino's film as the heroine finds herself victimized in both places.

The have/have not relationship is also unsettled in *Outrage*. As a city-dweller, Ann does not have power in the conventional sense of material wealth or high-flying career. Indeed, as the early scenes show, her life is ordinary (she lives with her parents and works in a factory as a clerk). As it is difficult to see her as a "have", what is it that she possesses that the rapist attempts to take? The narrative eventually makes it clear that what the rapist envies is Ann's "innocence" (he divests her of her virginity) – the innocence forcibly taken from him by the war. In common with the rape-revenge perpetrators, *Outrage*'s rapist is an impaired character, denoted by his obsessional behaviour and facial scar. Unlike them, he has a very small role, disappearing completely from the story after the rape, except insofar as he figures in Bruce's speech to the court, in which his actions are explained as the result of war damage (another way in which he differs from the low-budget rape-revenge rapists, whose deeds are given minimal, if any, explanation).

Like the heroine of *I Spit On Your Grave*, Ann looks to the country for refuge from the city. Like her, she discovers there is no such refuge. Forced to defend herself against the advances of Frank Marini, she takes up a wrench and uses it as a weapon to attack him, mirroring the violence of the man who first assaulted her. Unlike her late 1970s sister, however, she is not in fact empowered by taking the law into her own hands in this way. Her masculinisation is perceived as part of her neurosis and she is immediately pathologized and imprisoned. Her one attempt at turning the tables is thus a miserable failure – but every move Ann makes to take control of her destiny is punished or refused. The rape is simply the limit case of her powerlessness, and it recedes in importance as the film heaps humiliation upon humiliation. To make matters worse, she is "rescued" by a man who pleads on her behalf to the court, explaining her violence in terms of psychological disturbance, arguing that she is, like the rapist, a suitable case for treatment, and promising to take care of her. As in *The Accused*, masculinity is redeemed through Bruce's taking the side of the victim, in this case, of both rapist and raped.

Again as in *The Accused*, Ann's victory (better seen as "cure") is ambiguous. As already indicated, the rehabilitation scenario, suggesting that Ann is ready to return to "normal" life, is undercut by the implication of the ending that she has yet to find subjectivity. It is interesting that the last shot of *I Spit On Your Grave*, as described by Clover,[17] is of the victorious heroine speeding along in a motorboat. Like Ann, she is finally seen in transit – perhaps also unlikely, after her similar traumatic experiences, to find a resting place. *Outrage* straddles both sides of Clover's high/low dichotomy, sharing *The Accused*'s liberal critique of the legal system while allowing its heroine no retribution, and subscribing to *I Spit On Your Grave*'s relentless brutalization scenario without the gender-reversal pay off. In the light of Clover's revisionist reading of the rape-revenge genre, therefore, Lupino's rape film falls far short of the ideological disturbances detected by Clover in her 1970s and 1980s feminist-influenced examples. The rape-revenge reading produces a view of *Outrage* diametrically opposed to that produced by the melodrama reading. The first sees the film as endorsing the female victim position, while the second sees it as putting the drama of female subjectivity centre-stage. It is not my intention to argue for one reading over another, nor to suggest that both are equally viable. Rather, I want to keep both in play, so that each reveals the limits of the other.

Before settling for an antifeminist, prefeminist or feminist view of *Outrage*, however, it is worth looking more closely at the way it works through the male/female and country/city axes defined by Clover as the nub of rape-revenge. As Clover points out, the genre associates women with the city and men with the country. The move of the heroine (occasionally the hero) from city to country involves an encounter with impaired, "feminised" males who brutalize her in an attempt to restore their damaged masculinity. Confronted with her own powerless femininity, the victim evens the score by exacting retribution of the same order as that visited on her by her assailants, "feminising" them and by the same token "masculinising" herself. The fact that frequently she is the lone survivor suggests that the female to male transformation is more acceptable than the male to female one.

Outrage follows the pattern up to a point. Ann moves from city to country after she has been victimized by an impaired male, and once there, she discovers a "feminine", nurturing man and an apparently caring environment – at least for a while. The difference between *Outrage* and the 1970s rape-revenge films lies in the positive value it attaches to feminised masculinity, which it defines not just in terms of lack and impairment, or the juggling of the roles of victim and perpetrator, but as a sympathetic, woman-made transformation of traditional virile masculinity. Bruce's non-phallic sexuality, as the embodiment of this feminine ideal, is seen as a desirable option to the heterosexual power relations embedded in either marriage or rape. Ultimately, *Outrage* reneges on this promise of non-phallic masculinity, closing down on it the moment that desire between Ann and Bruce becomes a possibility; however, at least it is there as a question, breaking through the phallic régime characteristic of the rape-revenge scenario. Bruce is a different kind of "have-not", also damaged by the war but still capable of compassion; and his final relinquishing of Ann to her family and fiancé can be seen as an act of supreme self-sacrifice. The last shot of *Outrage* stands in stark contrast to that of *I Spit On Your Grave*. In the former, a feminised male reaps the ambivalent rewards of his transformation; in the latter, a masculinised female flees the scene of her own transmutation.

As I have already argued, *Outrage* reverses the city/country divide characteristic of rape-revenge by representing the country (specifically California) as a place where innocence might be regained. This pastoral myth, fundamental to US culture and national identity, was revived during the postwar period, when the agrarian West once again had particular resonance as the repository of utopian dreams. Laura Mulvey discusses the importance of this myth to Douglas Sirk's melodrama *All That Heaven Allows* (1955), quoting Jon Halliday on Rock Hudson's role as the idealised "natural man": "'Hudson and his trees are both America's past and America's ideals. They are ideals which are now unobtainable...'".[18] This might easily be applied to *Outrage*. Like Cary Scott, the heroine of *All That Heaven Allows*, Ann has happiness with a natural man within her grasp, only to have it snatched away; the pastoral idyll is revealed, precisely, as myth. The city, in the form of the law, follows Ann to the country, and there is no escape. The city/country axis is not specific to melodrama – it turns up in most genres from film noir (Nicholas Ray's *On Dangerous Ground*, 1952, made for RKO, in which Lupino starred with Robert Ryan, for example) to the western. The modern horror film, and the associated rape-revenge cycle, offer the most extreme versions of the pastoral dream-gone-bad, in that the country is demonised as the place where the protagonists' worst fears are realised. The specificity of the pastoral myth in melodrama and in the rape-revenge films described by Clover lies in the way these genres' heroines look to the country as the locus for the discovery of new sexual identities and gender power relations, or the rediscovery of earlier, less contaminated ones.

A focus on the city/country axis reveals classic melodrama and contemporary low-budget rape-revenge to have more in common than is immediately apparent. Yet Clover's revisionist reading of the modern horror film suggests that much has happened in the twenty or so years between *Outrage* and *I Spit On Your Grave*. Clover's approach depends on the idea that the interests of 1970s feminism are much more explicitly and overtly represented in low-budget rape-revenge than in adulterated mainstream versions of the genre. Thus, the assaulted heroines of rape-revenge are able to turn the tables on their attackers, take control of their destiny and survive, and in the process overturn existing gender power relations. With their stark, male/female binary oppositions, these films clearly owe something to one version of contemporary feminism – a radical feminism which sees heterosexual relationships as fundamentally non-egalitarian and imbued with the violence of oppressor against oppressed. But low-budget rape-revenge adopts the tenets of feminism only up to a point. There is, for example, no community of women to which the heroine can turn for refuge or support. Indeed, the bloody battles between victim and perpetrator usually take place outside any social, legal or political context. Clover claims that this allows the specificity of rape as a sexual crime against women, and the experience of the rape victim, to be foregrounded. But another version of contemporary feminism would argue that the act of rape itself is inseparable from the underpinning social and legal system which treats the victim herself as a criminal – as having provoked the act of sexual violence in some way, as delivering misleading signals, meaning "Yes" instead of "No", and so forth. This feminism sees rape and sexual violence as the limit case of violence against women and puts forward a transformation of social institutions as part of the solution. Mainstream films such as *The Accused*, with their focus on the inadequacies of the law and gestures towards feminism as a political movement, owe more to this version of feminism.

Clover's defence of low-budget rape-revenge against mainstream rape films thus puts us in the unenviable position of deciding which of these popular versions of feminism is preferable. It also leads to a predictable critical impasse in which mainstream Hollywood films are seen as more ideologically flawed than low-budget independent productions. Both these arguments beg a number of questions. Is there a coherent "feminism" against which we can measure these popular representations and arrive at definitive value judgments? Or is feminism better thought of in terms of multiple, conflicting positions which traverse popular fiction in a variety of ways? Clover is right to rescue "low" horror from critical opprobrium and incomprehension, feminist or otherwise; however, as I have already suggested, the high/low distinction does not hold up when a wider field of rape films is scrutinised. This implies the need for a more complex notion of the way feminist issues surface in popular texts, one which recognises the many faces of feminism.

Clover's high/low argument also begs the question of whether low-budget rape-revenge is less "compromised" than mainstream examples by virtue of being produced, distributed and exhibited outside the "middlebrow" quality circuits. Clearly, low-budget independent production enables filmmakers to take risks, but this does not mean that it is immune from ideological or economic pressures. Nor can low-budget exploitation, which exists on the periphery of mainstream film production, be seen as entirely independent. It is perhaps better conceived as negotiating a space on the boundaries between mainstream and independent production proper, capitalising on, yet keeping a distance from, the mainstream.

These questions are relevant to my attempt to produce conflicting readings of *Outrage*. In the period separating Lupino's film and 1970s rape-revenge movies, rape did, as Clover claims, move centre-stage and was transformed under the influence of 1970s feminism. It is also helpful to look at Lupino's 1950s social problem melodrama from the perspective of 1970s rape-revenge, not least in order to map historical changes in one of the few genres to place a female perspective, and a feminist sensibility, at the centre. One of the more obvious changes is the graphic detail in which 1970s rape-revenge represents the brutality of rape and sexual assault, albeit mostly, as Clover points out, from the point of view of the victim rather than the perpetrators. In *Outrage* the rape discreetly takes place out of frame, an elision which leads to some of the textual excesses described in my reading of the film as melodrama. It is almost as if the repression of the act of sexual violence produces hysterical symptoms in the body of the film itself,[19] as well as in that of its heroine. Although, as Clover argues, the explicit representation of rape in rape-revenge has the advantage of underlining the sexual nature of the crime and the experience of the victim, it is by no means clear that it can be argued that this represents a "progression" in feminist terms from *Outrage*'s use of melodramatic strategies to ensure the visibility of its heroine's psychological and emotional trauma.

Similarly, as I have argued above, the empowerment-through-masculinisation of the rape-revenge heroines is problematic and cannot be seen as inherently more feminist than the emphasis in *Outrage* on Ann's powerlessness. Nor do the circumstances of *Outrage*'s production, any more than those of low-budget rape-revenge, guarantee it progressive status. Lupino's film bears all the marks of having to straddle both independent and studio production: striving for authenticity and realism (outdoor location shooting, lesser known actors, true stories and so forth), while maintaining an "expressionist" *mise en scène* and use of sound characteristic of studio artificiality, particularly in the early city sequences. (Indeed, it would not be too fanciful to read *Outrage* in terms of its director's struggle to achieve an identity as a filmmaker at the edges of the studio system.) In this respect, *Outrage* is neither more nor less compromised than any other film on the margins of the mainstream that seeks a popular audience – and 1970s low-budget rape-revenge must also seek such an audience.

The sense of dissatisfaction with Lupino's The Filmakers movies expressed by some 1970s and post-1970s feminists evidences a common desire to recover the work of women in the past in the interests of present-day feminism. Yet, this is a project which is bound to disappoint, in that every feminism, including contemporary varieties, is marked by time and place and can only incompletely find itself in other feminisms. The quest for feminism in popular texts is in any case self-defeating, in the sense that these texts produce popular versions of feminism, rather than reproduce an "authentic" feminist politics. Overtly a hybrid of genres and production contexts, *Outrage* resists any single interpretation – indeed, significantly different versions of feminism are produced when different reading models are brought to bear on the film. Paradoxically, the film's quality of resistance to feminist interpretation is its strength. Rather than providing the illusory satisfaction of a coherent feminist discourse, it offers the opportunity to explore the limits of feminist enquiry by testing it against a text which refuses to conform easily to political or ideological categories we might wish to impose.

Notes

[1] Lucy Stewart, *Ida Lupino as Film Director, 1949-1953: an 'Auteur' Approach* (New York: Arno Press, 1980): 62.

[2] British Film Institute Library microfiche on Ida Lupino.

[3] Douglas Gomery, *The Hollywood Studio System* (London: British Film Institute/Macmillan, 1986): 9-10.

[4] The X certificate was introduced in the United Kingdom in 1951 in an attempt to stem the decline in cinema audiences by moving into previously forbidden areas of sex and violence. In the United States, too, censorship was beginning to be relaxed as the self-regulatory controls of the Motion Picture Producers and Distributors of America (MPPDA) started to break down with the major studios' loss of hegemony. See Gomery: 11.

[5] See *Evening News* 18 June 1953; Harold Conway, *Evening Standard* 29 November 1949; Richard Winnington, *News Chronicle* 9 November 1951.

[6] "WomanSense Goes to the Pictures: Men Will Hate This Film...", *Daily Herald* 28 November 1949.

[7] Molly Haskell, *From Reverence to Rape: the Treatment of Women in the Movies* (Harmondsworth: Penguin Books, 1974): 201.

[8] Patricia White, "Ida in Wonderland", *Village Voice* 5 February 1991: A64.

[9] Ronnie Scheib, "Ida Lupino", The Museum of Modern Art programme note accompanying the Ida Lupino retrospective 1 February-9 March 1991. See also Scheib, "Ida Lupino: Auteuress", *Film Comment* 16: 1 (1980): 54-64.

[10] See Thomas Elsaesser, "Tales of Sound and Fury: Observations on the Family Melodrama", and Laura Mulvey, "Notes on Sirk and Melodrama", in Christine Gledhill (ed), *Home Is Where the Heart Is: Studies in Melodrama and the Woman's Film* (London: British Film Institute, 1987): 43, 75, for discussion of the importance of visual codes in Hollywood melodrama.

[11] See Gomery: 141.

[12] Lynn Spigel, "Television in the Family Circle: The Popular Reception of a New Medium", in Patricia Mellencamp (ed), *Logics of Television: Essays in Cultural Criticism* (Bloomington and Indianapolis: Indiana University Press, 1990): 74.

[13] Lynn Spigel, "Installing the Television Set: Popular Discourses on Television and Domestic Space, 1948-1955", in Lynn Spigel and Denise Mann (eds), *Private Screenings: Television and the Female Consumer* (Minneapolis: University of Minnesota Press, 1992): 9.

[14] Ibid: 13.

[15] Carol J Clover, *Men, Women and Chain Saws: Gender in the Modern Horror Film* (London: British Film Institute, 1992).

[16] Linda Williams, *Hard Core: Power, Pleasure, and the "Frenzy of the Visible"* (London: Pandora Press, 1990): 208.

[17] Clover: 148.

[18] Mulvey, in Gledhill: 79.

[19] See Geoffrey Nowell-Smith, "Minnelli and Melodrama", in Gledhill: 73.

Hard, Fast and Beautiful (1951)

Mandy Merck

Florence Farley is a young woman just out of Santa Monica High School and a keen tennis player. As she practises her strokes against the garage door, her mother Milly trims the dress she is sewing for her. Florence's practice is interrupted by a young man, asking if she has seen a stray dog. He identifies himself as an assistant at the local country club and asks to use the telephone. Florence recognises him as a former schoolmate, Gordon McKay, and introduces him to her mother, who inquires about his family and offers lemonade. Gordon declines, but invites Florence to play tennis with him at the club.

That evening, Milly rejects her husband Will's advances and complains about their neighbourhood. As the couple prepare themselves for bed, Milly declares her ambitions for her daughter, but Will defends their homely circumstances. Florence enters and holds an excited conversation about her prospective match with Gordon. To her mother's disappointment, she reveals that he is not wealthy, but a student working his way through college. Will reminds Florence that her forthcoming match is "only a game". "Well, sure", Florence replies, "but maybe I can beat him".

Florence beats Gordon, who suggests that she should play doubles with him at the club. She begins to win local matches and is soon asked by the club president to represent it at the national junior championships in Philadelphia. When Milly refuses permission for Florence to travel there without her, she too is offered an expenses-paid trip. Before they depart, Gordon declares his love to Florence with an engraved pendant in the shape of a tennis racquet.

At the junior championships, tennis agent Fletcher Locke is impressed by Florence's ability and inquires about her to a colleague. Milly overhears and contrives to introduce herself to Fletcher by pretending not to understand the tournament draw sheet. Florence wins the tournament but defers to her mother in the post-match interview. Milly tells the press that they will "just go home and be ourselves for a while".

Florence, now wearing an expensive tennis outfit donated by a manufacturer, is picked up by Gordon after partnering a wealthy local woman. When Gordon angrily reproaches her for accepting $50 in payment, she protests that she is not endangering her amateur status. Meanwhile, her mother brushes aside Will's objections to a new car and declares that she has already bought one on a deal arranged for Florence. Fletcher Locke flies to California to persuade the Farleys to enter Florence in the national championships. Milly conducts the negotiations, as Will stands awkwardly by. Before leaving with her mother, Florence reconciles with Gordon and accepts his proposal of marriage.

Florence plays in several preliminary tournaments and loses one because of her weak backhand. Fletcher drills her on it exhaustively and impresses Milly with the prospective rewards of her daughter's success. Florence wins the national championship as her sick father listens to the radio broadcast and Gordon watches from the stands. After the match, Milly persuades Florence to marry Gordon on tour in Europe, where he can work writing newspaper articles for her. Gordon angrily refuses and ends their engagement.

Florence tours Europe over the winter and wins Wimbledon. After a drunken night out in London, she reveals to her mother that she now understands her unpopularity with the other players. She berates her for accepting illicit expense money and separating her from Gordon. In Paris, Florence takes control of her affairs, refuses to endorse a shoddy racquet, and ends her tour to return for the US championships.

There she responds to a journalist's questions about the amateur game with a sarcastic endorsement of the values of family and fair play. A telegram arrives with news of her father's illness, and Florence defies Milly to fly home on the eve of the final. Weak in hospital, Will is tender with his daughter but dismissive to his wife, telling her to "beat it". Exhausted from her flight, Florence struggles in the final, but ultimately wins as her father listens to the broadcast. Gordon is also watching from the stands and appears to rescue the dazed victor from a barrage of press questions about her intended retirement. He abruptly escorts her from the stadium, but Florence turns back to hand her mother the trophy, saying bitterly that she has "earned it". A panicked Milly appeals to Fletcher to intervene, but he is already approaching a new protégée. As darkness settles over the stadium, Milly sits alone in the stands.

*   *   *

Contemporary reviews of the fourth film directed by Ida Lupino, *Hard, Fast and Beautiful* (1951), were quick to acknowledge its dual interest in mother-daughter relations and in tennis "shamateurism". Some, such as the *Motion Picture Herald*, saw no contradiction in these themes:

Ida Lupino directed with fine focus on feminine values this stirring contemporary drama, which shows in highly exploitable fashion how commercialism invades the amateur sports field without the knowledge of innocent contenders. With Claire Trevor in a polished portrayal of an over-ambitious mother of an amateur tennis champion, brilliantly played by Sally Forrest, the production is powerful in its appeal to the distaff element.[1]

Others complained of a generic misfit in the combination of maternal melodrama and social criticism:

The film ignores most of the opportunities for satirical comment on the occasionally odd interpretations of amateurism in sport and concentrates on a rather novelettish study of the relationship between mother and daughter.[2]

The apparent incongruity of the film's title was noted by *Time* ("a title that conjures up visions of a wanton wench on the marquee"), but not its possible linkage with the spectacle of the athletic female body ("...turns out to apply to nothing more alluring than a tennis ball")[3] – let alone with the phantasmatic figure of the powerful mother. Where the film's source, a 1931 novel by John R Tunis, had foregrounded the dilemma of a *Mother of a Champion*, its screen adaptation was titled with a trio of adjectives ostensibly suggesting sex.

To those familiar with Lupino's œuvre, this suggestion comes twice as hard – echoing the 1943 melodrama, *The Hard Way* (Vincent Sherman, Warner Bros.), in which her character exploits the beauty of a younger sister to escape a tough mining town for show business. As Jeanine Basinger reminds us, the three words of that title are superimposed, not over the mean streets of the sisters' origins, but on the torso of an unidentified woman, "a set of breasts, shoulders, and fingernails"[4] meretriciously adorned with jewels, orchids and fur.

In the scenes which follow, we discover that this expensively clad figure has parlayed her sister's "natural resources" into Broadway stardom. But the *Hard Way* to Broadway requires the destruction of both women's marriages, as well as the career of a rival actress. The maternal function performed by the older sister in furthering her sibling's success is very like that of the madam, enriching herself by supplanting affective relations with those of commerce, by becoming – in the crudest sense – "hard".

Nine years after *The Hard Way* came *Hard, Fast and Beautiful*, and its remarkably similar story of a mother whose ambitions for her daughter threaten both her own marriage and that of her child. This

75

time, however, Lupino was the director rather than the lead, and the daughter's career not show business but sport. Between the two productions Simone de Beauvoir published *The Second Sex*, with its observations on the mother's idealisation of the daughter "she regards as her double",[5] as well as its provocative comparison of the cinema star and the courtesan – the latter "perhaps less a slave than the woman who makes a career of pleasing the public".[6] But if the female performer could already be identified with the prostitute, *Hard, Fast and Beautiful* extended *The Hard Way* to the woman athlete, whose amateur status becomes an object of the economic pressure seen to bear down on all aspects of American life.

Such pressure is pervasive in the maternal melodrama, whose struggling heroines typically strive for "something better" for their daughters. In *Hard, Fast and Beautiful* Milly Farley recalls this aspiration in her opening voice-over, addressed to the teenage girl hitting tennis balls against the garage door:

> From the very moment you were born, I knew you were different. I could see things in you that no one else could. And I knew that somehow I was going to get the very best there was out of life for you. Listening to you drive that ball used to drive me crazy. That's because I always wanted something better for you. And I made up my mind to get it, no matter what I had to do.

Milly is not visible until, at the end of her second sentence, the scene changes to her trimming the fabric of Florence's evening dress. As Ronnie Scheib[7] and Wendy Dozoretz[8] have stressed, the dissolve from the athletic daughter to the ambitious mother, busily fitting the dress to its "dummy", suggests that Florence's youthful energies will be brought under maternal identification and control. But the mutuality of their endeavours is also indicated by what the girl is aiming *at* – painted numbers at which she directs the ball, just as her mother tailors the dress to the requirements of the dummy and the paper pattern. From the outset, sport in this film is no more an act of spontaneous physical exuberance than sewing.

Like her mother's housework, the daughter's tennis practice is performed in an ostensibly free domestic space which is revealed to be as rigorously delimited as the chessboard which stands at her father's side when he listens to a radio broadcast of her match. The Farley home is divided between the contending parents, who even sleep facing apart on twin beds whose central headboard barrier could almost parody the Hays Code restrictions on conjugal intimacy. When, early in the film, they retire to their separate beds while discussing Florence's future, a close-up centres the headboard to split the screen, and the couple, as each speaks and reacts antagonistically to the other. Similarly, Florence and Gordon are twice separated in their initial encounter: by the picket fence which surrounds the Farley property, and by the cuckoo which suddenly emerges from its own little clock-house to fly between them. Finally, the garage door against which Florence rallies is divided into squares whose numbers anticipate the figures which will be offered to her in illicit payments. To hit each number as she calls it out, Florence adjusts her stance to "angle" her shot – just as her agent will play the "million angles" of financial opportunity opened up by her tennis success.

Thus, despite postwar aspirations for a suburban haven away from the pressured environs of the workplace, with sport as a form of recreative play on its grassy lawns and paved driveways, the opening scenes of *Hard, Fast and Beautiful* mark out its domestic *mise en scène* as one of contention and commerce. The frustrated Milly Farley has married at seventeen to escape privation, only to end up in a cramped house in Santa Monica with an unmarried daughter and a husband unable (and seemingly unwilling) to earn their way out to the classier precincts of the Pacific Palisades. In the face of Will Farley's apparent economic passivity (his employment is never seen or discussed), Milly takes over the paternal function – albeit in the vicarious manner with which she choreographs her daughter's personal life and career.

This pseudo-economic role seems the only one available to a woman in Milly's circumstances. Unlike her most celebrated cinema antecedent (and near namesake) Mildred Pierce, the diminutive "Milly" does not move formally into the sphere of commodity production by, for example, becoming a dressmaker or restaurateur. Instead, she seems to welcome commerce into the home, greeting the nephew of a prominent figure as a potentially advantageous match for her daughter, then the local businessman and country club president when he arrives to ask Florence to tour with the club's team, and finally the entrepreneur Fletcher Locke when he seeks permission to enter her in the national championships.

If this vicarious economic activity demonstrates the difference between the working woman of wartime and her housewife successor, it is not the argument of this film that the latter is exempted from commodity relations. On the contrary, Milly's dependence on Will encourages her to be constantly "at" him to improve the family's fortunes: in order to keep house she must be able to purchase the goods of postwar expansion. The key commodity here is, of course, the car (to which the title *Hard, Fast and Beautiful* might also apply), the new car which Florence's success will enable Milly to buy in the face of her husband's objections.

This is the California that inspired Theodor Adorno's *Minima Moralia* (written in Los Angeles during his 1940s exile there and published in the year of this film's release), whose habitations are described as "factory sites that have strayed into the consumption sphere"[9] and whose "leisure" pursuits are equally industrious.[10] Modern sports, Adorno cautions elsewhere, "seek to restore to the body some of the functions of which the machine has deprived it. But they do so only in order to train men all the more inexorably to serve the machine."[11]

To dramatise this striking convergence of work and play, industry and domesticity, there could be no better sport than the seemingly genteel game of tennis. The modern competition has evident precedents in the ball games of antiquity and the 16th century development of "real tennis", but their Victorian successor was launched as an unabashed commodity by its devisor, Major Walter Clopton Wingfield. Lawn tennis or "sphairistike" (as Wingfield christened it in a Greek locution freighted with a mercantile culture's fantasy of the nobler ideals of ancient athletics) was introduced at a party given by the Major in December 1873. By the following February, this gentleman-at-arms in the court of Queen Victoria had patented the game, its name and its equipment (nets, posts, rackets and balls), which were sold in a boxed set exclusively from Messrs French & Co of Pimlico for the not inconsiderable sum of five guineas.

The price suggests the intended market for Major Wingfield's product: the middle class, enriched by industry and recently possessed of country houses with extensive lawns. More athletic than croquet, but sufficiently gentle for the ladies, tennis became the new pastime of the new class, with a dress code (white outfits from the 1880s), an absence of physical contact and a disdain for time limits which wholly obscured the onerous labours on which its players' fortunes were founded. But if this sport was predicated on an almost wilful detachment from its material circumstances, the detachment which notoriously endows the commodity with its fetish character, it would not be so for long.

With the rapid rise of national and international competition came the prospect of full-time play, *paid* play on the exhibition circuit which the legendary French champion Suzanne Lenglen pioneered as early as 1926. Lenglen's decision to turn professional was regarded as scandalous in many quarters, but she replied with a telling criticism of the amateur rules, under which, she complained, "only a wealthy person can compete, and the fact of the matter is that only the wealthy people *do* compete".[12] Consequently, top amateurs, including the American star who supplanted Lenglen, Helen Wills Moody, were increasingly offered newspaper contracts and couture clothing, and more covertly rewarded with appearance fees for entering particular tournaments, and with "expenses" beyond the tiny maximum permitted by the amateur authorities.   "The only way now open for an amateur to avoid professionalism", wrote Wills Moody in 1931 – twenty years before *Hard, Fast and Beautiful* and thirty-seven before tennis finally went "open" – "is for him to be rolled in cotton wool and moth balls between tennis seasons".[13]

This contradictory combination of amateurism and professionalism – "shamateurism" as it became known – provoked particular difficulties for women players. If amateurism is understood as a form of devotion, an engagement in a pursuit for the love of it, tennis was also tailor-made for another form of love, the courtship rituals of the Victorian bourgeoisie, for whom its "matches", in twos and fours, were ideally structured. The latter gave the ladies an unprecedented entry into the sport, with the first women's singles championship played at Wimbledon only a decade after Major Wingfield's party, and three years later in the United States. But the culture which offered women an invitation into what became the pre-eminent professional sport of their sex would also inhibit their athleticism. As one commentator recently observed in a report on the current women's tour:

> I was constantly reminded of the balance that women were forced to strike between their ambition and society's expectations, between their determination to be unique – i.e., number one – and their wish to be "normal," between their desire to excel and their fear of losing their femininity.[14]

Two years before *Hard, Fast and Beautiful*, a player for whom the title might have been devised, Gertrude "Gorgeous Gussie" Moran, pushed those contradictions to their limits. Moran had reached the semi-finals of the US nationals in 1948, but she was more famous as the glamour girl of the tour, dating movie stars and releasing details of her 37-25-37½ measurements. For her 1949 Wimbledon debut, she asked tennis couturier Teddy Tinling for "something feminine".   His revolutionary creation was ultra-modest by today's standards, a white dress of satin-trimmed rayon hanging a few inches above the knee. Beneath it Moran wore the voluminous "panties" of the period, but edged for the first time with a tiny ribbon of lace. The result was a press sensation, record attendance figures, and an official Wimbledon rebuke to Tinling, for "unnecessarily attracting the eye to the sexual area".[15] On the eve of *Hard, Fast and Beautiful*, women's tennis did indeed have – notwithstanding *Time* – "a wanton wench on the marquee", and the film acknowledges this. In an allusion to the scandal, it includes a locker-room scene in which Florence's first opponent at the national junior championships shows off *her* lace-

79

trimmed panties to another player, who pronounces them "real wild". The incident, like the film's title, portrays tennis as an undeniably sexual spectacle.

Florence Farley enters this world as the classic ingénue – eager, unsophisticated, guileless. As her boyfriend Gordon McKay points out after their first match, she has *no backhand*. Florence will acquire this stroke under the tutelage of Fletcher Locke, described in the film as "a combination coach and promoter – if you know what I mean". (Milly knows, but innuendo is a language which Florence has yet to learn. The indirectness with which Fletcher is introduced underlines the deviousness which is his stock in trade.) A series of brief scenes, punctuated with montages of Florence's tournament play, establishes the links between her coach's financial contortions (accepting "backhanders" in exchange for Florence's favours) and her increasing expertise.

The series begins with Milly's voice ("It was hard, Florence, all the way, but my dream for you was coming true") over a montage of the girl in action at tournaments in New Jersey and Pennsylvania. (Lupino herself – in cap and dark glasses – is recognisable in a cut to a tournament audience.) After a loss to a reigning champion (in which the frightened Florence is literally marched on and off court by Fletcher and her mother), she is coldly instructed to "work" on her backhand. The next scene shows Florence, in a dark practice shirt, hitting backhands until a pan left reveals Fletcher shouting criticisms of her technique and insisting that Florence "do it until it's automatic". When the exhausted girl protests (in an echo of her mother's reproaches to Will) that she has been "at it and at it", the coach concedes a rest. A dissolve to a dark evening bag hints at the financial rewards of this forced labour, rewards which Fletcher outlines expansively to a smartly dressed Milly in the swish surroundings of a cocktail bar: "Hotel chains all over the world! Press syndicates! A million angles, and they all work!". The action returns to a brief scene of another tournament, and then to Fletcher drilling Florence again on her backhand ("Now let's do it until it's mechanical") while he sits and smokes. Two tournaments later, the series ends with a telling bedroom scene in which the pyjama-clad Florence sets aside the letters she has just written to Gordon and her father, dons an elaborate hat with a dark veil and strikes poses in the mirror.

Here we see Florence becoming, as Gordon will accuse her, "more like your mother every day". A marked departure from the sportswear she has favoured, the glamorous hat is the first garment to have anything in common with the gauzy evening dress which Milly has been preparing for her daughter since the film's beginning. The coy femininity with which Florence tries it on before the mirror is also that of her mother – a mask assumed as surely as Milly's own disguise of nail polish, dark glasses and elegant clothes. (In the absence of greater production values in this low-budget film,[16] the clothes which Milly continually sews, packs, recommends or poses in function not only as the film's central status symbols, but also as figures of deception, clothing as *costume*, the concealment of the "real self" which the popular wisdom of the 1950s endlessly counselled teenage girls like Florence to "be".)

In her analysis of another woman who assumed an exaggerated femininity to conceal her guilty appropriation of the masculine prerogative, Joan Riviere famously refused to exempt any "womanly" behaviour from the function of what she termed "masquerade".[17] It is not surprising that a film as interested in performance as this one, a film which is set next door to Hollywood and whose central character is clearly modelled on the pushy "stage mother", should foreground the performative aspect of femininity. What *is* remarkable is the connection it draws between the playing of this role, the playing of competitive sport, and work.

Florence learns her backhand, that difficult and deceptive stroke, by sheer, repetitive work. If modern sport, as Adorno argued, trains the weekend enthusiast to serve the machine, this film insists that the serious competitor must *become* a machine to win championships. The strangely mechanical quality of tennis, the metronomic tick-tock of its strokes and its comically "coercive"[18] swivel of the spectator's head to follow the ball, depend upon abilities which must also become "automatic". Like the cuckoo which springs from the clock to interrupt her first tête-à-tête with Gordon, or the wind-up dog she toys with as she later berates her mother, the practised Florence becomes something of an automaton – *hard, fast, beautiful* – machine-like in her strength and her speed, but also in a kind of patent prettiness. Where a more conventional story might have taken her athleticism as a departure from femininity, Lupino's film insists on the relation between the two.

Florence's mastery of the backhand is matched by her acquisition of other skills of indirection. (Her strategically delayed announcement to Gordon of their European wedding plans is one example. So, in a subsequent scene, is her newfound command of sarcasm.) The most emblematic of these skills is femininity, "womanliness" as a masquerade learned as mimetically from Milly as the high follow-through is from Locke. Florence's hat and veil, her beaded gown and elaborately decorated décolletage, are the costume of a new role, a form of simulation achieved through practice. In Florence's case the labour involved is sometimes made explicit: she can have the beaded gown, her mother explains, if she will just "pose for a few publicity pictures". Both sport and dressing up, those quintessential leisure pursuits, are revealed to be work. Together, these two forms of labour combine to produce the spectacle of the woman tennis star – athlete and erotic object. (The two terms are fatefully united on the engraved necklace which Gordon gives Florence: "I love you champ".)

However obscure to *Time*, the sexual discourse in this film is at the heart of its condemnation of commodity culture. As de Beauvoir argued in *The Second Sex*, the division between any female performer and the prostitute is at best uncertain:

> All occupations in which women are on exhibition can be used for gallantry...frequently a woman who goes before the public to earn her living is tempted to trade more intimately in her charms.[19]

If we (as de Beauvoir wryly notes of the misogynist Henri Millon de Montherlant) attempt to exempt female athletes from this objection ("by the independent exercising of the body they can win a spirit, a soul"),[20] the commercialization of sport makes them as vulnerable as any celebrity to the lure of treating "not only their bodies but their entire personalities as capital to be exploited".[21]

In *Hard, Fast and Beautiful* this function is significantly divided: Florence is exploited, not by herself, but by her mother. The taint of prostitution is displaced onto Milly, who conducts the film's financial transactions and keeps as much information as she can from her daughter. And unlike Sally Forrest, who brings the bruised innocence of Lupino's earlier heroines (the unwed mother in the 1949 *Not Wanted* and the polio victim in the 1950 *Never Fear*) to the role of Florence, Claire Trevor had her greatest successes in the role of prostitute (for which she won an Academy Award® nomination in *Dead End* (William Wyler, 1937) and the bar-room "moll" (her 1948 Academy Award®-winning performance in *Key Largo*, John Huston).[22]

Yet these apparently differing roles – of the naïve competitor and her controlling mother – have been aptly described as "two aspects of the same woman",[23] a splitting which enables the double entendre of the film's title: the virtues of the strong, swift athlete, and the vices of sexual experience and desire. At their most polarised, these are the characteristics of an extreme virginity and an extreme promiscuity – of impenetrable chastity and unfeeling corruption. They are also, and not insignificantly, figures of a transcendent masculinity and a grossly carnal femininity, the absence of the latter which – de Beauvoir argues – leads de Montherlant to exempt the female athlete from the opprobrium in which he holds women. Finally, in psychoanalytic terms, these ostensible antinomies are simply different stages in the sexual development of women.

In Freud's narrative of this development, children of both sexes share a phallic phase prior to puberty, in which "the little girl is a little man"[24] with a clitoral focus of erotic pleasure and a primary attachment to the mother she endows with a phallic perfection. In order to achieve "femininity" (in order to become the mother rather than desire her), the girl is faced with two tasks. She must transfer her erotic sensitivity from the (active) clitoris to the (passive) vagina and her object choice from the maternal to the paternal. This double move is said to originate in the girl's successive discovery of her own "castration" and that of her mother, with the former failing bitterly blamed on the latter:

> The turning away from the mother is accompanied by hostility; the attachment to the mother ends in hate... the more passionately a child loves its object the more sensitive does it become to disappointments and frustrations from that object....[25]

So profound a repudiation of the mother, and its psycho-functionalist defence, has attracted extensive feminist criticism, not least Wendy Dozoretz's elegy for "The Mother's Lost Voice in *Hard, Fast and Beautiful*":

> By the end of the film, the mother's place is totally subsumed by Gordon and Mr. Farley. They assume the positive characteristics of both mother and father, leaving no need for an actual mother. Accordingly, Mrs. Farley's voiceover disappears halfway through the film, a typical occurrence in films with female narrators.(17) Furthermore, Gordon literally replaces Mrs. Farley as Florence's voice.[26]

Countering Freud's account with a Chodorowian analysis emphasizing the durability of the girl's early attachment to her mother,[27] Dozoretz attributes the film's savage demolition of Milly Farley to the ideological imperatives of postwar familialism (under which Tunis's original story was revised not only to separate the ambitious mother from her daughter, but also to marry the latter off to Gordon).

Without denying the force of this reading, it should be noted that the film's denouement is hardly the "happy ending" that the RKO executives prescribed.[28] As at least one dissenting review complained, "Mom seems to be in for a beating in Hollywood these days".[29] And the severity of Milly's punishment is nowhere compensated for by Florence's nuptial joy. Instead, the daughter grimly confers the championship cup on the mother who "earned" it and disappears with Gordon from the screen. Far from representing some happy domesticity, the film's final shots stay in the stadium, where the abandoned Milly sits in the gathering darkness.

This humbling of the mother is not specific to *Hard, Fast and Beautiful* or to its era. As Ann Kaplan has observed, *Now, Voyager* (Irving Rapper, 1942) offers a precursor to Milly in the oppressive mother of Charlotte Vale.[30] Although Kaplan does not discuss Lupino's film, the similarity is notable. Like Milly, Mrs Vale speaks for her daughter and separates her from a lover, and, like her, she is in turn demoted through the double agency of a younger suitor and an older paternal figure, Dr Jaquith. (Kaplan notes that Dr Jaquith personifies the psychoanalytic ideology which later texts – including *Hard, Fast and Beautiful* – will simply assimilate.) Kaplan traces *Now, Voyager*'s subordination of the mother to its opposite – the phallic power attributed to the female parent in early childhood, and its phantasmatic revival as women entered the US workforce during the Second World War. The monstrous Mrs Vale is merely the obverse of the adored mother. The daughter's fear masks her desire, a longing which is made explicit in Kaplan's final film example, *Marnie* (Alfred Hitchcock, 1964) and recapitulated in that recent epitome of the woman's film, *The Piano* (Jane Campion, 1993).

This "arrested desire for the mother" takes us back to *Hard, Fast and Beautiful* and the complex connections it establishes between professionalism, prostitution and the maternal object. The film's manifest transgression – accepting money for amateur competition – is repeatedly associated with sexual misconduct. When Gordon is offered employment ghosting newspaper articles for Florence he replies, in one of the film's most conspicuous euphemisms: "What you're asking me to do is become something there's a name for, and it's not for me".

The name for the profession Gordon rejects is clearly not "ghostwriter" but "gigolo", the paid male sexual companion he fears becoming if Florence, rather than he, is the family breadwinner. Gordon, the poor relation of a wealthy family and temporary skivvy for the "impossible" club president ("What a way to make a living!"), is appalled by such a prospect. "Do I look like a ghost?", he demands indignantly. And, indeed, the film posits masculine subordination as potentially lethal. Florence's father, who has accepted the secondary status which Gordon refuses, becomes sicker and sicker during his family's absences, until he lies in hospital listening to his exhausted daughter struggling to retain her national championship. As the radio announcer comments "The champion is fighting for her life", and Fletcher declares to Milly, "She's fading fast", a cut to the hospital matches the father with Florence much as the film's earlier sequences identified her with her mother. But it is Milly herself who is the film's ultimate ghost, and its most vivid figure of prostitution.

The equation of the mother with the prostitute is the theme of

Freud's study of the compulsive attraction to women of ill repute. There he attributes this apparently bewildering passion to the Oedipal child's discovery of parental intercourse, and his (sic) jealous realisation "that the difference between his mother and a whore is not after all so very great, since basically they do the same thing".[31] This apprehension of maternal infidelity comes late to Florence Farley, for whom Fletcher and Milly form a far more sexual, and more secretive, couple than her parents. The high point of their conspiratorial romance occurs in the scene discussed earlier, when Fletcher regales a raptly attentive Milly with the aphrodisiac prospects of Florence's European earnings – a scene whose erotic tenor is signalled at its opening by his intimate foray into Milly's handbag in search of a lighter, and at its closing by his oleaginous compliment on her appearance.

Fletcher's wooing of Milly to ensure Florence's agreement to the tour underlies the convergence of economics and erotics in this film, a convergence which does not exclude its primary couple. At their climactic confrontation, Florence returns drunk to her London hotel suite at 4 am and accuses her mother of deliberately separating her from Gordon in order to play "it dirty for money". As Milly anxiously attempts to calm her daughter and help her undress for bed, Florence decries her situation in terms which further sexualize both her exploitation and the filial bond which facilitated it: "Then I'll finish the tour. I'll play the game the way you play it, for money. You've made our bed – now we'll both lie in it." Here the circuit of erotics, economics and athletics is closed, for to be "on the game", in the venerable English usage with which the London-born Lupino could not have been unfamiliar, is to be a prostitute.[32]

If the mother's breast is, in Freud's evocation, "the place where love and hunger meet",[33] the prostitute has been described as the point where "sexuality and exchange value coincide".[34] To Walter Benjamin, the prostitute represented the way in which "[T]he commodity attempts to look itself in the face. It celebrates its becoming human in the whore."[35] The cinema has had its share in this personification, from *Pandora's Box* (1929) to *Pretty Woman* (1990). However, as Mary Ann Doane has observed, the figure of the prostitute is far more common in art and literature than on film. Neither censorship nor notoriety wholly explains this scarcity, since the movie tart is almost invariably endowed with a heart. Yet, ironically, this rehabilitation of the prostitute may correspond with her obsolescence as a character. For *the* task of the cinema, in Doane's view, is to effect what she represents:

the humanization of the commodity. Perhaps this is why her literal representation in the cinema is unnecessary as such and the fascination with the figure of the prostitute declines in the twentieth century (in comparison with the obsessions of the nineteenth). The process of characterization now endows the commodity with speech, with emotions, with a moral psychology which strives to give the lie to both alienation and commodification.[36]

What is striking about *Hard, Fast and Beautiful* is its resistance to this project. Far from rendering commodification in any way congenial, it stresses its depredation of American family life. Intimacy is invaded, play is proletarianized and the female body bartered twice over – in athletic competition and sexual spectacle. What is worst is that the prostitute returns, not as a golden-hearted heroine, but as a *mother*. The fact that she sells not her own services but those of her daughter underlines the parasitism of an already vicarious enterprise, while the sexuality which she deploys to do so makes her both adulterous and incestuous.

That all this happens in the unlikely setting of a sport story only serves to emphasize the pervasiveness of exchange relations in this film. As its ending suggests, there is no other place to go. ("You can't fly home again, Milly", Will declares from his sickbed, calling to mind the domestic conflagration which greets the errant ladybird in the rhyme.) Florence disappears into an unrepresentable marriage with Gordon. Will sickens (and, in some critics' extrapolations,[37] dies). Fletcher pursues a new protégée. And Milly sits motionless in the dark stadium, arms folded iconically across her breast, her white garments and fair hair lit with a ghostly pallor.

Ironically, the film's intransigent (*hard and fast*) condemnation of commercial culture precludes the feminist endings which have been desired for it. Florence will no more be allowed "career and marriage", in Dozoretz's wish, than Milly will be permitted to finish her narration. In the first instance, the film's denunciation of exchange relations militates against the representation of emancipatory employment as effectively as it does that of domestic bliss. (When Florence and Milly finally return to Will, it is to a hospital, not to their home.) In the second instance, the termination of Milly's voice-over halfway through the film can itself be attributed to the commodification of culture.

The narration which the film, as a woman's picture, conventionally offers the mother (unlike Tunis's novel) and equally conventionally rescinds before the end (like *Mildred Pierce*), is not assigned to Will or Gordon. The first may sum up Milly's moral failings from his hospital bed ("You never gave love..."); the second may speak for Florence at her final press conference ("That's enough. Let's go home."). However, the narrative functions which Milly initially performs are assumed by the radio commentator who broadcasts Florence's tournaments. As the film's action shifts from the domestic sphere to a series of national tournaments, it is he (in an on-camera role for an actual sportscaster of the period, Arthur Little, Jr) who establishes time and place, recounts many of the film's most dramatic moments, and ultimately calls the score. In a move which appropriates Milly's story, while obliterating her enunciation, the mother's voice is literally *mediated*.

The formal advantages of this device are obvious. Writing the match commentator into the diegesis is an easy way to tell a sports story, and also to transform existing tournament footage intercut with shots of Forrest into some semblance of actual competition. But the move from the maternal to the media also consigns this story to the world of commercial spectacle – the stadium strewn with discarded programmes and newspapers which Milly, in a fate redolent of Dante, cannot leave.[38] There she sits, no longer a housewife, but no career woman either. Unable to return to a private life despoiled by commercial imperatives, but stranded in the public arena, Milly is the casualty of her age – an age which both incited and proscribed maternal ambition, and then turned the consequences of that conflict into its own statuesque (and manifestly commercial) spectacle, the sorrowful mother of melodrama, *hard, fast and beautiful*.

Notes

1   *Motion Picture Herald* 183: 8 (26 May 1951): 861.

2   *Monthly Film Bulletin* 18: 213 (1951): 347.

3   *Time* 6 June 1951.

4   Jeanine Basinger, *A Woman's View: How Hollywood Spoke to Women, 1930-1960* (New York: Alfred A Knopf, 1993): 436.

5   Simone de Beauvoir, *The Second Sex*, translated and edited by H M Parshley (Harmondsworth: Penguin Books, 1972): 533.

6   Ibid: 583.

7   Ronnie Scheib, "Ida Lupino: Auteuress", *Film Comment* 16: 1 (1980): 61.

8   Wendy Dozoretz, "The Mother's Lost Voice in *Hard, Fast and Beautiful*", *Wide Angle* 6: 3 (1984): 52.

9   Theodor Adorno, *Minima Moralia: Reflections from a Damaged Life* (1951), translated by E F N Jephcott (London: NLB, 1974): 38.

10 See Theodor Adorno, "Free time", in *The Culture Industry: Selected Essays on Mass Culture*, edited with an introduction by J M Bernstein (London: Routledge, 1991): 164: "Just as the term 'show business' is today taken utterly

seriously, the irony in the expression 'leisure industry' has now been quite forgotten".

[11] Theodor Adorno, "Veblen's Attack on Culture", in *Prisms*, trans. Samuel and Shierry Weber (Cambridge, MA: MIT Press, 1981): 81. See also Adorno's "Free time": 168: "The accepted reason for playing sport is that it makes believe that fitness itself is the sole, independent end of sport: whereas fitness for work is certainly one of the covert ends of sport".

[12] Quoted in Billie Jean King with Cynthia Starr, *We Have Come a Long Way: The Story of Women's Tennis* (New York and London: McGraw-Hill, 1988): 41.

[13] Quoted in ibid. Wills Moody's observation was made in the year that John R Tunis published *Mother of a Champion*.

[14] Michael Mewshaw, *Ladies of the Court: Grace and Disgrace on the Women's Tennis Tour* (London: Little, Brown and Co, 1993): 204-205. Mewshaw also discusses the deleterious effects of parental ambition on the players, particularly Jennifer Capriati and Mary Pierce. In today's multi-million-dollar game, however, the offending parents are *fathers*.

[15] John Haylett and Richard Evans, *The Illustrated Encyclopedia of World Tennis* (Basingstoke: Marshall Cavendish, 1989): 229.

[16] See *Saturday Review* 30 June 1951: "the shoestring budget keeps showing through, and the colorful backgrounds that might have been obtained for it with (I hate to say this) more money are simply not in evidence".

[17] See Joan Riviere, "Womanliness as a Masquerade" (1929), in Victor Burgin, James Donald and Cora Kaplan (eds), *Formations of Fantasy* (London: Methuen, 1986): 35-44.

[18] Sabrina Barton, in "'Crisscross': Paranoia and Projection in *Strangers on a Train*", *Camera Obscura* 25-26 (1991): 88, notes that in the famous tennis sequence in *Strangers on a Train* a "reverse angle of the spectators' heads rhythmically following the back-and-forth movement of the ball invites the film audience to laugh at their coerced looking".

[19] de Beauvoir: 579.

[20] Ibid: 233.

[21] Ibid: 580.

[22] Hank Whitemore, "My Life in Hollywood's Golden Age", *Parade Magazine* 20 February 1994: 14: "'See, Claire usually played the 'tough' girls.'"

[23] Scheib: 62.

[24] Sigmund Freud, "Femininity", *New Introductory Lectures on Psychoanalysis* (1933 [1932]), volume 2, Pelican Freud Library (Harmondsworth: Penguin Books, 1977): 151.

[25] Ibid: 155-157.

[26] Dozoretz: 56.

[27] See Nancy Chodorow, *The Reproduction of Mothering: Psychoanalysis and the Sociology of Gender* (Berkeley: University of California Press, 1978).

[28] Dozoretz cites a 28 March 1950 memo from producer William Fadiman to Gordon Youngman, insisting that "The screen play demands and requires a happy ending in which the heroine relinquishes any idea she might have had of turning professional and decides to marry the boy she has always loved".

[29] *The Commonweal* 54 (27 July 1951): 380.

[30] E Ann Kaplan, "Motherhood and Representation: From Postwar Freudian Figurations to Postmodernism", in E Ann Kaplan (ed), *Psychoanalysis & Cinema* (New York: Routledge, 1990): 128-142.

[31] Sigmund Freud, "A Special Type of Choice of Object Made by Men" (1910), *On Sexuality*, volume 7, Pelican Freud Library (Harmondsworth: Penguin Books, 1977): 238.

[32] This usage dates from at least the late 19th century, via the medieval meaning of "game" as "amorous sport or play" and "on the game" as an 18th century phrase for robbery. See the *Oxford English Dictionary*.

[33] Cited in Angela Carter, *The Sadeian Woman: An Exercise in Cultural History* (London: Virago, 1979): 134.

[34] Mary Ann Doane, *Femmes Fatales: Feminism, Film Theory, Psychoanalysis* (New York: Routledge, 1991): 265.

[35] Walter Benjamin, "Central Park", *New German Critique* 34 (1985): 42.

[36] Doane: 265.

[37] See, for example, Basinger: 435.

[38] That this is also the world of the film's director has not gone unremarked by Lupino's critics. See Barbara Koenig Quart, *Women Directors: The Emergence of a New Cinema* (New York and Westport, CT: Praeger, 1988): 27: "The anti-feminist content of her work becomes more explicit, and the gap between what Lupino herself did and the values she promulgated more dramatic....The unambitious, decent ordinariness of the average loving American family is pitted against the pursuit of the best, the competitiveness that Hollywood itself was made of, that the directors of these films lived by – and the kind of drive a woman like Lupino would have had to have".

The Hitch-Hiker (1953)

Lauren Rabinovitz

Once the pre-credit sequence warns the audience that "the facts are actual", the grim, gritty melodrama spins out its realistic "facts" in two murder-robberies accomplished by an anonymous hitch-hiker. His victims are the motorists who pick him up along the side of the highway. Newspaper headlines relay that there is a national manhunt for the killer, Emmett Myers. Unaware of the danger, two suburban husbands, out for a weekend of fishing, pick up the hitch-hiker. He holds them at gunpoint and forces them to drive him across the Mexican desert. The remainder of the film traces their journey down the Baja Peninsula towards the town of Santa Rosalia, where the killer plans to catch a ferry in order to escape. Along the way, he sadistically plays cat-and-mouse with his two captives, and they wait nervously for opportunities to escape during their numerous stops to buy food and petrol, to make minor car repairs, or to camp overnight. While the trio heads towards Santa Rosalia, the film periodically keeps the viewer apprised of the police dragnet as it closes in on the group. The police lure the killer into a trap with a false radio report received by the men on their car radio. As they move closer to their destination, the men attempt an escape but are recaptured. When the car breaks down, the three walk the final miles across the desert to Santa Rosalia. On the outskirts of town, the killer changes clothes with one of the hostages and sends him into the police trap. In the ensuing shoot-out, the kidnapped man is unharmed, and the other captive overpowers the real killer. The right man is arrested, and the freed hostages walk away arm-in-arm into the darkness.

* * *

Lupino's films, like those of Nicholas Ray, Sam Fuller, and Robert Aldrich, are very much the product of a postwar consciousness, left, in the disjunctive transition between trauma and a possibly even more traumatic return to normality, to reconstruct or re-destruct the suddenly tenuous connections between an alienated subjectivity and the too-stable structures through which it can no longer define itself.[1]

Not Wanted

Not Wanted

Never Fear

Never Fear

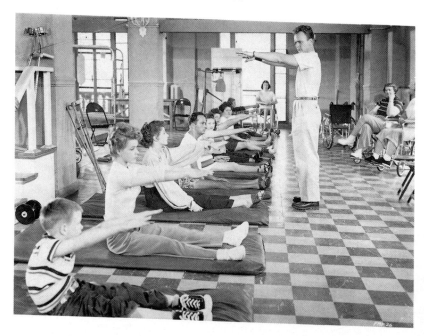

Never Fear

Outrage

Outrage

Hard, Fast and Beautiful

Hard, Fast and Beautiful

The Hitch-Hiker

The Hitch-Hiker

The Bigamist

The Bigamist

The Trouble With Angels

The Trouble With Angels

What is most interesting about her films are not her stories of unwed motherhood or the tribulations of career women, but the way in which she uses male actors: particularly in *The Bigamist* and *The Hitch-Hiker*, Lupino was able to reduce the male to the same sort of dangerous, irrational force that woman represented in most male-directed examples of Hollywood *film noir*.[2]

In the 1950s...there was a firm expectation (or as we would now say, 'role') that required men to grow up, marry and support their wives. To do anything else was less than grown-up, and the man who willfully deviated was judged to be somehow 'less than a man.' This expectation was supported by an enormous weight of expert opinion, moral sentiment and public bias, both within popular culture and the elite centers of academic wisdom.[3]

* * *

The few film critics who have taken Ida Lupino's films seriously, such as Ronnie Scheib and Richard Koszarski, note as a common thread not the women of her plots but her *male* characters – who are restless, anxious but unable to alter their fates, unable either to remake the structures through which they lead their lives or effectively to reconfigure their places within them. Ronnie Scheib suggests that Lupino's films are about the "essential passivity of ready-made lives". Nowhere is this more emphatically so than in the films Lupino directed in the early 1950s, which are usually considered to be her best work.

Within this constellation of films, however, *The Hitch-Hiker* (1953) is a particularly troublesome entry for those who have attempted to resuscitate Lupino's auteurist reputation, and especially her reputation as a feminist or at least a protofeminist director. How does one critically explain a woman's sensibility in a film that features no female characters and no typically feminine situations? In an all-male film, how does one excavate a pro-feminist auteur when there is no masculine-feminine tension and an absence of male heterosexual desire? In this instance it is impossible to resort to comparisons with Dorothy Arzner, the Hollywood director of the 1930s and 1940s whose auteurism was significant for first-generation feminists because she subverted women's gender prescriptions and sensitively hinted at social critiques in her melodramas that focused on women's lives, spaces and occupations.[4] Nor is it possible to compare Lupino's 'B' movie portrayal of suburban husbands on a weekend fishing trip gone awry with any of the female independent documentary and feature directors of the 1950s and 1960s

(Shirley Clarke and Helen Levitt, for example) in the quest for a woman's identification with socially alienated "Others", such as Beats, drug addicts, juvenile delinquents or African-Americans.[5]

What Lupino offers in *The Hitch-Hiker* is a vision of hell that is masculinity fragmented into neurotic components of maladjustment in a world that orders adjustment. It is the story of two middle-class, married Second World War veterans on a fishing holiday who pick up a hitch-hiker, a killer on the loose, who forces them to drive him across the Mexican desert. Its rhythms are those of a three-way dance of death, a *No Exit* of masculinity confronting its constituent parts as the film alternates between the claustrophobia of the men trapped inside the moving vehicle and wide-angle exterior shots of the vehicle moving through the desert wasteland of northern Mexico. In this scenario, two conformist husbands must confront their own conformity as it is pitted against the pathological deviancy of the killer. *Their* normality, however, likewise comes under scrutiny and investigation, since their presence in the barren landscape – a world outside the order of suburbia – is made possible only because they seek flight from their normal world. Lupino's forte here is that the manifest content of the film is less a crisis in postwar masculinity than a suspenseful film noir ideologically organised through a cultural crisis in masculinity where the protagonists, by confronting the masculinity run amok of a psychopathic killer, must face (or avoid) what they fear most – their own desire to revolt.

What is all the more interesting is that if US Cold War culture generally depended upon a plethora of medical and scientific experts to identify, define and pathologize (through psychology and sociology) the narrow parameters of normal masculinity according to rigid gender roles, Lupino's film depends no less upon the same expertise to define the realism of its case. *The Hitch-Hiker* was based on a notorious real-life case, that of William Edward Cook Jr, a 22-year-old Missouri ex-convict who killed six people on a murder spree while hitch-hiking in the Southwest in December 1950. His victims included a family of five held hostage for three days, and a travelling salesman from Seattle. He was eventually captured by Mexican police at Santa Rosalia (the same location used for the final destination and capture in the film) in the Baja Peninsula, together with two El Centro, California prospectors he had kidnapped, taken prisoner, and forced to drive him across Mexico. Cook's crimes, capture, subsequent trial, and death a year later in the California gas chamber were all covered in detail by the major news magazines of the day – *Time, Newsweek, Life* – and by wire services that sent the stories to local newspapers across the country.[6] Newspaper headlines labelled Cook a "desperado", and *Time* called him a "desperado [who] would just as soon kill".[7] Indeed, Cook's story was so well-known and his notoriety so great that when he died in December 1952, a rather ghoulish but enterprising undertaker in Oklahoma obtained legal claim to the body from Cook's "ne'er-do-well" father and put it on display for an admission charge before burying it.[8]

Cook and the roots or causes of his criminal acts became a subject for much speculation among both journalists and psychology experts. For example, *Time* laid out Cook's story twice for its readers: once upon his capture in January 1951 and again in December 1952 when he died in the gas chamber.[9] In the former story, he was dubbed the "young man with a gun" and the manhunt for him likened to the one for gangster John Dillinger in the 1930s. Both stories reiterate the details of his childhood, providing a ready-made explanation for his life in crime and deviant behaviour. Cook and his seven brothers and sisters were abandoned by his father in a deserted mine cave when he was five. Without the nurturing environment of a middle-class family, he eventually spent his adolescence in reform schools and then ended up in the state penitentiary: "Most of [his siblings] found foster parents, but only 'the county' would take William, a small, ugly child with a deformed right eyelid. William bit like a caged wildcat at the institutional hand that fed him. When the county put him in a boarding home, he threw tantrums and complained.... At twelve, he quit school; when he was hauled before a judge he sullenly asked to be sent to the reformatory."[10] The emblem for his past was summed up in tattooed letters on the knuckles of his left hand: HARD LUCK.[11] The rhetoric credits both the environment and a bestial nature as the cause for his decline, the outcome of which is reflected in Cook's words at the time of his arrest: "I hate everybody's guts and everybody hates mine".[12] It is a succinct statement of a boy-turned-psychopath.

The photojournal *Life* depended upon the same information and cause-and-effect criminal psychologizing, but outdid *Time*. With its voracious need for visual material as the predominant means for representation, it photographically narrativized Cook's life and crimes.[13] *Life* displayed a photograph of a hand with the letters H-A-R-D L-U-C-K imprinted on the knuckles over two thirds of a page, and pictured Cook in a mug shot from his reform school days. It began his story with "He was born in penury" and traced the origins of Cook's misanthropy to his mother's death when he was a young child. The narrative of Cook's abandonment is similar to the one that *Time* ran, except that the small, ugly child sent to the county home is here a "resentful, squinty-eyed 5 year old" whom "no one wanted".[14] It ended the Cook story with a full-page photograph of him in close-up being restrained at the throat and surrounded. His face and hands are prominently highlighted. His wrists are in shackles, and his face, with one eye closed, stares out blankly.

In between the story of his youth and his capture are three pages of photographs of the victims in a family portrait – their family home, their car, the site where the bodies were found, their next of kin, their coffins at the cemetery – as well as photos of the other murder victim and released hostages, law enforcement officials who aided in the manhunt, and Cook's elderly father. The portrayal of the victims' life represents what was missing in Cook's life, a conclusion further elaborated by the article's author, who calls Cook's multiple murder "a savagely symbolic and probably unconscious gesture of revenge on the family life he himself had never had".[15] Nowhere does Cook himself articulate such a self-aware motive for killing the family of five, either at the time of his capture or during the trial coverage. However, at a time when juvenile delinquency was increasingly popularized as the result of inadequate family attentiveness, and particularly as a loss of maternal nurturing, the events of Cook's life fit neatly into current popular beliefs about the role of the family in developmental psychology, while also serving ideologically to reinforce the family as the structural centre for postwar America. A crime against the family achieves recognition as one of society's most heinous acts.

Lupino and co-screenwriter Collier Young relied upon Cook's story as it was constructed in public discourse for the basis of their film. Throughout the film, the same geographical locations repeat Cook's trail. Over the opening credits a car pulls alongside the highway to pick up the anonymous hitch-hiker who is seen only in shadow and from the legs down; and, before the car drives away, the camera tracks in to a close-up of the rear licence plate that prominently displays its state of origin: Illinois. Such information serves no narrative purpose here and only provides an intertextual reference to Cook's murdered family whose Illinois residency was well-established in the press.

It is interesting, however, that if Cook murdered an Illinois family of five, Lupino and Young reconfigure the victims as a young couple – a man and a woman. These victims are glimpsed only briefly in long shot as the car pulls away. Their primary cinematic inscription occurs not through their visual incorporation into the film but through the screams of a woman on the soundtrack that accompany a shot of the anonymous hitch-hiker holding the raised gun. We then see and hear the gun fired and watch a handbag fall to the ground beside the car whereupon the gunman's hands rifle through it for money. The female voice saturates the soundtrack and effectively contrasts the inscription of the gun as a malevolent object enunciated through its unified acoustical and visual agency. In the final shot in the sequence, a flashlight's white beam of light travels across the side of a car at night to focus on and to highlight the splayed legs of the woman and to pan up and across her still torso to the limp hand of her male partner on the steering wheel. The image spins out in a sequence of three front-page newspaper banner headlines: "Couple Found Murdered", "Nationwide Search for Hitch-Hike Slayer", "Ex-Convict Myers Suspected in Hitchhike Atrocities" with a photographic portrait of actor William Talman. The children from the original family have become wholly unrepresentable, and the cruel attack on the family becomes displaced in the film as an attack on heterosexual partners.

The next sequence shows a second murder-robbery, a second crime that duplicates Cook's, its cinematic retelling a duplicate of the iconic style of presentation of the first crime. A car stops along a sunlit highway, a man leans across and beckons from the passenger side of the car, the anonymous hitch-hiker gets in, and the car pulls off. The image dissolves to an extreme long shot of the headlights cutting through the desert at night and then to a night-time point of view shot of the road from the car's front seat. Then, a man holding a gun crouches over a dead man's body and rifles through the victim's wallet. The camera tracks with him as he walks to the car, gets in and drives away.

These two murders establish an intertextual framework as an important prelude of realist referentiality for the only significant change that the film effects – turning Cook's kidnapped victim-prospectors into middle-class husbands on a weekend getaway.[16] Thus, the shots that immediately follow of Gil and Roy in the front seat of their car revolve around their discussion of leisure in homosocial bonding rather than in the signification of their identities through their labour or work. Gil and Roy choose a destination different from the one they told their wives, implying that they are embarking on a new route for the sheer thrill of defying the women they left behind. But this rebellion is quite tame, since, as Roy notes, their new destination still offers only fishing and no other entertainment. Roy reminisces about their adventures together at a border town bar and girlie show before they were married, suggesting that they reacquaint themselves with the saloon on their way to the fishing site. Gil reluctantly agrees, and then says wistfully that this is the first time – except during the war – that he has been away from his wife and children. In short order, the men's self-identities are established in relationship to wives and family, and their desire organised through a binary opposition of carefree bachelorhood and the responsibilities of marriage. The point is visually underscored when the car reaches Mexicali, the border town whose night-time neon signs of bars and strip-tease joints alternate with close-ups of Roy's beaming face from the interior of the car. Sticking his head in the car window, a local invites the men into a nearby bar to watch a woman dancer. Roy is interested but Gil is now asleep, and so he drives out of town.

Even before meeting the hitch-hiker, Gil and Roy are figures in flight from their family responsibilities. They are representative of what

Barbara Ehrenreich calls the "breadwinner ethic", an adult masculinity indistinguishable from the familial economic role.[17] In the early 1950s any man who did not achieve "breadwinner" status acquired the taint of homosexuality, a man neither fully masculine nor mature. When masculinity itself was tied to such a rigid gender categorization, there was an inevitable rebellion. Ehrenreich describes the forms of such a male revolt against the constraints of patriarchal identification either in the corporate absorption ("the gray flannel suit") or through methods of escape into alcoholism, adultery and/or popular culture (movies, the pulp novels of Mickey Spillane, westerns).[18] The weekend fishing holiday of fraternity becomes yet another means of escape, a structure of containment that allows for temporary flight from and abandonment of the "breadwinner" identity for a defined period of carnivalesque revelry.

While there is a significant difference between Myers's active murderous revolt and the two husbands' more contained rebellion, it is through the contrasts and similarities between the two that *The Hitch-Hiker* is able to remake Cook's highly publicised crime against the family into an investigation into the tensions of masculinity in postwar America. Certainly the film sets up Myers/Cook as a figure of "deviant" manhood, masculinity run amok, because, as a killer on the loose, he is marked consistently at the level of plot and narrative as socially "deviant". But what is expressed through the inscription of cultural values specific to the 1950s is that such social deviance is a condition of the same conflations between sexual and gender expectations as those about which Roy and Gil offer some long repressed doubts.

Here, the hitch-hiker as such becomes an apt metaphor for the masculine figure ungrounded in either familial or suburban structures – a solitary, rootless, nomadic man. The viewer's first glimpses of him are as an anonymous elongated shadow on the highway. The first inscription of the hitch-hiker's physical likeness occurs not along the road or in a car – his "natural" terrain – but as a "wanted" photograph that stares out from the front page of a newspaper. It is a frozen image detached from any semblance of such naturalistic effects as motion or gesture.

It becomes interesting to note therefore that the hitch-hiker becomes a specifically postwar construction. He is a shadowy figure, made possible through the new automobile highway system of the United States in the 1950s and dependent on a parasitic relationship to that system. He not only requires the transportation apparatus for his nomadic activities, his wandering; but also preys upon those who depend upon the highways – the travelling salesman (the man from Seattle killed by Cook); the family en route to a Christmas reunion; law enforcement officials who roam the roads surveying and regulating the highways; and the men in flight from their families.

However much Gil and Roy stand in contrast to Myers, the two husbands also represent a further contrast between each other. Their masculine difference from each other is not only quickly established in their contrasting reactions to their absence from their families and desire for women and drink. But once they pick up the hitch-hiker and identify themselves to their captor, they are further defined in class terms. Gil is a draughtsman whereas Roy is a mechanic. Even Myers understands that there is a distance between the two, and says as much to Gil: "That makes you smarter, or does it?". It is a biting retort about class hierarchy and the questionable possibility of becoming a member of the bourgeoisie.

The class difference between Gil and Roy – small as it may be – is important for articulating the parameters of the new masculine toughness and the men's troubled relationship to it. In this new world it is other people, rather than the material environment as such, that present problems. Thus, the ability to pay "close attention to the signals of others" – what David Riesman tagged in 1950 as "other-directedness" – became an important characteristic of the successful breadwinner.[19] While one could say that women are stereotypically supposed to be able to read others for emotional purpose, the "other-directedness" that Riesman widely spread as *the* desirable personality of the 1950s is not ever understood as such – that is to say, as feminine. Perhaps this is because other-directedness means restyling oneself to conform with others more than trying to meet another person's needs, more mimicry than responsiveness. Indeed, it was "other-directedness" that characterised the salesman/businessman as the stereotypically ideal personality of the 1950s. According to Ehrenreich, the "other-directedness" that characterised the breadwinner ethic simultaneously worked to devalue blue collar work (because this called for a man to work with his hands and so to have no need to practise skills of "other-directedness") while overvaluing white collar occupations as the successful product of the more mature, "other-directed" personality.[20] Such hierarchical categorization clearly spelled out and defined important boundaries for identifying a new professional-managerial class. While such class difference is not itself an indicator of difference in consumer power, it indicates the power of psychology and sociology in defining and supporting an ideology of idealised masculinity that was specifically class-tied. In *The Hitch-Hiker* this is an order to which one of the male protagonists, the one identified as the more deeply dissatisfied and neurotic, clearly does not belong. Although both protagonists are in flight, only Gil is coded as the "adequately" masculine hero of the film; and indeed it is his "other-directedness" that better enables him to read Myers like a book throughout the film. Thus, even within the articulation of the limitations of masculine conformity, the film provides more than one kind of disjuncture.

All this implies that the film is not a philosophical diatribe about the male's existential crisis of gender-rigid sexuality in the early 1950s, but that the terms by which the narrative evokes conflict and crisis are dependent upon values steeped in just such a crisis. It is this crisis that sets the terms for what constitutes conflict, identity and anxiety. To those critics of two decades later who were to wonder where in Ida Lupino's œuvre as a potentially feminist auteur a film containing no women at all could be fitted, the answer is simple. While this film does not actively critique gender roles, it does unsettle, and foreground the alienation of, rigidly defined gender roles for constituting binary sexualities of either masculinity or femininity. The remainder of the film articulates this nervousness about masculinity – through its *mise en scène*, characterisations and narrative.

Much of the men's flight across the desert alternates long shots or extreme long shots of the small car passing across and through the sun-drenched wasteland of the Mexican desert with close shots of the three men locked together in the interior of the car. Within conventions of classical Hollywood cinema, the drama of such a situation might be expected to build through increasing the pace of cutting between shots and reaction shots of the individuals. But here Lupino follows a more leisurely pattern of editing rhythms, one that corresponds with those more usually associated with melodrama. The very tight close-ups and the slow, even "sluggish" pacing (as Carrie Rickey dubbed it) allow facial expressions to build.[21] The stylisation conveys the importance of slow reactions and characters' faces as the symptomatic surfaces for interior psychological states. The editing style shifts emphasis from mounting suspense through crisp action to the strain on the characters of passively waiting.

The only things that happen in this film are the small breaks in the routine of the drive across the desert – stopping for supplies and petrol, evening camp-outs, a flat tyre. These are the moments where the three men must leave the car and where the tension of their confinement together in a claustrophobic space shifts to a wider field of action in which there are implicitly potential opportunities for escape. However, in each instance where escape is blocked, the wide spatial field is narrowed to a series of very tight close-ups between the men, reproducing the same constriction of space as in the interior scenes in the car. For example, after the first few stops to eat and to acquire a map, Myers turns the time spent outside the car into a psychological extension of the cramped hell of the interior. He forces a game of marksmanship onto Gil or insists that he will shoot Roy. Gil must shoot a can out of Roy's hand from a great distance, and while he prepares to do so, Myers taunts both men with the jeer that it is "just a game" and asks Gil, "Whatsamatter, you scared?". Gil's visible tenseness and agitation are reinforced by the delayed anticipation of Gil's shot and by the editing pattern which shortens the wide space separating the men into a series of tight facial close-ups that alternate between the three. Gil's success results not in any expressions of relief or satisfaction between any of the men but in a cross-cut between close-ups of Myers and Roy that produces menacing glares at each other. The challenge to Gil, who responds somewhat emotionally but nonetheless efficiently, is transformed into the beginning of an escalating emotional showdown between Myers and Roy.

A second stop in the journey functions similarly. The men get out of the car at a rural *abarrote* (small store) where they stock up on groceries while a small girl plays on the floor. Roy stops his lunge towards Myers when the girl gets in the way, and Gil picks her up and hugs her tightly. In a choked voice he tells her, "vaya con dios [go with God]". In response to Myers, he replies in an emotion-laden voice, "You wouldn't understand". The effect of this sequence, which emphasizes close-ups of Gil's distressed face, is that it brings Gil to the brink of emotional excitability. After this "break" involving the child, Gil reverses his responses; he becomes increasingly cool and vigilant, whereas Roy becomes progressively more agitated.

As Roy expresses greater frustration over their inactivity and the wait to be killed, killer Myers becomes more verbally menacing. When they camp out in the dark, Myers tells them, "You guys are soft....You're suckers! You're up to your necks in IOUs. You're scared to get out on your own." There is some truth in what he says, since their weekend trip is just such a limited attempt to get out on their own. Myers even reminds them later that they lied to their wives about where they were going, and he somewhat accurately suspects that they turned towards Mexico "for dames".

Roy's mounting frustration and his visible agitation may be seen as the product of Myers's escalating taunts and the flaunting of his deviancy. The more each is disconcerted by the picture of the other, the more each becomes driven by a menacing bravado. For Myers it is increasingly to bully Roy; and for Roy it is to assert impulsively to Gil that he is going to escape, to take action. Roy and Myers are linked by a code of machismo in which they both make desperate moves to show each other that they are men. But each move is either ineffectual or empty swaggering. Their play off each other and its escalating emotional expressivity counters Gil's trajectory from initial overwrought reactions to a more stoical presence.

Roy's descent into an increasingly edgy, neurotic manliness is merely the logical outcome of the behaviour of a man who nostalgically remembers the philandering days before his marriage and his current desire both to get away from home and to get drunk in a house of ill repute. It is Gil who advises Roy not to be impetuous and to think through their situation in a rational fashion. It is Gil, not Roy, who advises that they break the car radio so that Myers will not hear if the police have located them, thereby prompting Myers to "bump them off". It is Gil, not Roy, who leaves behind his watch at a petrol station as a clue that his wife will recognise. Gil is the man of responsibility in this situation, as well as Roy's protector. When Roy can take no more and angrily yells at Myers, "Why, you dirty –", it is Gil who knocks him out to prevent his being killed. In this way, Roy's repeated empty challenges to Myers appear immature. Compared with Gil, Roy does not exhibit important adult masculine characteristics, since, although it is a crisis, he is restless, anxious and constantly angry at their impotence.

Roy's descent into infantile regression is most pointed in a scene where the car's breakdown has forced them to walk across the desert. It is midday and they are resting among the rocks. When Roy spies an overhead plane, he jumps up. Dirty, bedraggled, and limping from a twisted ankle, he yells at the plane and tries ineffectually to catch the pilot's attention. Exhausted and overwrought, he collapses crying on the ground, and the high-angle overhead view of him reduces him physically to the state of a small, frustrated child.

His frustration about their passivity is the inversion of Myers's twisted logic of living by the gun as the ultimate means of being constantly powerful. Such a mirroring culminates in Myers's insistence that the two men switch clothing – that Roy become him. The physical transfer of their jackets and Roy's hat merely completes what the film has suggested all along – that Roy, too, is damaged goods. His adult role of brave self-assurance has been revealed as a pretence, a façade. Once he is in Myers's clothing, Roy taunts Myers, "You haven't got a thing without that gun. Without it, you're nothing." Myers tells him to shut up. In this exchange, which occurs during daylight on the rocky beach of Santa Rosalia, the men have come as far as they can go, both physically and psychologically. Roy's worst nightmare has come true: he must now act out the finale as Myers and his own psychic fear that lays bare the heart of this film – the fear that it will be found out that underneath he is not really "a man". The trip across the desert accomplished the stripping away of that façade, and it functions thus all the more effectively because, by contrast, Gil's façade has become strengthened.

The night-time finale occurs when Roy, dressed as Myers, walks out to the end of the pier to see whether the fishing boat in which Myers will escape is there or whether the police have laid a trap. The scene is less a suspenseful climax in the noir tradition than the denouement to a morality play. The Hades-like *mise en scène* is so dark that one can barely see the movements of the principals. Across the murky images of the pier and the water, the spectator can only focus on Roy saying, "I'm not Myers. Do you hear me? I'm not Myers". While Roy protests – ostensibly to the arresting police officers but theoretically also to himself – Gil punches the real Myers and heroically wrestles the gun away from him. Myers is caught and handcuffed by the police. Realising that he has been shackled, a spotlit Myers, in close-up, reacts hysterically. Only at this moment does Roy confront him and repeatedly beat him about the face. If the power roles have become reversed, the reversal functions to negate Roy's words "I'm not Myers" and to reveal the shared aspects of their natures – their violent outbursts, their hysteria when rendered impotent, and their bullying when they have the upper hand.

If the trip makes Roy come unglued and reduces him to an immature state of masculinity, it teaches Gil the emptiness of masculine toughness and that passivity is a capitulation to fatality. If Gil's façade remains intact, the lingering close-ups throughout the film register less his stoical fortitude than an increasing blankness, which may indeed also signify interior emptiness. That is to say, the lack of Gil's emotional responsiveness as the journey wears on is not "natural" for him, since, at their stop at the Mexican store, he showed an excess of "feminised" emotion as he tried to hold back tears and hugged a child in a spectacular burst of feeling. After this, his "empty" responses to each new situation outside the car are more a product of the journey itself. Waiting makes him less a heroic protagonist who is self-controlled, a solid citizen and man, and more a passive shell of endurance. As Ronnie Scheib says of Lupino's protagonists, "Passivity in Lupino's films is no comfortable sinking into despair, no well-fed suffering spiced with revolt or self-abnegation, but a stark, stock-still simultaneous inevitability and impossibility of consciousness".[22] Thus, in the concluding shot, Gil's final words, "It's all right now, Roy", as he wraps his arm protectively around his companion as they walk away into the darkness, ring particularly hollow. Within this threesome, there is no heroic manly way out.

* * *

My gratitude to Alison MacCracken for research assistance.

Notes

[1] Ronnie Scheib, "Ida Lupino: Auteuress", *Film Comment* 16: 1 (1980): 55.

[2] Richard Koszarski (ed), *Hollywood Directors 1941-1976* (New York: Oxford University Press, 1977): 371.

[3] Barbara Ehrenreich, *The Hearts of Men: American Dreams and the Flight from Commitment* (New York: Doubleday, 1983): 11-12.

[4] In this capacity, the landmark publication was Claire Johnston (ed), *The Work of Dorothy Arzner: Towards a Feminist Cinema* (London: British Film Institute, 1975).

[5] For a discussion of such women filmmakers (emphasizing Shirley Clarke) see Lauren Rabinovitz, *Points of Resistance: Women, Power & Politics in the New York Avant-garde Cinema, 1943-71* (Champaign: University of Illinois Press, 1991), particularly 92-149.

[6] See, especially: "Young Man with a Gun", *Time* 22 January 1951: 19-20; "Killer on a rampage", *Newsweek* 22 January 1951: 21; "The Kid with the Bad Eye", *Life* 30: 5 (29 January 1951): 17-21.

[7] See, in particular: Gladwin Hill, "Desperado Seized, Called Killer of 8", *The New York Times* 16 January 1951: 2; "Desperado Admits Killing Family of 5", *The New York Times* 20 January 1951: 8; "Young Man with a Gun": 20.

[8] "Billy's Last Fling", *Time* 29 December 1952: 15.

[9] "Young Man with a Gun": 19-20; "Billy's Last Words", *Time* 22 December 1952: 18.

[10] "Young Man with a Gun": 19-20.

[11] Ibid: 20.

[12] "Billy's Last Words": 18.

[13] "The Kid with the Bad Eye": 17-21.

[14] Ibid: 17.

[15] Ibid: 18.

[16] The film even duplicates Cook's deformed right eyelid, which the prospectors said made it impossible for them to tell when he was asleep. This very detail also becomes a plot element in *The Hitch-Hiker*.

[17] Ehrenreich: 30.

[18] Ibid: 14-41.

[19] David Riesman, *The Lonely Crowd: A Study of the Changing American Character* (New Haven: Yale University Press, 1950): 21.

[20] Ehrenreich: 33-35.

[21] Carrie Rickey, "Lupino Noir", *Village Voice* 29 October-4 November 1980: 45.

[22] Scheib: 57.

The Bigamist (1953)

Ellen Seiter

San Francisco. Social worker Mr Jordan interviews Eve and Harry
Graham about their application to adopt a child. As they conclude the
discussion, he gives the couple one last form to sign, one which grants
the agency permission "to check into every detail of your private life".
After the Grahams leave, Mr Jordan reports into his dictaphone – the
Grahams have been married eight years, income $20 000 a year, work
in company owned by the Grahams, Mrs Graham very capable – but
something seems odd about Mr Graham and his hesitation to sign the
release form. When the cleaning woman, who has been eavesdropping
on Mr Jordan while she cleans his office, accuses him of being an old
fusspot, Mr Jordan tells her that he once made a mistake and now
believes he "can't be too thorough" where a child is concerned.

At home, Eve wakes Harry from an afternoon nap to show him a
toy soldier she has bought for the child she hopes to adopt. She
wonders if Harry has had any second thoughts, having noticed that his
behaviour was a little strange in the social worker's office. He assures
her that he wants the child, if she does. They embrace tenderly and Eve
wistfully recalls "other Saturday afternoons like this". Dinner guests are
coming that evening and she urges Harry to dress.

Later Mr Jordan drops in to visit Harry at the couple's glamorous
high-rise apartment. Mr Jordan questions Harry about his business
associates in Los Angeles, where he often travels on business. Harry is
openly resentful of Mr Jordan's intrusions. Eve arrives home carrying
shopping and warmly welcomes Mr Jordan. After Mr Jordan leaves it
is time for Harry to prepare to depart for a business trip to Los Angeles
the next day. Eve offers to pack for him, teasing him about why he
never brings home dirty laundry or needs any buttons sewn on his
shirts. Harry seems uncomfortable, answering that he has found a good
laundry in Los Angeles and leaves his things there.

Los Angeles. Mr Jordan pays a surprise visit to Harry's office.
Harry is out and Mr Jordan asks the secretary to find out which hotel he
is staying at. A co-worker wanders by, offering some hard liquor to
celebrate the coming of Friday afternoon. He refers to Harry jokingly
as "Mr Exclusive" and "The Invisible Man", because he is never seen at
hotels, restaurants or nightclubs in town. After some time on the

telephone, the secretary tells Mr Jordan that Harry is not registered at any of the usual hotels, and that the hotel clerks reported that they had not seen Harry Graham for several months.

Mr Jordan finds the address for a Harrison Graham in the telephone book and takes a taxi there. Harry answers the door, looking haggard. He tries to end the conversation hurriedly, suggesting they meet for lunch the following day, when suddenly a baby's cry rings out from the back of the house. Mr Jordan follows Harry into the house where he tenderly comforts the baby and tucks him back in his cot. Mr Jordan's taxi begins honking. Harry urgently presses him to send the taxi away, blurting out, "My wife's been up two nights in a row with the baby". "How long has this double life of yours been going on?", Mr Jordan asks indignantly, "How could a man like you, successful, admired, get into a position as vile as this?". Harry begs for a chance to explain before Mr Jordan calls the police.

Harry's story begins four years earlier – at the time Eve first became a partner in the business, at his suggestion. Disappointed when the doctor informs her she cannot bear children, Eve has become distant, too focused on the business. Harry feels lonely, spending several weeks each month in Los Angeles. One day on a Hollywood bus tour of the stars' homes, he begins to flirt with a stranger, Phyllis Martin. Cool and sarcastic at first, Phyllis softens when she recognises Harry's loneliness. Harry begins spending time with her at the shabby Canton Café, where Phyllis works as a waitress. On his birthday Harry impulsively takes Phyllis on a quick trip to Acapulco, and sex presumably follows their evening at a nightclub. Afterwards, Harry resolves not to see Phyllis again. When he returns to San Francisco, Eve is packing for a trip to her parents' home – her father has had a heart attack. Harry gives her a diamond bracelet and reaffirms his commitment to their marriage. Eve tells Harry that she is ready to adopt a child and apologises for her emotional distance. Harry tells Eve he wants to hire another salesman for the travelling and stay at home full-time.

Harry remains in San Francisco for three months, taking care of the office while Eve is obliged to stay with her parents. Finally returning to Los Angeles on a brief trip, Harry stops in at the Canton Café, where he is told Phyllis is sick and has stopped working. When he goes to Phyllis's boarding-house to say goodbye, he discovers that she is pregnant. The doctor and landlady tell Harry how much Phyllis needs him. Phyllis insists that Harry has no obligation to her but he wants to get married. "I'll take care of everything", he tells Phyllis.

On the day Harry resolves to inform Eve of his predicament over the telephone, she calls him with the news that her father has just died. Later in San Francisco he tells Eve there are things they must talk about, but Eve presents Harry with her grandfather's watch and tells him how much the adopted child means to her. Henry becomes increasingly panicky after Phyllis gives birth to their son. When Eve flies to Los Angeles to surprise Harry for their wedding anniversary, neighbours spot Harry strolling with Eve on his arm. When Harry returns, Phyllis, thinking he is having an affair, kicks him out. Harry suggests to Phyllis that they should separate, but he immediately withdraws the idea when Phyllis asks him to stay.

When Harry ends his story, Mr Jordan is stunned and befuddled. "I admire you and yet I pity you", he tells Harry, "I don't even want to shake your hand and yet I almost wish you luck". Mr Jordan decides not to call the police. Harry leaves Phyllis a note revealing his marriage to Eve and leaves before she wakes in the morning. Back in San Francisco, Harry turns himself in to the police, saying a hurried goodbye to Eve and leaving his lawyer to explain everything to her. In the courtroom Eve and Phyllis watch as Harry is lectured by the judge, who takes the view that the situation is the result of a tragic mistake by a basically decent man. The question, according to the judge, is which woman will take him back. Sentencing is postponed. The courtroom empties, and Eve watches as Harry, still in custody, is led out by the police.

* * *

The Bigamist fuses two divergent genres: the film noir and the domestic melodrama. The investigative flashback structure of *The Bigamist*, its visual style, its despairing tone and its focus on the man's story suggest the noir tradition. The predicament facing the protagonist is the stuff of those melodramas of the 1930s and 1940s that focus on a lover's choice between two partners; however, the situation of bigamy, rather than courtship, presents such choice in a radically new light. The mixture of genres produces a particularly unsettling result: an exceptionally pessimistic view of marriage and domestic life, and a departure from the conventional representation of women in both genres.

Christine Gledhill has cited "the investigative structure of the narrative and plot devices of voice-over and flashback" among these features of film noir that "produce a specific location for women and somewhat ambiguous ideological effects".[1] *The Bigamist*'s narrative structure suggests its connections with noir: an investigation by an authority figure (albeit a social worker rather than a private detective or police officer) leads the film off. The title of the film informs us of the hero's guilt; we simply await its inexorable uncovering. The hero is paranoid, hunted, subjected to a surveillance that is certain to uncover his crime. Once Mr Jordan discovers Harry's second wife, the story is told using flashbacks narrated by Harry, an account of his escalating duplicity. His fall – precipitated by his relations with women – will be retold in the course of this flashback. Harry Graham is a hero well suited to film noir: a travelling salesman, not particularly intelligent or attractive, who is dependent on women.

As in other noir narrations, Harry's voice-over is full of despair and ennui. The voice-over is also riddled with resentment towards Eve for outstripping him in their business partnership, for being so "perfect". The undertone of hostility in Harry's voice-over belies his claims that the only thing he ever wanted was to make Eve (and later also Phyllis) happy: "It was my idea – coming in to the business. She caught on fast, so fast she doubled our sales in no time". Through the voice-over Harry shifts the guilt from himself to Eve, whose excessive involvement in the business, and inattention to Harry's emotional, psychological and sexual needs are presented as the cause of his tragic error – a single night of love with Phyllis. Harry's tone is sarcastic when he tells his business associates that Eve is "the perfect wife, good in the office, great in the home". "Eve was in one of her executive moods that night – career woman – you wouldn't recognise her, she's not like that now", he recalls about a dinner party where we witness Eve selling to a potential client – one that Harry had never been able to sell to. Harry sarcastically remarks to the dinner guests, "Didn't you know, Eve's the brains, I'm just the brawn?". Eve rushes in to contradict him: "I'm just Harry's little secretary", she claims disingenuously, shortly before giving an impressive description of the complex mechanical functioning of their new model of freezer. In another scene Harry telephones Eve from his lonely hotel room the day he meets Phyllis. "Eve was all business that night", Harry wearily complains.

Harry expects a sympathetic audience from Mr Jordan as he elaborates the premise of the film: the natural place for Eve is at home with a baby. Normally, film noir focuses its moral condemnation and alarmism on female sexuality; instead, in *The Bigamist* a therapeutic discourse – signified by the presence of the social worker as investigator – condemns Eve for being a bad wife, uninterested in the world of feelings. This therapeutic discourse is more typical of domestic melodrama than of film noir, but it is common to other Lupino films (*Outrage* and *The Hitch-Hiker*, for example). Harry's long evening's talk with Mr Jordan sounds like a marriage counselling session and, as a good therapist, Mr Jordan withholds moral judgment. The interrogation of the hero shifts to the interrogation of the heroine, herself denied a voice-over or other opportunity to narrate her side of the story, and thus the film seems to fall solidly within a noir tradition seeking to punish the woman heroine. Lupino's own remark that *The Bigamist* was "definitely...the man's story"[2] is an acknowledgement of this structural element.

Harry's flashback dichotomizes his life in San Francisco with Eve, where all scenes take place within bourgeois domestic space, and his life in Los Angeles, set in public, working-class milieux, such as restaurants, parks and city streets, some of them typical film noir settings. Although only one cinematographer, George Diskant, receives credit in the film, Lupino used two different cameramen to film the scenes of Eve in San Francisco and Phyllis in Los Angeles, according to Ronnie Scheib.[3] The Los Angeles scenes are suffused with urban alienation and despair. Harry's life as a travelling salesman is the tawdry shadow underside to Harry and Eve's glamorous upmarket apartment in San Francisco. Urban life is not depicted as threatening and dangerous, but as claustrophobic and lonely. "Have you spent half your life staying in hotels, eating in restaurants, walking the streets looking for a movie you haven't seen?", Harry asks Mr Jordan.

Harry takes the fateful bus tour of movie stars' homes only because "here were people going somewhere and I was going with them". While Phyllis tries to sleep, the driver chatters on about the excitement and glamour of the movie stars: starkly contrasting with the banality of real life. Exhausted from her job, she takes the tour just to get off her feet on her one day off work each week. As Carrie Rickey has noted, "Pick-ups are a leitmotif of a Lupino/Collier [sic] script: they always begin awkwardly and proceed in an excruciatingly laconic way".[4] Edmond O'Brien's performance as Harry abruptly changes direction here, as his depressive demeanour disappears and he suddenly becomes energetic, even leering. "This is the first time I've tried to pick up a girl", Harry tells Phyllis. "Well, you're learning fast", Phyllis replies sarcastically. After the bus tour ends, Phyllis says a quick goodbye, but Harry follows her: "There's something you should know about travelling salesmen: they have very large expense accounts and frequently buy dinner for pretty girls". While Harry's own account of himself is as an innocent victim of circumstance, he is seen here avidly pursuing Phyllis, something which contradicts his story that he merely stumbled into the affair.

Phyllis works as a waitress at the Canton Café, a failing Chinese restaurant owned by an Irishman, and lives at a seedy boarding-house. Both locations are extremely dark and lit in the low-key lighting style typical of film noir. Harry and Phyllis's courtship is set in an ethnic Los Angeles (unlike Eve's WASP petit bourgeois world) and watched over by Sam, the Chinese host at the restaurant (who interrupts their conversations to call Phyllis away to serve other customers) and Phyllis's British landlady. Phyllis and Harry's first kiss takes place at the boarding-house. Their faces are hardly seen, thus breaking the convention, noted by Virginia Wright Wexman, of the movie kiss as "a privileged moment of romantic bonding, the prelude to which is designed to foreground the emotional expressivity of the actor's face".[5] The kiss is followed by a low-angle shot of Phyllis ascending the stairs, the bars of the railing casting stark shadows across the set. On the fateful night when Phyllis becomes pregnant, the two of them have gone to Acapulco. The illegitimacy of their developing relationship is underscored by this association with racial and ethnic otherness. In contrast, Eve and Harry's relationship belongs exclusively to a white, bourgeois world.

Scenes of Harry alone in Los Angeles also mirror a noir visual style. Alone in his hotel room, Harry is silhouetted by neon signs flashing outside his window. Walking the streets of Los Angeles, he passes closed shopping districts with their frozen shopfront mannequins. The film's lighting is not consistently expressionistic – possibly due to the low budget and short shooting schedule. Instead, dim lighting creates a dreary darkness in all the domestic interiors, and claustrophobia is created by the repeated use of door and window frames and other enclosing structures. These elements run throughout Lupino's work, something that led critic Carrie Rickey to dub the films she directed "Lupino *noir*":

> The basic look of a Lupino movie is shabby genteel; the characters take buses; when they're on vacation they go fishing; when they eat out it's at a diner or lunch counter. ... They're ... all dreaming for Mr. Right to save them, only to discover painfully there's no Mr. Right. No other Hollywood movies of the time promoted such bitter wisdom. Not *film noir*, but Lupino *noir*: a dimly lit, low-budget world where everyone lives sadder-but-wiser-ever after.[6]

Missing from Lupino *noir* is the treacherous femme fatale, the unstable characterisation of the heroine, and the emphasis on sexuality in the photographing of women that Gledhill has also identified as typifying film noir.[7] Phyllis is tough and cynical. She describes herself as a farmer's daughter who "wanted to see the world". Her job, as a waitress in the Canton Café, is similar to those of other noir heroines, such as nightclub performers and hostesses, who work for a living and are paid to be attractive to the customers. Yet Phyllis is no sexual temptress, and the photography does not emphasize her body. Phyllis is the femme fatale hostess with every speck of glamour stripped away: struggling to make ends meet, living on the brink financially, and physically exhausted by her job of waiting at tables. Far from the evil castrating manipulative villainess, she turns out to be simply an intelligent, somewhat world-weary woman. There is no seduction here; only an evening with too much champagne. Throughout their relationship she has been straightforward and candid with Harry: "I don't want anything from you and I'm afraid of being in love again". Harry refers to her as "a funny little mouse" when telling Eve about her after their first encounter. When we see Phyllis after the night in Acapulco, she appears as nothing more than a poor woman in a scrape. She insists Harry has no responsibility to her: "Yes, it's yours if that's what you mean, but I don't trap my men that way". She wants the baby because she has never had anything of her own – and has feared telling Harry about it in case he might not want her to have it.

When more than one female character appears in film noir, the second woman usually serves as a basis for comparison with the femme fatale. The two women represent the good and bad sides of femininity – the one sexual, the other virginal; the one seductive and destructive, the other nurturing and passive. *The Bigamist* introduces Eve and Phyllis using some conventions of this noir representation of women, but, as the film progresses the differences between the two women are minimised. Visually and narratively, Eve and Phyllis appear at first to be the classic feminine noir duo. The domestic, loving, blonde wife juxtaposed with the mysterious, unattached, dark-haired mistress. Throughout the film Phyllis wears cinched waist dresses with flared, crinoline skirts. At work, her uniform consists of a tightly fitting embroidered silk Chinese jacket. Eve, on the other hand, dresses mostly in white and pearls, her hair tightly pulled back in a bun during her "career woman" phase, let down on her shoulders once she has decided to adopt a baby. Ultimately, however, the film fails to uncover any female duplicity. Rather, it reveals both women to be sincere and good-hearted, both extremely capable and strong, and wise in the ways of the world.

The Bigamist bears comparison with *Mildred Pierce* (Michael Curtiz, 1945), since both films share a mixture of elements from melodrama and film noir.[8] Eight years separate the two films, and each had radically different production circumstances. *Mildred Pierce* was a major studio production adapted from a best-selling novel; *The Bigamist* was a low-budget independent film. Yet, both films are preoccupied with the instability caused by career women who neglect the domestic sphere and misdirect their maternal energies. Both Mildred and Eve turn their homes into places of work, become far more successful at business than their husbands, and their success alienates their husbands. *The Bigamist*'s treatment of Los Angeles is indebted to the tradition of noir fiction set in that city epitomized by James M Cain, author of the novel *Mildred Pierce*. According to Los Angeles historian Mike Davis, the motifs of this fiction include "the moral phenomenology of the depraved or ruined middle classes...and the parasitical nature of Southern

California".[9] Both films portray two kinds of domestic world: a lower-middle-class home, and a much more glamorous, opulent one. In *The Bigamist* the lower-middle-class milieu, where the father has authority and the atmosphere is homey if unglamorous, is nevertheless tainted by its association with a venal Los Angeles – an association that helps to naturalize the inevitable breakup of Harry and Phyllis's home.

Bert in *Mildred Pierce* and Harry in *The Bigamist* are brothers of the postwar era film: underemployed, somewhat ineffectual, silently resentful of their wives' ambitions and dominance. Like Mildred, Eve Graham is guilty of having too much talent for business. The theme of emasculation is much milder in *The Bigamist*, partly due to the starkly different performance styles of Joan Fontaine and Joan Crawford (Fontaine is rather unbelievable as a castrating powerhouse). Emasculation nevertheless motivates Harry's effective departure from their home, just as it causes Bert to leave Mildred. Bert's humiliation and Mildred's transgression are exacerbated by her choice of the decadent, womanizing Monty – a professional man of leisure – as her lover. The dangers of women overpowering men was a discourse acute in 1945 when GIs were returning home from war. It had continued relevance throughout the 1950s when many women continued to work, often because two incomes were needed to maintain the level of consumerism the family desired. Mildred's ambition for her daughter Veda expresses itself as a need to provide nothing but the best of everything for her. In a similar vein, Eve ignores Harry's desperate plea that they go away together immediately – Eve prefers to wait and save: "Someday we'll go to all those glamorous places *Holiday* writes about, and we'll go first cabin, too".

Pam Cook has suggested that *Mildred Pierce* seems to be driven by the "historical need to re-construct an economy based on a division of labour by which men command the means of production and women remain within the family, in other words the need to re-construct a failing patriarchal order".[10] Cook has argued that in *Mildred Pierce* the resolution is achieved by replacing Mildred's point of view, told in the style of melodrama, with the patriarchal tones of film noir, in which she is found guilty and punished. *The Bigamist* seems to operate in the reverse fashion, replacing the noir world with melodrama, and translating Harry's account of his crime into a discourse on feelings. Because Eve and Phyllis are both sexually unthreatening (and both remain faithful to the bigamous Harry), the narrative does not demand the kind of interrogation or punishment of either woman that Mildred receives.

Film noir often lures its hero from the normalcy of the bourgeois family to the underworld with its evil and corruption. But Harry's "other" life in Los Angeles – his illicit, exciting one – gradually shifts from the world of restaurants and nightclubs to just another average-looking domestic scene. This is the crime: not murder, blackmail, drugs or extortion, just the keeping of one family too many. Thus, any expectations of a sexually charged, forbidden, exotic, criminal noir world – of the kind suggested by the Canton Café – are disappointed. When Mr Jordan arrives at Harry's door in Los Angeles, he walks in on a scene of stark, everyday domestic wear and tear. The baby is crying in the back; the wife is sleeping after being up all night. The living room is small and cluttered. There is nothing titillating about the discovery Mr Jordan makes: the very mundaneness of the scene is what proves so shocking.

The Bigamist shares with domestic melodrama and its most familiar form in contemporary media, the made-for-television movie, an exclusive focus on the problems besetting heterosexual couples, especially the difficulty of communication. Harry's voice-over highlights his own emotional desires and the ways these have been frustrated in marriage, as well as his own suffering in his attempt to avoid hurting either Phyllis or Eve. Like all good melodramas, *The Bigamist* relies heavily on coincidence in the timing of crucial narrative events, and these unlucky accidents serve to maximize the hero's distress. The predominance of facial close-ups and a musical track that punctuates the emotional import of phrases and events also place *The Bigamist* in the melodramatic tradition.

In many ways Harry embodies the conventional values of the domestic melodrama – as does the father in Lupino's *Hard, Fast and Beautiful*. But where the father in that film is pushed to the margins of his daughter's life by the overbearing mother, Harry holds the centre of *The Bigamist*. He narrates the emotional significance of events, expressing an overriding need for communication, companionship and togetherness with Eve. He desires to place emotional needs ahead of financial ones: "Let's go away together, Eve, it doesn't matter where as long as we're together!". The language of emotionalism permeates Harry's speech: "How can you hurt someone so much...?"; "I loved Eve but I never felt she needed me..."; "I loved Phyllis and that child. I hated to give them pain". By contrast, Eve and Phyllis are less sentimental. When Harry tells Eve, "It's no good being away from each other", Eve replies, "I didn't realise how much that meant to you". Phyllis is cast as a woman who has suffered for love in the past and wishes to avoid being in love again. When Harry tries to flirt with her, Phyllis cynically suggests a better pick-up line to him: "How about, 'I'm sad and lonely, don't know anyone in this big old town'".

As with the heroines of the classic women's films of the 1930s and 1940s, Harry is at the centre of the film's love triangle. Women's films that rely on a triangular configuration tell their tales from the woman's point of view, with the lover often oblivious to the heroine's suffering and loneliness, in films such as *Back Street* (John M Stahl, 1932), *Camille* (George Cukor, 1936), *Gilda* (Charles Vidor, 1946), *Love Affair* (Leo McCarey, 1939) and *Letter from an Unknown Woman* (Max Ophuls, 1947). *The Bigamist*, however, spares us scenes of lonely female suffering. The film lacks the masochistic edge of many women's films because the story is told from the man's point of view and because the hero is already married to both women. Because Eve and Phyllis are oblivious to the bigamy, Harry is left to suffer alone for his mistakes. Harry is placed in the more masochistic position: suffering interminably for his one night's mistake, and yet unable to take any action to change his circumstances. He describes "months of panic and fear", feeling "sick of lies and deceit" and times when he was "afraid every step of the way".

The Bigamist never draws the audience into the characters' belief in romantic love: indeed, it hardly draws the audience in at all. Desire lacks intensity here, and *The Bigamist* is directed in a matter-of-fact way, producing a remarkably humdrum account of a love triangle. Phyllis is faced with pregnancy, but she holds no romantic illusions about Harry, although she lacks the crucial piece of information that he is already married. Sacrifice is not an option for either Eve or Phyllis, and neither woman is dependent on Harry, emotionally or otherwise. Once both women are married to Harry, *The Bigamist* stresses their similarity as women who are limited not by individual choices but by their respective class positions – Eve wedded to a notion of being "the perfect wife", determined to move ahead in business, throwing dinner parties, saving for expensive holidays; Phyllis constrained by her low-paying job and diminishing prospects, a woman who waited for her lover to come home from war, only to lose him to a "little Fräulein".

In the woman's film, matrimony is proffered as the solution (even if unattainable) to the heroine's suffering. *The Bigamist* gives a radical twist to this scenario by allowing both of Harry's marriages a chance to settle in, to become suffused with ennui. Both women get the man, as it were, and no one is happy. It is not clear that the bigamous situation *per se*, however, is responsible for this unhappiness. Eve and Harry's marriage is riddled with tension over their business, their childlessness and anxiety over adoption. Phyllis, on the other hand, is very ill from her pregnancy, and she and Harry are never seen to enjoy a single moment's happiness together after they marry.

The Bigamist also breaks with the woman's film's notions of romantic love, insisting on marriage as a social arrangement, not a mystery of heterosexual attraction. Eve's marriage is firmly grounded in financial stability. Harry and Eve's partnership has secured an elegant lifestyle: china and silver at every meal, a posh apartment, fashionable clothing. Their marriage is literally a corporation. Phyllis secures legitimacy for her child through marriage and avoids the negative sanctions against childbirth out of wedlock. For Harry the second marriage provides him with a home in Los Angeles, a respite from the chain of hotels and restaurants, someone to do his laundry and sew the buttons back on his shirts. Harry and Phyllis's home is much more modest – and more "homey" – than Eve's: toys strewn around the room, pictures cluttering the walls, a baby carriage parked in the living room. But the class difference is laid out in stark financial terms. Harry and Eve earn about $20 000 a year; when Harry suggests the separation from Phyllis, he offers her $85 per week (about $4500 a year).

In *The Bigamist* the limiting conditions are not individual choice and sacrifice, but the class positions of the protagonists. The plot suggests that both roads lead to the same dead end: the dilemma of domestic travail, of struggling to get along. Both marriages reach a crisis, although a profoundly unsentimentalized and relatively unemotional one. The iceboxes, in which Harry and Eve's refrigeration business specialise, serve as the perfect symbol for the film's view of marriage: the icebox is familiar, domestic, mundane – and a mechanism for isolation and coldness. Bigamy is a normal, even tedious, reality for Harry Graham: it has not doubled his pleasure, merely plunged him deeper into the freeze.

The Filmakers prepared their own publicity for *The Bigamist* and distributed the film through the Filmakers Releasing Organization. The pressbook neatly represents the mixture of film noir (in its depiction of Harry) and "woman's picture" (in its depiction of Phyllis and Eve), promising a degree of high drama and titillation lacking in the film itself.[11] Harry Graham is shown in full-length long shot: dressed in suit and hat, his back turned, his face heavily shadowed, in three-quarters profile. Flanking him are profile close-ups of Eve and Phyllis. The contrast of scale is such that the woman's faces are as large as Harry's entire body. Eve's caption reads "When I found out I couldn't have a child I hated you, myself – everybody". Phyllis's reads "It's yours, if that's what you mean, but I don't trap my men this way". "Wanted by Two Women", boasts the poster's headline.

Harry appears alone in a head and shoulders shot in some quarter-page advertisements. Immediately beside his face is a graphic of the pointing index finger of a gloved hand, encircling the word "The" in the film's title, and so removing any doubt as to the character's guilt. Dialogue from the film poses the question of Harry's guilt in different versions of the ad: "How can a man call his wife of eight years and tell her that he's been unfaithful?"; "Some men escape their loneliness with women who are easy to get. But that didn't work with me...Eve was my whole life"; "If he had taken Phyllis Martin as his mistress, people would have winked a wicked eye...".

The film was positioned by The Filmakers as adult entertainment – a cut above the teen pic. *The Bigamist* boasted material that could not be seen on the television screen, content that passed the censors for good taste but still appealed to adult sensibilities. This positioning clearly reflects the anxieties of the declining film industry of the early 1950s and the attempt by independents such as The Filmakers to establish a niche. The pressbook refers to the threat of imports that promised more adult themes ("Not so long ago this kind of adult entertainment came to you from a few 'foreign' producers. But here is proof on film that Hollywood is growing up!"); caters to teenage audiences ("We don't go along with the idea that American movie patrons are equal to the 'Twelve-Year-Old-Mind'") and implies censorship battles ("Yes, the screen is more than ever free for grown-up entertainment. Therefore, we in Hollywood, proudly submit 80 minutes that only a few years ago we would not have dared offer you.").

The Bigamist, the last film Lupino directed in The Filmakers cycle, had a remarkably complex backstage story, even by Hollywood's standards. Lupino directed the film from a script by her ex-husband Collier Young, who also receives credit for producing the film. She also played the role of Phyllis. Lupino's co-star, Joan Fontaine, was at the time married to Young. Young's successive marriage and the Lupino/Young business partnership provide a fascinating subtext to the film's narrative. The fact of Lupino's previous marriage to Collier Young is conspicuously absent from the pressbook, despite the prominent placement of a photograph of Lupino and Young watching a love scene between Fontaine and Edmond O'Brien (as Harry) which bears the caption "One of 1953's most famous photographs". These circumstances were known to the public at the time, however: they are mentioned, for example, in *The New York Times* review of the film.

The publicity nevertheless emphasizes that the film is a "family affair". Articles discuss the fact that Young had to talk Fontaine into taking the role of Eve, and Fontaine's insistence that Lupino direct ("Hubby Sells Joan 'Bigamist' Lead"); mention visits from Lupino's infant daughter to the set, and the child's relationship to Fontaine and Young as godparents; discuss the casting of Fontaine's mother, Lillian Fontaine, as the landlady ("Star's Mother in Top Film Role"). Throughout the pressbook, Young's role as producer and screenwriter is given more space than Lupino's as director. Furthermore, Lupino's direction is downplayed in favour of her acting performance. A brief feature, "Star Breaks Vow; Directs Self", explains that Lupino had sworn never to act and direct in the same film, but that her "double duty on the picture came about as the result of a sudden, lucky accident" – namely, because Fontaine made it one of the terms of her participation in the film that Lupino both act the part of Phyllis and direct. Another feature article, entitled "New Experience", casts Lupino's role as director in a jokingly misogynistic light. The story reports Edmund Gwenn's feelings about "taking orders from Miss Lupino" – the first time in his 58-year career that he has had a woman director:

> "I don't mind a bit," Gwenn replied. "In fact, it's thrilling coming up against my very first woman director, especially when she's so talented." Then, as an afterthought, the 77 year old performer chuckled: "Actually there's nothing new to being told what to do and how to do it by a woman. Women have been doing it to men since time began."

There is no attempt in the publicity to claim for Lupino any special insight into sensitive subject-matter, the drama of the female characters or "a woman's touch".

Ronnie Scheib has described the tension in Lupino's films as based on "the interreaction of a claustrophobic 'woman's picture' emotionalism and a full-frame documentary realism (complete with extensively researched detail, non-professional actors, and, in many instances, true stories)".[12] The understatement of emotion in the film, especially Lupino's performance, is particularly interesting in this regard. Lupino spoke in an interview of the difficulty of directing under these circumstances, adding that she had her cameraman observe her acting and signal to her when her performance was too emotional.[13] The scant critical praise that Lupino received for *The Bigamist* acknowledges her restrained, low-key directorial style. Here was Lupino's solution to her confinement to what Rickey has dubbed "the populist potboiler": to reduce the emotionalism, particularly in the women characters, and to dignify them with reserve, endurance and toughness.

Surprisingly, the film was denigrated by means of the usual association with soap opera. *Films in Review* called the film "a trifle" and commented of Lupino that "her directorial skill saves a sudsy tale from some of its lack of substance".[14] *Newsweek* concluded that the film "suggests a moralistic diagram, with overtones of sermon and, at its worst, of soap opera".[15] Similarly, the *Time* reviewer explicitly linked the film with soap opera and *The New York Times* described the plot as "the perfect format for the soap opera of them all".[16] The latter reviewer admires the unemotional performance, however: "the incidents of deadlock and discovery are calmly devoid of any sound and fury".

The Filmakers had specialised in topics unusual for the 1950s, so much so that *The New York Times* could describe the company as showing "a penchant for such somber, unorthodox themes as illegitimacy, rape, maternal ruthlessness and pathological vagrancy with an estimable batting average".[17] These were precisely the kinds of topics that migrated to the small screen as made-for-television movies. *The Bigamist* presages many aspects of the made-for-television movie, with its focus on illicit behaviours within the family and on the complex patterns of kinship resulting from multiple marriages and divorce, and its presentation of a therapeutic discourse.[18] Like the television movie, *The Bigamist* moves from investigation to courtroom scene, calling in such witnesses as social workers, psychologists and judges to police the familial crisis, while at the same time expressing a deep-seated unease with these interventions into private life. Precisely the same topics that The Filmakers brought to the screen – including bigamy – have been made into numerous made-for-television movies in the past decade. Lupino's experience and her directorial style suited her well to the extended career in television direction she would later pursue.

The banal courtroom scene that ends *The Bigamist* belongs neither to film noir nor to melodrama, but is a precursor of countless endings of the made-for-television movie. While the film seems to question the adequacy of medical, criminal and psychological institutions to "cure" this situation, or to bring justice for female complainants, Lupino ultimately refrains from any kind of feminist statement. Harry is treated as an individual case and the fate of the characters is placed in the hands of the paternalistic judge. Like Mr Jordan, the judge favours Harry's own version of events and postpones sentencing, arguing that the worst punishment will be the emotional consequences of his actions, not the court's sentence. It is a perfect ending for Lupino, in that it resolutely refuses to assign moral culpability. Such a lack of narrative closure, a feature of the made-for-television movie, may be a necessary component of narratives that are so potentially subversive of the ideology of the nuclear family. The only certainty is that Eve and Phyllis will be alone again. Lupino grants Eve no angry scene of recrimination, and completely frustrates the urge of the melodrama devotee to break down in tears. Phyllis and Eve refrain from weeping, from any display of desperation. Phyllis simply flashes Harry a short, brave smile and walks out of the courtroom; Eve watches Harry as he is led out by the police. Both women are on their own again.

Notes

[1]   Christine Gledhill, "*Klute* 1: A contemporary film noir and feminist criticism", in E Ann Kaplan (ed), *Women in Film Noir* (London: British Film Institute, 1980): 14.

2   Debra Weiner, "Interview with Ida Lupino", in Karyn Kay and Gerald Peary (eds), *Women and the Cinema: A Critical Anthology* (New York: E P Dutton, 1977): 174.

3   Ronnie Scheib, "Ida Lupino: Auteuress", *Film Comment* 16: 1 (1980): 64.

4   Carrie Rickey, "Lupino Noir", *Village Voice* 29 October-4 November 1980: 44.

5   Virginia Wright Wexman, *Creating the Couple: Love, Marriage, and Hollywood Performance* (Princeton: Princeton University Press, 1993): 18.

6   Rickey: 43

7   Gledhill: 14.

8   For a discussion of the blend of melodrama and film noir and the opposition of male and female discourses see: Joyce Nelson, "*Mildred Pierce* Reconsidered", *Film Reader* 2 (1977): 65-70; Pam Cook, "Duplicity in *Mildred Pierce*", in E Ann Kaplan (ed), *Women in Film Noir* (London: British Film Institute, 1980): 68-82; Linda Williams, "Feminist Film Theory: *Mildred Pierce* and the Second World War", in E Deidre Pribram (ed), *Female Spectators: Looking At Film and Television* (London: Verso, 1988): 12-30.

9   Mike Davis, *City of Quartz: Excavating the Future in Los Angeles* (London: Vintage Books, 1992): 40.

10   Cook: 68.

11   *The Bigamist* pressbook, Filmakers Releasing Organization, 1953, courtesy of the Center for Motion Picture Study, Margaret Herrick Library, Academy of Motion Picture Arts and Sciences, Beverly Hills, CA.   Special thanks to archivist Val Almendarez for his assistance.

12   Scheib: 58.

13   Louise Heck-Rabi, *Women Filmmakers: a Critical Reception* (Metuchen, NJ: Scarecrow Press, 1984): 237.

14   *Films in Review* 5 February 1954: 96.

15   *Newsweek* 4 January 1954: 61.

16   *The New York Times* 26 December 1953, 10: 4.

17   Ibid.

18   See Mimi White, *Tele-Advising: Therapeutic Discourse in American Television* (Chapel Hill: University of North Carolina, 1992).

The Trouble With Angels (1966)

Mary Beth Haralovich, Janet Jakobsen and Susan White

The action takes place over three years in the lives of Mary and Rachel at St Francis Academy, a convent school for girls.[1] Mary, an orphan, has been sent to the school by her uncle in the hope that the nuns can reform her. Rachel has been taken out of the New Trends Progressive School whose curriculum would not prepare her for life. In addition to being a girls' school, St Francis Academy is also the mother house for the nuns, the place where novices enter the Order and nuns retire.

Mary and Rachel play a series of schoolgirl pranks, "scathingly brilliant ideas" conceived by Mary, for which they are reprimanded by Reverend Mother. Mary and Rachel organise a tour of the nuns' cloister, an area forbidden to the girls. They put bubble bath crystals in the nuns' sugar bowls, and try to create a plaster cast of another girl's face. Reverend Mother reaches the end of her patience when Mary and Rachel smoke cigars in the basement, setting off a fire alarm. On the verge of expelling the girls, Reverend Mother relents when she meets Mary's uncle, his "secretary", and Rachel's father. She realises that the girls are better off with her and that Mary is much like she herself once was.

As the years pass, the girls grow older and more mature. During summer breaks from St Francis, Mary and Rachel both have adventures with boys. Unable to comprehend why a woman would become a nun, Mary is drawn to watching Reverend Mother in her more spiritual and intimate moments. Mary strives to understand the nuns and their choice of life, asking why a beautiful nun would volunteer to teach in a leper colony and why Reverend Mother would give up a career in the fashion industry for a religious vocation.

Although its grand appearance suggests financial security, St Francis Academy is in need of a new boiler for the antiquated heating system, which continually creaks and sputters. Reverend Mother sees an opportunity to win the money for the boiler through a school band competition. Mary and Rachel, in a "scathingly brilliant idea" which this time benefits the school, spy on the New Trends band. They discover that New Trends is as musically inept as St Francis, but that they have costumes. Reverend Mother arranges for band costumes to be loaned to the school. She is shocked to see the girls marching in glittering, short, red uniforms, with feathers on their heads. But the girls are happy. St Francis wins the contest and looks forward to having a new boiler.

This resolved, the girls gather in the entrance hall in white gowns for graduation. Reverend Mother announces the names of those who have decided to join the Order. Rachel is stunned and angered to learn that Mary will become a novice upon graduation. At the St Francisville railway station, Rachel refuses to speak to Mary, despite Reverend Mother's assurances that Mary made the decision on her own. Mary begs Rachel to speak to her. Finally, the girls have a tearful reconciliation and Rachel leaves. Mary and Reverend Mother return to St Francis.

* * *

With its generational conflict led by America's favourite teenager, Hayley Mills, *The Trouble With Angels* appears to address religious conversion and a young girl's growth into adulthood. The 1966 Easter release of *The Trouble With Angels* and the contemporaneous proliferation of films about nuns highlight the role of religion, and particularly of Catholicism, in the popular imagination of the 1960s (Vatican II reforms were widely discussed; the Catholic John F Kennedy was elected President, and assassinated; Pope John XXIII had recently died). Although the coming of age of a novice in the convent was a fashionable subject for mid-1960s Hollywood, in *The Trouble With Angels* the familiar story of a girl's decision to turn away from the world, to "give up" (hetero)sexuality by embracing a religious vocation, is transformed into a film about woman-woman identification and the attractions of a community of women. Through a redefinition of male-female authority and the female gaze, *The Trouble With Angels* suggests the possibility that at St Francis Mary Clancy may find something more than spiritual union with God.

Religions, which exist in a dynamic interplay between tradition and innovation, often provide a backdrop for exploring fears and hopes with regard to social change. By 1966 Americans were faced with dramatic changes within the Catholic Church which had begun in the Second Vatican Council (Vatican II), 1962-65. Catholicism, frequently seen as the icon of tradition in contrast to the adaptable acculturation of US Protestantism, was losing some of the identifying markers which made it both different from, and reassuring to, dominant US culture. Americans had also witnessed dramatic transformations in the public role of religion, particularly through the civil disobedience of the Civil Rights Movement. Protestant clergy of the Southern Christian Leadership Conference, in conjunction with radical Jews and Catholic clergy and nuns in religious garb, were visible on the nightly news and in the morning papers as agents of change rather than as the protectors of tradition. In the mid-1960s, with change occurring both in gender roles and in religions, the visible place of women in religion became a site where tradition and change could modulate each other. Nuns could go to non-traditional places and take up non-traditional roles provided they wore the traditional habit of religious garb which also signalled commitment to patriarchal authority.[2]

Films about nuns provide a terrain on which these issues are worked out. While films such as *The Nun's Story* (Fred Zinnemann, 1959), *The Sound of Music* (Robert Wise, 1965), *The Singing Nun* (Henry Koster, 1966) and *Change of Habit* (William Graham, 1969) depict male sexuality as potential saviour and/or looming menace, *The Trouble With Angels* suggests that even in a world that exploits women it is possible to find comfort and meaning in a life lived among them. Yet *The Trouble With Angels* is not only about choosing a vocation. In fact, the Catholic press of the time did not see the film as truly representing a calling to a religious vocation. Many details of the film do not "cohere" unless one positions it as addressing young women's questions about how love and sexuality between women can be played out in their lives. *The Trouble With Angels* is based on a series of looks between women, beginning with Reverend Mother's looks of approbation, then shifting to Mary's gaze of interest and desire. Unlike Maria in *The Sound of Music*, Mary does not explicitly state her efforts to understand her vocation. Instead, key scenes which present Mary's struggle are silent and intimate, even sensual in their tranquillity, as she secretly watches Reverend Mother in her most spiritual moments.

The very fact that the film depicts a strongly self-sufficient homosocial community of women in itself queries heterosexual assumptions about what gives rise to happiness.[3] In this context, Alexander Doty has pointed to the necessity of bringing queerness (lesbian, gay, bisexual and other "alternative" perspectives) out of the oppressive "closet" of the "connotative" or "*sub*-textual" realm of film analysis to which it has generally been assigned:

> I've got news for straight culture: your readings of texts are usually 'alternative' ones for me, and they often seem like desperate attempts to deny the queerness that is so clearly a part of mass culture.

Doty suggests that "the queerness of mass culture develops in three areas: (1) influences during the production of texts; (2) historically specific cultural readings and uses of texts by self-identified gays, lesbians, bisexuals, queers; and (3) adopting reception positions that can be considered 'queer' in some way, regardless of a person's declared sexual and gender allegiances".[4]

The Trouble With Angels engages the coming of age and sexual identity of its adolescent women viewers. The circumstances of the film's production contribute to its focus on the community of women. *The Trouble With Angels* was one among other films with religious themes released for the Easter week 1966 box office. However, Hollywood's secularity deflects the representation of religious beliefs. The narrative site of the convent functions as a means of reconciling women's work to women's lives, a place where working does not mean taking a "masculine" role, and where women's stories and romances can be removed from masculine domination.

Director Ida Lupino may have been attracted to the film project, which brought her back to film work after a hiatus in television, because its script provided a means of working through many of the issues of gender identity that troubled her own career and private life. Lupino faced numerous difficulties regarding gender identity, and occasionally laments not being given "women's films" or romances to direct. In an article entitled "Me, Mother Directress", published soon after the release of *The Trouble With Angels*, Lupino describes how she took the role of "mother" with her crews in order to avoid being a "bossy woman" "shoving" men around on the set. For a woman taking on a double role in filmmaking – those of director (commonly associated with masculinity) and of star (more easily reconciled with the norms of femininity) – Lupino's complex persona allowed her to negotiate and appear to reconcile the demands of directing, those of her image as screen idol, and those of wife and mother. Perhaps this process of negotiation makes itself felt as a palpable tension between different kinds of "women's roles" in *The Trouble With Angels*.[5]

The film's star, Hayley Mills, bears a strong resemblance to the actresses in Lupino's earlier films, who in turn resemble the young Lupino; in addition, Mills's acting background and early career in many respects parallel Lupino's own. When *The Trouble With Angels* was made, Mills's career was at a tenuous point, poised between her child-star days with Disney and the adult roles she desperately wanted to undertake.[6] Mills was 20 years old in 1966. With the release of each new Mills film in the early 1960s, magazine stories rehearsed her star image: her acting talent and natural scene-stealing; the efforts of her parents to give their children a "normal British" family life; and the fact that Mills was older than the characters she played. This publicity presents Mills as well-adjusted and at ease with parental authority ("the world's greatest teen-ager"), but as continually looking forward to playing older characters (that is, girls her own age). Typical is this example from *Senior Scholastic* magazine which asked Mills at the release of *The Chalk Garden* (Ronald Neame, 1963): "Now that she was in her late teens, did she think it would become increasingly difficult to get suitable roles? Would the film-going public tend to reject her – as they did Shirley Temple and Mickey Rooney – in anything but the 'kid' parts in which she had proved her popularity?". In response, "Hayley became very contemplative. 'Frankly, I'll be a better actress if I can act my age, on screen and off.'"[7] Mills's continually deferred screen womanhood, discussed in her publicity stories, underscores the gender/ sexual tension in the film which at the end resolves itself in favour of female activity and companionship.

When *The Trouble With Angels* opened in New York in April 1966, it was one of several religious-theme films playing during an Easter week of record box office activity in New York City. The mainstream Hollywood hit of the season was *The Singing Nun* (1966) in a record-breaking seven-week run at Radio City Music Hall with its "Glory of Easter ... cathedral pageant" stage show. Cecil B De Mille's *The Ten Commandments* (1956) established box office records for a reissue film. *The Greatest Story Ever Told* (George Stevens, 1965) returned for a "limited 14-day engagement". Pier Paolo Pasolini's *Il Vangelo secondo Matteo* (*The Gospel According to St Matthew*, 1964) continued an extended run in New York. Furthermore, the film which popularized nun stories on film, *The Sound of Music* (1965), began the second year of what was to become one of the top box office performances in history. In April 1966 the Academy Awards® for 1965 were announced. *The Sound of Music* was nominated for ten awards and won five (Best Film, Direction, Editing, Music Scoring – Adaptation or Treatment, Sound).[8]

Among this spectacular company, *The Trouble With Angels* was certainly a respectable film and was much more favourably received by Catholic reviewers than *The Singing Nun*. The promotional campaign for *The Trouble With Angels* paralleled that of *The Singing Nun* in presenting nuns in positions of undignified mobility. A large alliterative advertisement in *The New York Times* promised that *The Trouble With Angels* would be "A Story of Faith, Hope and Hellarity!!!!" about "A Hip Headmistress and two Heavenly Hellions Hit Head-on in a Hilarious Heart-warming Honey of a movie!" – "the perfect Easter holiday entertainment". *The Singing Nun* ad offers Debbie Reynolds in nun habit smiling and waving from a motor scooter, guitar slung on her back. For *The Trouble With Angels*, Rosalind Russell in nun habit sits astride a bicycle, legs akimbo, while Hayley Mills and June Harding smile behind her. While *The Singing Nun* ads could promise songs ("Dominique", "Brother John", "It's A Miracle"), *The Trouble With Angels* ad shows Hayley Mills in band costume with drum: "Everybody's beating the drums for *The Trouble With Angels*".[9]

Although *The Singing Nun* garnered more box office attention, reviews in Catholic journals found *The Trouble With Angels* to be less egregious in its presentation of religious life. Writing in *America*, Moira Walsh is "filled with foreboding" about nun films "because it is frighteningly easy to get nuns all wrong on the screen and terribly difficult to do them justice". Philip T Hartung in *Commonweal* calls *The Singing Nun* "the usual guff ... with so many tired cliches" and wishes that films "could capture the honesty and intelligence" of nuns. He finds *The Trouble With Angels* to be "the best of recent nun pictures" because its focus is on the girls instead of on nuns, but also because the Mother Superior "is no stereotype". Walsh is disturbed that nun films "radiate a sentimental rosy glow at all costs" and feels that *The Singing Nun* presents the "view that nuns are so naive, unrealistic and lacking in self-knowledge that they cannot possibly cope with the world". While Walsh finds *The Trouble With Angels* "so much better", she criticises its handling of "the matter of emerging nuns and changing convents". Like the book on which the film was based, the St Francis Academy represents the convent school of "thirty years ago ... in that the movie portrays uncritically ... many of the rigid and ill-considered practices of convent school that have long since been softened or eliminated". The film's comedy becomes "an impenetrable barrier to getting below the surface of the characters or conveying any real insight into religion or the religious vocation", with the result that Walsh is unconvinced by Mary's religious calling.

As Walsh observes, Mary's call to a religious vocation is not represented in terms of Catholicism or closeness to God. The male hierarchy of the Catholic Church is strikingly absent from her decision. God is not mentioned, nor does Mary pray for guidance. The only time Mary is seen on her knees in Chapel she is pretending to pray as part of a punishment. She is given a pillow by Sister Liguori, who knows that Mary is talking to Rachel rather than actually praying. Each of the key scenes leading to Mary's acceptance of her vocation involves her understanding relationships between women, the work embraced by nuns, and the dangers of the heterosexual world outside the convent. Mary's vocation is thus a locus for resolving the conflicts of young womanhood in the arenas of work, family, sexuality *and* spirituality.[10]

The Trouble With Angels opens with a direct reference to *Pollyanna* (David Swift, 1960), as the orphaned girl arrives by train in the community of St Francisville where she will begin her training in female self-sacrifice. Catholic nuns are frequently thought to embody the epitome of female self-sacrifice, having given up even the pleasures of sexuality in order better to fulfil the demands of (virgin) motherhood. There is, however, another side to the commitment of Catholic sisters who, freed from the strictures of marriage and child-rearing, are able to pursue roles otherwise unavailable to women. By abstaining from the sacrifices necessary to heterosexuality, sisters may find a life among women with new opportunities and even alternative forms of desire. In *The Trouble With Angels* the convent is presented as a "sanctorium" (to quote one of the convent students who seems to confuse the convent with an asylum) for women pledged to love and serve other women.

As is often the case with convents in fiction, the convent in *The Trouble With Angels* functions as the site of female passage into adulthood. In works as diverse as *Les Lettres de la religieuse portugaise* (*The Letters of the Portuguese Nun*, 17th century), Michael Powell and Emeric Pressburger's *Black Narcissus* (1946), and Su Friedrich's lesbian reworking of that film in *Damned If You Don't* (1987), the convent serves as a place where the achievement of sexual and spiritual maturity involves an overt or covert decision about, or a coming to terms with, sexual preference and/or gender allegiance. The imperative towards chastity carries with it an implicit assumption of heterosexuality, both in terms of the sexuality from which one abstains, and in the vow of faithfulness which sisters make in their marriage to Jesus. However, the social space of the convent opens more possibilities, providing for relationships between and among women which are relatively protected from the strictures of heterosexuality and male intervention.

The vow of chastity opens onto multiple relational possibilities for the exploration of various registers of spiritual, emotional and sexual feeling and interaction between women.[11] Historically, in predominantly Christian societies, the sisterhood provided women with one of the few available alternatives to heterosexual marriage, an alternative which at some points in history was significantly empowering, providing access to education and economic and political power, as well as the opportunity to live primarily among women in communities which buffered some of the direct expressions of patriarchal power. In *The Trouble With Angels* the male hierarchy of the Church is strikingly absent. Priests do not appear to hear the sisters' confessions, administer communion or assert institutional authority over the school. A scene with Mr Petrie, Rachel's teacher from the progressive school, reiterates Reverend Mother's appropriation of the position of male authority in a community of women relatively removed from direct male oversight. Upset with Reverend Mother, Rachel makes an appeal for male support when she writes to Mr Petrie: "I'm a captive in a nunnery". Reverend Mother stands down the idealistic young teacher, saying with authority that in the matter of progressive education "God is on our side". Reverend Mother's direct appeal to God allows her a power which effectively emasculates Mr Petrie without need for the intervention of a priestly representative of the Church hierarchy.

The convent in *The Trouble With Angels* allows a space of possibility which is not always already overwritten with heterosexuality.

The film's animated opening credits feature schematized figures representing the various characters as well as three issues central to the film: the relationship between Mary and Reverend Mother as Mary disrupts St Francis's protocols; the embodiment and display of the female body which re-emerges in the form of women exploring the "secret places" of other women, in particular Mary's curiosity about the nuns who supervise her; and the marginalization of male authority through a group of "outsiders", mostly male, who gaze through an arched doorway which Mary closes, blocking their view. The credits begin with an angel flying out of the haloed "a" in Columbia. She is a winged girl in uniform (obviously Mary). A nun (Reverend Mother) lights a candle, prays, crosses herself, and places the candle in a niche. The angel flies in and uses the candle to light a cigar. A lightning strike leaves her and the cigar singed. A giant hand descends from above, poking at the annoyed Mary and tying her wings.

A "bubble dancer", mostly naked behind her large pink balloon, descends between a pair of nuns holding balloons. The "angel" Mary pops all three balloons, forcing the dancer to flee. Gypsy Rose Lee's name appears in pink lettering that contrasts with the otherwise black script. What is a stripper doing in a film about a convent?[12] In response to parental complaints about the "singular clumsiness" of their daughters, Reverend Mother has called upon the services of a flamboyant dance instructor, Mrs Mabel Dowling Phipps, who is played by Lee. Shown wriggling in from the rear in a pink dress and immense picture hat, Mrs Phipps is a great hit with the girls, teaching them to be "as graceful as young willows" – "fluid! fluid! fluid! fluid!" Reverend Mother wanders into the room unobserved and is appalled by what she sees – young women's bodies in a state of "fluidity".

She tolerates this incursion of normative femininity, in which women construct "proper" images of other women, as a necessary evil. Reverend Mother is in fact quite knowledgeable about women's clothing, for the issue of image-construction for women proves to have been a strongly cathected element of her own past as a fashion designer. Lee's part in the film is not flamboyantly sexual, but brings up associations around the inadequacy of both traditional and "progressive" ideas about heterosexual femininity, which is as often comically dismissed as it is "threatening". Perhaps because she does not want to confront again the comically sensual spectacle of young women's bodies, Reverend Mother insists that Sister Rose Marie take the girls to pick out (as the young sister says) "binders". "Brassieres, sister, brassieres", Reverend Mother corrects her. Sister Rose Marie loses control of the girls in the lingerie shop. Mary tries on a bustier while comparing herself to Jayne Mansfield and gives a lavender one to Rachel, who looks despairingly at her bust: "Rock Hudson". Reverend Mother eventually appears, choosing plain cotton bras for the girls.

The first scene of the film sets up the basic triangular joke structure of the film's character interactions: Mary takes the lead; Rachel follows, awestruck by her friend's daring; another woman looks on censoriously or becomes a victim of their pranks. Mary and her soon-to-be bosom buddy Rachel Devery spot one another as "fellow travellers", both riding the train on the way to incarceration in the convent at St Francisville. As the supposedly world-weary Mary lights a cigarette, a lady across the aisle reproaches the girl for smoking at her age. Mary answers that she is actually "a midget with bad habits". In this case the joke is on the disapproving adult. Mary also makes a prescient pun when she says that she has bad "habits". When at the end of the film she decides to join the Order, Mary will of course acquire another kind of "habit" – a "good" one, one supposes.

This triangular joke structure prevails when Sister Clarissa picks up the new scholars in a yellow school bus.[13] Mary has already organised her classmates, who have assumed false names, including "Pearl Ring", "Fleur de Lys" and, for Mary herself, "Kim Novak". Such names play on the ambiguity of the "nunnery" as locus of chastity or as place of ill repute. The intervention of the star name implicitly compares the glamour of the assumed identity of the star with that of the nun, both of whom take on another identity and a new name.[14] Sister Clarissa fails to see through the girls' charade, but Reverend Mother immediately detects not only the falsehood, but also, through quick visual inspection, the ringleaders, Mary and Rachel.

Sister Clarissa is the first nun introduced in the film. The stereotypical awkward, likeable, and completely unromantic gym teacher, Sister Clarissa is the site of the classic schoolgirl crush and comic relief. Alexander Doty discusses the need for films to provide escape routes which offer the possibility of a straight reading so that people will not be overly threatened by the possibilities of queer pleasures. The "butch" gym teacher in nun's habit acts as an emissary to a world where pleasing men is not the goal of its inhabitants. Although Sister Clarissa may also seem to be a negative model – the mannish woman, one who is both a bit repugnant to and easily dismissed by "boy-crazy" teenage girls, *The Trouble With Angels* assigns even this stereotype a place of respect as a lovable character in a spectrum of women-identified women.

However, Sister Clarissa is not the nun to whom Mary is drawn. In fact, Mary and Rachel spend the film avoiding Sister Clarissa's activities. They lag behind when jogging and avoid wearing swimsuits and learning to swim by claiming to have various rare diseases. In order to graduate, they must jump into the water and one girl must "save" the other. In this rite of passage into the world of adult womanhood, the girls are called upon to make a declaration of their mutual dependence, trust and love. They fail the test and learn to "swim" in different waters, as Mary decides to plunge into convent life while Rachel stays on the shores of heterosexual secularity.

In an expository scene set in the convent's dining hall, Reverend Mother introduces the nuns and the St Francis Academy. This scene represents the entire span of nuns' lives, post-Vatican II possibilities for social change, as well as some of the questions of gender and sexuality that will be worked through in the film. Because St Francis is the mother house, nuns of all ages and conditions live there, from novices to the retired Sister Prudence, who is almost deaf. Sister Constance is a "flawless beauty", as Mary describes her. Sister Liguori is Reverend Mother's assistant and the mathematics teacher whose methods Mother describes as "newer than new". Reverend Mother also explains the history of the mother house and the rules for living within its confines. Each of these rules will, of course, be violated by the students.

Reverend Mother's brief speech about the Order is interrupted by a loud knocking from the radiator. She begins to speak about the house itself (a "positively medieval" structure, as Mary observes), both acknowledging and ironizing the "patrimony" that has benefited and controlled the Order. The impressive castle-like dwelling was donated by Mr Walter Gaffney, to whom Reverend Mother expresses due gratitude. However, she also admits that this patrimony is insufficient and must be supplemented by the sisters and their pupils. The boiler itself is a multivalent sign. Its state of disrepair represents the need for renewal and change in the patriarchal Church; its loud noise and threats to explode seem linked to the noisy and disruptive presence of the girls, especially Mary and Rachel.

The need for the Order to earn money is mischievously paralleled by Mary's first major prank in the convent (after she and Rachel have been caught smoking in the toilets by the observant Reverend Mother): selling "tours" of the cloister where the nuns reside. This prank establishes the motives for Mary's gaze, which eventually becomes her route towards a vocation: her desire to look at forbidden or secret places; the silence and intimacy of the tranquil space of nuns' lives, in this case the cloister; and Mary's desire to expose and embody what it is to be a nun.

As the girls sneak into the cloister, Mary salaciously promises a look at that "mystery of mysteries", where Reverend Mother sleeps. Mary knows which cell belongs to Reverend Mother by its "king-size crucifix", and challenges one girl's disappointment with the tour by asking "What'd you expect? Hair shirts?". Mary's cousin, Marvel Ann, who also attends the convent school, and upon whose body Mary and Rachel carry out some of their most dangerous practical jokes, is unimpressed by the cloister and complains loudly. Meanwhile, not surprisingly, Reverend Mother has come up the backstairs and heard the girls' voices. As the students attempt to leave, they find the door locked. One of the girls, Charlotte, faints (which she threatens to do repeatedly throughout the film), falling on top of Marvel Ann, who is trapped under her body: "Get her off of me!". The bodily contact between Charlotte and Marvel Ann is also an initial signal for the possibility that women's bodies can touch within the walls of the cloister, a possibility which is both fearful and one of the pleasures offered by the tour.

In his psychoanalytical study of the effects of voice in cinema, Michel Chion describes the maternal voice as a place of enclosure within an "umbilical net" ("toile ombilicale").[15] Thus, sounds – murmured prayers, snores, plainchant, silences – as well as vision produce this womb-like space of the cloister as one of entrapment, engendered in this scene by the sound of the girls' voices within the silent reaches of this mysterious realm. The "student body" has penetrated the cloister, indeed, and finds itself trapped in its suffocating confines. The double valence of fear and pleasure continues for Mary as she explores desires while remaining hidden.

A major crisis erupts following the smoking theme introduced in the opening credits. The girls have been at the convent school for two years and by this time have developed a fondness for the chains that bind them. Nevertheless, they persist in pulling pranks, and at one point retire to the cellar where they smoke large cigars. There is a certain gender ambiguity in girls in uniform clutching large cigars, evoking the possibility that homosocial relations are also homosexual relations. Smoking is the signifier of implied sexuality in the closeness of Mary and Rachel. As smoke pours from the window and the fire engines arrive, Reverend Mother gazes down at the two astonished girls. What *have* the girls been doing that created such heat and smoke and loud signals of alarm? A prank based on the genre conventions of the Catholic girls' school? Their rebellion against Mother here takes the form of overt female-female "sexual" behaviour.

This scene echoes the one earlier in the film, showing smoking in the toilets, which establishes a number of possibilities for queer relationships in the film. Reverend Mother makes her appearance in the mirror, thus establishing the complex dynamic of identification and difference between Mary and Reverend Mother and the triangulation between the three. Mary confides in Rachel that she has been sent to St Francis because her uncle thinks the nuns will be able to "straighten her out", while Rachel declares that she and Mary are "definitely simpatico". Once Reverend Mother makes her presence known, she declares that "smoking, drinking and s...imilar extra-curricular activities are not permitted at St Francis". Thus, smoking becomes one indicator of the possibility of s...exual activities which cannot otherwise be spoken at St Francis. In the second smoking scene, when Reverend Mother catches the girls, Rachel has her arm around Mary, thus connoting the possibility of those unnameable s...extra-curricular activities. The scene also oddly echoes a story Mother tells Rachel and Mary about Sister Ursula and the Jewish children hidden in the cellar. In this case Reverend Mother takes the place of the Gestapo breaking into the cellar, trying to put out a fire that her own female community has lit.

The second smoking scene also presages the future direction of Rachel and Mary's relationship and the eventual breakup of girlhood romance. As Mary blows smoke rings, Rachel declares, "I'm not sure I like this". Later, when both girls are assigned an essay on "The Evils of Smoking and Why I Gave It Up", Rachel muses, "I was going to give up smoking anyway. I never did like it". Reverend Mother is determined to expel the girls, and Rachel's parents and Mary's uncle are called in. As Mother explains why she must expel Mary, and listens to the uncle babble about his devotion to the girl, she moves over to the window and glances outside. Leaning seductively against a large convertible is the uncle's "secretary", a typical mid-1960s glamour puss. Reverend Mother's tone becomes more and more ironic as she forces the uncle to continue with his half-baked expressions of concern. She has adopted the "male gaze" towards the woman outside and is thoroughly disgusted by its implications.

The Trouble With Angels raises complex issues about the desiring gaze and how that gaze can be represented. For Reverend Mother, contraints on overt looking come from the generation of nuns she represents, but also relate to the need for the film to provide opportunities for straight readings. Mary has a more openly desiring gaze and promises to be active in the more progressive Catholic Church. Indeed, Mary has brought a "male", or at least a worldly, appreciation of women into the convent. She moves towards her vocation through watching Sister Constance, the "flawless beauty" who will soon travel to the "exotic" Philippines to work in a leper colony. Mary claims that it is unfair for Sister Constance not to use her beauty in the service of a heterosexual narrative (Rachel has suggested one involving a long-lost lover), but Constance expresses happiness at her alternative path.

Although Mary has offscreen encounters with a boy on a motor scooter she had met on a holiday, he is never mentioned again, nor are there any further boyfriends. Her object of desire upon return from a later holiday seems to be one of her uncle's secretaries, of whom she has photos in a "black mesh bikini". It is precisely this kind of aesthetic and desiring look at the woman's body that Reverend Mother left behind (or had to avert) upon entering the Order. Even as Mary brings into the convent what seem to be disruptive and uncontrollable heterosexual and homosexual impulses, she raises the spectre of Mother's own suppressed desire to look at women and the need for a potential nun to cope with the desiring gaze.

As Mary moves towards the sacrifice she fears, she also gains a new power to look, one which couples spirituality and sensuality. As Mary becomes increasingly aware of the spiritual qualities of Reverend Mother, the film shifts from Reverend Mother's gaze of discipline and guidance to Mary's gaze of interest and desire. Four key scenes show Mary's gaze as she begins to watch the Mother Superior more carefully and is drawn towards the life of "sacrifice": at the grotto where Reverend Mother prays at a statue of the Virgin Mary; Mary's silent observation of Reverend Mother with the statue of St Francis; Mary's encounter with Reverend Mother and elderly women at a retirement home; and Mary's silent observation of Reverend Mother mourning Sister Liguori. Mary's emotional state alternates between anger and intense desire as she confronts Reverend Mother directly but without being observed.

Rachel and Mary encounter a pensive Reverend Mother sitting in a grotto dominated by a large statue of the Virgin Mary. The exchange between the three is abrupt. Mother asks if the girls have permission from Sister Ursula to be outside. Mary answers with an imitation of the nun's German accent. Angered by Mary's levity, Mother informs the girls "that during the war, Sister Ursula kept thirty-four Jewish children hidden ... in the cellar of a destroyed convent outside of Munich .... When this was finally discovered she was imprisoned. She suffered untold indignities and she – she – ...". Unable to tell the remainder of what seems to be the story of Sister Ursula's rape, Mother breaks down and turns back towards the statue of Mary. The other Mary, obviously touched, declares that she "hates" the Reverend Mother, who has revealed to her the realities of violence inflicted upon women and nuns. From within a grotto guarded by the Virgin, Reverend Mother speaks of the forcible penetration of other spaces – a cellar, Sister Ursula's body. It is not that nuns do not have knowledge of sexuality. Perhaps they know about it all too well and have chosen the community of women rather than the potentially hostile heterosexual world outside.

In the second key scene, Mary observes Reverend Mother placing bread on the shoulders of the statue of St Francis. The mood is tranquil, nocturnal, snow-covered, moving. In its silence and peace, and in Mary's quiet yet intense gaze at Reverend Mother, this scene evokes both spirituality and sensuality. In contrast, Mary is also disturbed by Reverend Mother when the girls are "blackmailed" (as Mary says) into going to a retirement home, which in fact houses only elderly women.

Each old woman has a sad tale to tell, and is waiting for someone to listen to her story of neglect and abandonment by husbands and family – loss of beauty, love, money. Distraught, Mary observes, as Reverend Mother holds an old woman who is sobbing that "her children didn't come", although they had promised. "I did everything for them when they were little; nothing was too hard". "Then do one thing more", says Reverend Mother, "Be happy". The woman goes upstairs to put on her make-up in order to act the part of an older woman comfortable with the price of female self-sacrifice. Mary, obviously excruciated with this view of a woman's fate if she chooses the heterosexual world, blurts to Reverend Mother: "I hope I die young and very wealthy". Reverend Mother smiles, understanding that this is the beginning of the girl's awareness that the convent offers more. This third crucial scene lays forth the "melancholy" of women's lives. The question raised here is less whether to enter or leave a convent than how to escape the lot of women in general. Mary is angered by the melancholic state of women's lives and holds "mother" personally responsible. The eternal question is posed as to whether the condition of loss and melancholy (so well described by Kaja Silverman in *The Acoustic Mirror*) in which our foremothers find themselves, is inevitable.

Mary's understanding of the depth of Reverend Mother's emotional life reaches a new level on the occasion of Sister Liguori's death from heart failure. Rachel wonders how Mother "can be so cold" when she announces the death of her closest friend in a controlled manner. Soon afterwards, Mary goes to the chapel, where the Superior bids Sister Liguori's family goodbye and is then left alone with the casket. In a scene reminiscent of the poignant ending of *Imitation of Life* (Douglas Sirk, 1959), Reverend Mother bends down to embrace the casket and weeps over her dead companion. Mary (who remains unseen) is deeply moved. When, at the end of the film, Mary decides to remain in the convent, the decision seems well motivated by these earlier scenes. Yet, even as it confirms Mary's desire for the kind of emotional attachment to women which Reverend Mother expresses in her grief, the films adopt a standard trope of (implied) lesbian relationships, separation by death.

The band uniforms scene indicates the degree of complexity of the issue of the "desiring gaze" in this film, as well as drawing together the association of "noise" with both discordant outbursts and the healthy sexuality of the "younger generation". Reverend Mother visits the band practice to announce that a contest is imminent and that despite stiff competition, especially from the New Trends Progressive School, she hopes that St Francis can win the prize money desperately needed for a new boiler. Yet another "scathingly brilliant idea" occurs to Mary. Playing truant from a class trip to the art museum, she and Rachel spy on the latter's *alma mater*.   Breathlessly, they return to face a reproachful Mother Superior, who quickly realises that *this* prank – one that has required Mary and Rachel to assume an illicit gaze – was carried out in the service of St Francis.   Before the girls leave, she pauses significantly, giving them their opening to tell her that the other band is just as bad, but that they have *uniforms*.   Reverend Mother refuses to consider the idea, but as soon as the girls leave the radiator begins to bang and she picks up the telephone.

The next scene takes place in the entrance hall, where Reverend Mother is in the act of thanking the owner of a uniform store, Mr Gottschalk, for contributing to the effort.   The girls come marching out, holding a school banner beneath which nothing is visible but naked legs.   As they advance, row upon row, it becomes apparent that they are wearing bright red, extremely short, uniforms, the bottoms of which are nothing more than panties.   Mr Gottschalk looks on approvingly, as Reverend Mother protests that "It's a Catholic school!".   Mr Gottschalk replies that band uniforms are non-denominational, while Mary and Rachel march at the back of the pack, grinning and thanking Mother enthusiastically.   She succumbs and, naturally, St Francis wins the competition.

A "straight" reading of this sequence might describe it as simply the softening of Reverend Mother's unnecessarily strict morality in the light of the changes coming about in the Church and US culture in the mid-1960s.   To some extent this is true, but a more precise analysis of the vicissitudes of looking reveals that a "queer" approach to spectator response is perhaps even more "available" than the straight one.   Mary and Rachel act as the eyes of the Mother Superior, who takes on the gaze of the man admiring the young bodies in "his" uniforms ("fem" ones as opposed to the "butch" ones required by the school – the girls were to have worn their gym clothes to the competition).   The "male" gaze found so reprehensible when Mother adopted it to look at the secretary from her window is being appropriated – for profit – but perhaps also as part of a larger aesthetic appreciation of the female body that Mother has forcibly suppressed or averted, and which is also represented by the irrepressible cacophony of the band.

This is not to say that the female desiring look *must* be tutored by the "male gaze" (which has also been created and perpetrated by women) – obviously not – but that because this gaze is ubiquitous the lesbian gaze must to some degree come to terms with it.   "Straight" women also inevitably look "queerly" at the female body partly because that body has traditionally been made to stand in for all visually-oriented sexuality.   Mr Gottschalk's presence and his obvious appreciation of the girls (and their uniforms) serve to disguise Reverend Mother's desiring gaze at women.   But Mary's "progressive" ideas and bolder sexuality are important lessons for the older woman: although she struggles against the ultimate implications of her own desires, Mary seems relatively at ease with her own enthusiastic appreciation of the female body.

Further evidence that such a repression has taken place can be found in the context of yet another competition – a sewing contest in which the soon-to-graduate students must all make cocktail dresses. Rachel, whose lack of sewing (or of any artistic) talent has already been established, is working late to finish hers. Reverend Mother comes upon her in the sewing room near midnight, and finds the girl unhappy with the product of her efforts. Pity for the tired girl and the challenge of making the dress inspire Mother to stay up until dawn to finish it, long after Rachel has fallen asleep. Mary enters and finds the Superior clucking contentedly over the lovely dress on a shapely dress form. Mother tells Mary of her own girlhood – like Mary she was an orphan in the custody of an uncle. As a young girl she crossed the ocean from Quebec to Paris where she apprenticed as a dressmaker, watching models on the catwalk and dreaming of launching her own line of clothing. Mary asks why she quit. "Because", Reverend Mother intones, "I found something better". Certainly her spiritual relationship with God can be read as the basis of that better life, but there is also a strong indication that Mother's aesthetic interest in women has been transformed into a more satisfying one in the companionship of her sisters. Reverend Mother is comfortable with the desiring gaze of her past and with that of her present. The appropriation and reworking of the "male" gaze has been a part of the process of becoming a nun.

The triangular structure of the film's relationships – two women against another – reasserts itself at the end of the film but in a new configuration. Before the graduation ceremony, a newly appreciative Mother Superior tells the girls that they are all beautiful. She also announces the names of the two girls who will remain as novices: one of them is Mary. Rachel feels hurt and betrayed that Mary has made such a crucial decision without telling her friend. During the final scene at the railway station, Mary stands with Reverend Mother to bid the young women goodbye. Rachel is reluctant to talk to Mary, especially when Reverend Mother mentions that Mary has "scathingly brilliant ideas" for improving the convent. Although Reverend Mother has opened the door for a progressive Church ("people in high places will know that Mary Clancy was at St Francis"), this seems more than anything to strike Rachel as a betrayal of their friendship and their intimacy.

The requisite breakup of girlhood romance, like the grieving scene, provides some of the most moving moments of the film. At the end of the film, Rachel still feels this attachment, need and closeness, but she is not sure which life calls her – the convent or the heterosexual outside world. Mary, on the other hand, is convinced that her choice is to stay.[16] It is clear that Mary is the one who has achieved spiritual and psychological maturity. Reverend Mother has equally benefited from the younger woman's intervention in the life of the convent. Mary is Sister Liguori's replacement, Mother's new companion in the community of women. The old place has a new, well-regulated but powerful, boiler energizing it.

Despite the apparent oppressiveness of her star image and the confines of the girlish roles she played, Hayley Mills's star image from her Disney years also permits *The Trouble With Angels* to contemplate change and tradition in the Catholic Church of the mid-1960s. While the Church offers a certain tolerance ("Can I be less tolerant of Mary than the Church has been of me?" asks Reverend Mother), Mary's strong will and leadership (echoes from Mills's Disney roles) are the characteristics which ultimately distinguish her from Rachel and make her "like" Reverend Mother. She will be bent but not broken by her life in the Church, and her pride will be tempered with humility. Just as the generational differences of the two women combine within a Church opened by Vatican II, *The Trouble With Angels* prefigures the generational shift to pride which was to erupt a few years later at Stonewall.

Notes

[1]   St Francis Academy is also the name of the school where Whoopi Goldberg teaches/hides out in *Sister Act* (1993) and *Sister Act II* (1994).

[2]   The habits in *The Flying Nun* (ABC, 1967-70) remained traditional specifically so that Sister Bertrille could fly. For a history of *The Flying Nun*, a television programme which "highlighted the tensions between nuns given to traditionalist and modernist affinities", see Rick Wolff, "*The Flying Nun* and Post-Vatican II Catholicism", *Journal of Popular Film & Television* 19: 2 (1991): 72-80.

[3]   Eve Kosofsky Sedgwick discusses the emotional range of the homosocial-homoerotic-homosexual continuum in *Between Men: English Literature and Male Homosocial Desire* (New York: Columbia University Press, 1985). See also her *Epistemology of the Closet* (Berkeley: University of California Press, 1993).

[4]   Alexander Doty, *Making Things Perfectly Queer: Interpreting Mass Culture* (Minnesota: University of Minneapolis Press, 1993): xi-xii.

[5]   Ida Lupino, "Me, Mother Directress", in *Action* 2: 3 (1967): 14, reprinted in Richard Koszarski, *Hollywood Directors 1941-1976* (New York: Oxford University Press, 1977). Thanks are due to Mary Celeste Kearney and James M Moran, whose essay, "Ida Lupino as director of television", in this volume

brought this and other materials on Lupino's television work to our attention. In their work behind the scenes to form and motivate characters, Reverend Mother (Rosalind Russell, whose Hollywood career roughly parallels that of Lupino) and Lupino play parallel directorial roles, especially in such moments where Mother concerns herself with the costuming, make-up, and "blocking" of the other actors'/characters' movements in the film.

6 Mills's six Disney films – *Pollyanna* (1960), *The Parent Trap* (1961), *In Search of the Castaways* (1961), *Summer Magic* (1963), *The Moon Spinners* (1964), and *That Darn Cat* (1965) – grossed $62 million, more than the combined first release grosses of *Snow White and the Seven Dwarfs* (1937), *Fantasia* (1940), *Pinocchio* (1940), *Dumbo* (1941), *Bambi* (1942) and *Cinderella* (1950). Jack Hamilton, "Hayley Mills: 'My Life Has Just Begun'", *Look* 28 May 1968: 101. The Mills-Disney influence continued in television. *The Patty Duke Show* (ABC, 1963-66) reprised the identical twin role made popular in *The Parent Trap*, and Sally Field cruised the skies as novice Sister Bertrille in *The Flying Nun*.

7 See, for example, "Hayley Mills, An English Pixie Chases Stardom", *Look* 1 August 1961: 87-90; Peter Martin, "Backstage with Hayley Mills", *Saturday Evening Post* 28 July 1962: 20-21 and ff.; Graham and Heather Fisher, "The World's Favorite Teen-ager", *Ladies' Home Journal* December 1962: 45, 76-77; Margaret Ronan, "Chip Off the Old Block", *Senior Scholastic* 25 October 1963: 10; Hayley Mills, "I'm Growing Up", *Seventeen* January 1964: 70-71 and ff. In her autobiography, Rosalind Russell remembered Mills as "another overripe adolescent ... bursting at the seams with repressed sexuality. Hayley was eighteen or nineteen, but she had that baby face, so Disney kept hiring her to play children's parts. Her talent was enormous, but it was only a question of time until she would break out". Rosalind Russell and Chris Chase, *Life Is a Banquet* (New York: Random House, 1977): 219; Hamilton: 102.

8 "National Boxoffice Survey", *Variety* 6 April 1966: 7; "The Music Hall's Great Easter Show!" ad, *The New York Times* 7 April 1966: 46; "Academy Awards", *Variety* 20 April 1966: 6. *The Singing Nun* was in its fifth week at Radio City Music Hall when *The Trouble With Angels* opened as a "major newcomer ... (also a nun pic)". *The Trouble With Angels* screened at smaller cinemas where it was held over "with a wham $55,000" in its second week, "big $26,000" in its third, and "solid $29,000" in its fourth. See "N.Y. Area Take", *Variety* 13 April 1966: 9; "B'way Holds Well", *Variety* 20 April 1966: 8; "B'way Turns Spotty", *Variety* 4 May 1966: 9. The week after Easter, movie receipts dropped considerably "as the vacation period ended and thousands of visitors left the city". See "B'way Holds Well".

9 *The Trouble With Angels* ads, *The New York Times* 5 April 1966: 43; 8 April 1966: 23; 9 April 1966: 12. *The Singing Nun* ad, *The New York Times* 7 April 1966: 46.

10 Moira Walsh, *The Trouble With Angels* review, *America* 16 April 1966: 568; Philip T Hartung, "Get Them to a Nunnery", *Commonweal* 15 April 1966: 114-118; Walsh, *The Singing Nun* review, *America* 16 April 1966: 567.

[11] The publication of Rosemary Curb and Nancy Manahan (eds), *Lesbian Nuns: Breaking Silence* (Tallahassee: Naiad Press, 1985) confirmed the multiple registers of relationships within the sisterhood, including lifelong emotional partnerships and sexual relationships.

[12] Rosalind Russell played Lee's mother in *Gypsy* (1962).

[13] In *Jokes and their Relation to the Unconscious* Freud refers to the "triangular structure" of most jokes. His theory is that most jokes have as their basis salacious and aggressive remarks that men would like to make to women. Because, he claims, men are or were socially inhibited from doing so (at least towards women of the middle and upper classes), jokes became a three-party matter in which a man would address a joke to another man and the woman would act as the butt of the joke. The assumptions about male "ownership" of joke structure in Freud's theory are, of course, open to question. See Sigmund Freud, *Jokes and their Relation to the Unconscious* (1905), in *The Standard Edition of the Complete Psychological Works of Sigmund Freud*, volume 8, translated and edited by James Strachey (London: Hogarth Press, 1953-74). Our discussion of the film's "triangular structure", in which a third party is either the butt or, alternatively, the master of the joke derives in part from Freud's theory, as well as from Eve Kosofsky Sedgwick's discussion of "triangular desire" (in which women act as the mediator of male homosocial/homoerotic impulses): see *Between Men: English Literature and Male Homosocial Desire* (New York: Columbia University Press, 1985).

[14] Mary's choice of Kim Novak's name as her pseudonym suggests interesting twists about self-identity for Mary and for Hayley Mills. Mary adopts a glamorous name which identifies a star who was famous for insisting on retaining her identity. Novak actually fought to keep "Novak" (her real name) as her professional name. Producers at Columbia thought that the name sounded too "Polish" to be accepted by the American public and they kept her hostage in her dressing room trying to make her slim down. See Virginia Wright Wexman, "The Critic as Consumer: Film Study in the University, *Vertigo*, and the Film Canon", *Film Quarterly* 39: 3 (1986): 32-41. The fact that Novak played adult film characters comments on Mills's view that she was coerced into taking on roles younger than herself. See Hamilton. *Life* magazine ran a "spotlight" on "gifted girls" of "fathers famous in entertainment", profiling Hayley and John Mills, Vanessa and Michael Redgrave, Susan and Lee Strasberg, Brooke and Leland Hayward, Sarah and Herbert Marshall, Anna and Raymond Massey and Jane and Henry Fonda. The story's title, ironic in retrospect, is "Don't Let the Old Man Down", *Life* 27 October 1961: 113 and ff.

[15] See Michel Chion, *La voix au cinéma* (Paris: Editions de l'Etoile, 1982): 63, cited in Kaja Silverman, *The Acoustic Mirror: The Female Voice in Psychoanalysis and Cinema* (Bloomington: Indiana University Press, 1988): 74.

[16] In some ways, this leave-taking follows a stereotyped view of lesbian relationships in which one woman decides to move on as her homosexual investment is just part of a passing phase.

Ida Lupino as director of television

Mary Celeste Kearney and James M Moran

> I never planned to become a director. The fates and a combination of luck—good and bad—were responsible.[1]

Ida Lupino's career in television plays something like her career in the cinema. Originally charting her course in each medium primarily as an actress, she apparently fell into directing as a matter of circumstance, like a "guest who came to dinner" and unwittingly found herself at the head of the table.[2] Making her debut on CBS Television's *Four Star Playhouse* in December of 1953 as a performer, only later was Lupino commissioned to direct – as if by chance, as she would tell it. According to one of many stories, it was George Diskant, the cameraman on *The Bigamist*, who first offered her an invitation to leave theatrical filmmaking and try her hand as a television actress: "'I'm in with a group called "Four Star" with some old buddies of yours, David Niven, Charles Boyer and Dick Powell. Why don't you come over and go into television?'".[3] Although at first snobbish towards the new medium, Lupino eventually succumbed to their overtures and became the fourth star of the series: "I...loved every minute of it – and never missed directing. Then, during a summer hiatus, [ex-husband] Collier Young asked me to direct Joseph Cotten in *On Trial*, and having been inactive as a director for so long I could not believe the offer."[4]

Over the next two decades Lupino would demonstrate a fondness for such informal anecdotes about her official entrance into television directing, sometimes elaborating details, at other times forgetting them. What has remained constant throughout her self-representation in the popular press, however, is Lupino's implied denial of her own agency, the insistence on her passive acceptance of the capricious nature of her role in the industry, and on her donning of the director's hat as yet another instance of public role playing in the career of a multifaceted celebrity. The tone of her anecdotes and the connotations of her diction (guests, dinner parties, invitations, old buddies) are revealing: they couch what may have been Lupino's recognition of the nascent television industry's opportunities for career advancement in the polite language of society columns, wherein traits of hospitality and glamour would be considered more suitable than blatant directorial ambition to describe an established female star working in Hollywood. These tensions – between public image and private aspiration, between a fading motion picture career and a new future in television, between stereotypes of feminine and masculine propriety in the work place – would continue to shape Lupino's uncertain tenure as a television director.

Despite Lupino's public remarks that would often colour the reason for her transition from cinema to television as her desire to "keep busy" between theatrical film projects, by the mid-1950s the star took fewer leading roles, and her activities as a film director had diminished. It would seem that economic necessity played as much a part as creative opportunities in Lupino's decision to work almost exclusively within television for the remainder of her career as a director. Although she would continue to act in even more episodes than she would direct, Lupino's unique position as the most active woman behind the television cameras rests more upon her reputation as a filmmaker than as a leading lady, and in particular upon the critical and commercial success of her most widely seen cinematic work, *The Hitch-Hiker*.

In fact, after 1960 Lupino earned the nickname "the female Hitch" for her speciality work in action-oriented genres that employed her talent at creating suspense. Richard Boone, the star of the popular *Have Gun, Will Travel* series (CBS, 1957-62), of which Lupino eventually directed at least four episodes, had admired her hardboiled style and offered her a script by Harry Julian Fink, "famed for his graphic descriptions of physical violence".[5] From then onwards and for the next decade, although she would direct a handful of sitcoms and various drama programmes, Lupino would be commissioned primarily for westerns (*The Rifleman*, *The Virginian*, *Dundee and the Culhane*, *Daniel Boone*, *Tate*), crime dramas (*The Untouchables*, *The Fugitive*, *77 Sunset Strip*), and mysteries (*Thriller*, *The Twilight Zone*, *Kraft Suspense Theater*, *Alfred Hitchcock Presents*). At times lamenting that she ultimately had become so "type-cast" as an action director that she "couldn't get a job directing a love story",[6] Lupino apparently relished her anomalous stature as a woman specialising in shootouts and car chases, at one point turning down Hitchcock's offer of a leading role in one episode of his series in order to replace him at the helm as its director.[7]

This figure of Lupino as a "female Hitch", whose nomenclature suggests the freedom to call her own shots and the status of an auteur, is rather misleading within the context of a television industry whose creative efforts are shaped and controlled almost exclusively by producers rather than by directors.[8] Hitchcock himself, while directing several episodes of his series, served primarily as its producer, guiding the programme whose established look, tone and content would in general override the individual contributions of its crew and various directors. Thus, although series such as *The Untouchables* and *The Fugitive*, whose intricate weekly subplots and relatively large guest casts required more creative input from Lupino, on formulaic series such as *Gilligan's Island* or *Bewitched*, her influence was minimal.[9]

For this reason, in contrast to her body of cinematic directorial work, most of which she also co-wrote or co-produced, Lupino's scattered work in television must, by the very nature of the industry, resist any auteurist approach. More of a freelance substitute than a series regular, Lupino established her career with an accumulation of random "guest" spots rather than by pursuing long-term contracts with any particular programme or network. Such job security was generally reserved for her male colleagues. On the other hand, Lupino's continued interest in acting[10] may have been equally responsible for her irregular directing schedule, at the same time as strengthening her reputation as a director who worked well with fellow actors. Although praised for her abilities to link scenes smoothly, to cooperate with the crew, and to come in on time and under budget,[11] Lupino's most "endearing" capacities apparently were her skill at handling players of both sexes and a sensitivity to the problems and needs of her cast which derived from her own training as an actress.

Although Lupino would continue to act at least as frequently as she would direct, she appeared unsure about her preferences, at least according to her contradictory public comments. In 1955, for instance, when first embarking upon her television directing career, she asserted: "Directing is much easier than acting ... . The actor deals in false emotions, produced on cue. The director has his problems, but they're all normal."[12] By 1970, however, near the end of her tenure in television, Lupino felt quite the opposite: "I think directing is much harder than acting. An actor is only expected to interpret one role at a time. A director has to interpret—and help actors interpret—any number of roles at the same time. It's a little bit like juggling; you can't afford to miss a beat."[13]

Nor has Lupino been consistent in her remarks about her preference for directing either films for the cinema or television programmes. Once again, early on she praised television "as exciting because it moves so fast ... . You film a television picture in three days and a week later you can see the finished product. It is not like making motion pictures which take months to film and then more months to complete editing and scoring. By the time a motion picture is finished you've forgotten it."[14] Years later, however, she complained that it is "harder to direct TV than movies. TV people want quality and they prefer it to be done in a short time. Sometimes that's impossible. I want to go back to movies because it would be like a vacation."[15]

Does Lupino's desire for a "vacation" indicate an exhaustion with the television industry that might in part explain her eventual withdrawal from directing in the early 1970s? After a decade of work spanning all three television networks, a variety of genres, and an irregular schedule, Lupino's commitment to directing, like acting, could not be said to have been total: "Directing takes all your time, all your energy. And, love, there are other things I want to do."[16] At a period in her life and in our social history during which her desire for a career chafed at her equally strong desire to raise and care for her family, Lupino suffered the dilemma of the average woman of the time who was forced to negotiate a notion of "work" that must threaten neither the spheres over which patriarchy dominated, such as the television industry, nor her identity as a wife and mother, whose "natural" place belonged in the home rather than in the studio.

Although Ida Lupino was the first (and perhaps the only) woman director during the early years of US television production, it is odd that she is rarely listed as a "groundbreaker" for other women entering the industry.[17] Recognising that she might be seen in this way, Lupino has indicated: "I really just thought that a woman directing was an oddity, but I never felt like I was on a crusade for a cause".[18] Perhaps the displacement of her importance as the first woman director in television is best contextualized not in terms of "female firsts", but in relation to the television production process itself, which privileges the creative role of the producer over that of the director.[19] Unlike Lucille Ball, Loretta Young, Joan Davis and other women who were involved as producers in early television programming, Lupino rarely had primary creative control over the programmes she directed.[20]

To contextualize Lupino's role as a director in relation to other women working contemporaneously as producers is not meant to suggest, however, that a critical analysis of Lupino as a woman director is irrelevant to television history and feminist inquiry. What remains significant about Lupino as a woman director was her integration into an occupation which was (and still is) dominantly coded as "masculine".[21] Assumed to be an outsider and an anomaly in this male-dominated position, Lupino was more often than not represented merely *as* a woman, while her directorial skill was either de-emphasized or ignored altogether. The contradictions which exist in various representations of Lupino as a woman director thus demonstrate how postwar oppositions to patriarchal ideology (especially women working outside the home)[22] produced various discursive negotiations of gender. We would like to consider, therefore, the ways in which the media (and Lupino herself) may have functioned to contain the potential threat of her gender to the privilege and power associated with the masculine job of television directing.

Of the various attempts to negotiate this threat, the media initially focused on Lupino's introduction to television directing. While her entry into this field can be considered a somewhat "natural" extension of her career in film directing, comments from journalists and from Lupino herself appear to associate her directorial debut in television with nepotism via her marriages to Collier Young and Howard Duff, or through connections to various producers in the industry. In turn, Lupino resisted being labelled pejoratively as a "crusader" who actively pursued such a career by insisting instead that she "fell into" directing. When contrasted with descriptions of how men enter this industry (through "networking"), representations of Lupino being "helped" speak to the misogynistic stereotype of women as too weak, passive and unintelligent (that is, technologically illiterate and unskilled) to get ahead on their own merit, a stereotype which has worked for many years to keep women out of "men's work".

While some articles regarding Lupino's directorial skill remain free of comments about her gender,[23] most media representations of the director focus on how her approach was gendered (as either masculine or feminine). The contradictions which surface regarding Lupino's gendered directorial perspective or style are illustrative of the negotiation of tensions arising from challenges to traditional gender roles in the 1950s and 1960s. The ideological tensions arising over working women appear, for example, in the title of Richard Gehman and Michael McFadden's 1963 article on women actresses who have begun to work behind the camera: "The Golden Sex: They Use Beauty, Brains to Produce TV".[24] In their article, the writers detail the main differences they perceive between men and women entering the more technical and managerial aspects of television broadcasting:

> Bitten nails and gray hair are standard physical equipment on most producer-directors, for the immense responsibilities keep them all a-jitter. In recent years, these two characteristics have been replaced, in certain instances, by carefully-enameled and unbitten nails and by bouffant hair-dos teased into the strata of haute couture. Very slowly, but nonetheless relentlessly, women are slipping behind producers' desks and into directors' chairs.[25]

Focusing on the physical and behavioural differences between male and female producer-directors, the writers demonstrate a sexist negotiation of women's changing roles in the workplace: "Women no longer are content to take orders from those who make TV and feature films.

Increasingly they are being gripped by the urge to give orders themselves ... . [A]pparently acting did not supply enough stimulation or satisfaction for them. They now say that they are happier behind the cameras than they were when they were before them."[26]

In an effort to make sense out of these women "gripped by the urge to give orders", the writers code them as androgynous: no longer "simply" women (that is, those who take orders), these new producers-directors are represented as adopting both feminine and masculine attributes in their work practices ("beauty and brains"). For example, when describing Lupino's reputation as a television director, Gehman and McFadden note: "The present Mrs Howard Duff is known to actors and actresses as one of the most sensitive—and the toughest—directors in the business".[27] Here, the writers legitimize Lupino both as a "good" director and as a working woman, firstly by linking her to her husband, and secondly by noting that she is able to demonstrate the best qualities of both femininity and masculinity.

While Gehman and McFadden evoke androgyny to explain these women's behaviour behind the camera, other journalists who note Lupino's ability in directing television typically gender her skill as masculine.[28] For example, in an article by critic Hal Humphrey, Lupino indicates that, of the two categories used to describe directors' postures while working in the studio – "standers" and "sitters" – she classifies herself as a "stander" due to her "high strung" nature.[29] Although she makes no connection in her comments here between gender and the posture of directors – noting at one point that Alfred Hitchcock was a "sitter" and John Huston a "stander" – several biographers, by ignoring her comment about Hitchcock and Huston, have implied that Lupino's "standing" directorial style is more demonstrative of an "active" masculinity than a passive, sedentary femininity.[30]

Later in this same article, Humphrey notes that Lupino brings a collapsible stool with her to the set in case she becomes tired. While some may see this as an attempt to code Lupino as a "fragile woman" (indeed, the stool is referred to as "dainty" by another journalist),[31] it is important to note that fatigue from prolonged physical labour is a human, and not a uniquely feminine, characteristic.[32] The faulty logic which connects the hard work of directing with masculinity reappears in a statement made by Lupino almost twenty years later: "Look. A man is a man and a woman is a woman, and I believe that. All right, so you probably might consider directing a man's job. Well, it is. Physically, directing is extremely rough."[33] Perhaps upset that some gender confusion on her part was being implied, Lupino seems unaware that there might be alternative ways to describe labour than using gender stereotypes.

While the coding of Lupino's directing as masculine is most

certainly related to the conventional masculinisation of the director's position, as well as to the ideological tensions over gender in the postwar years, Lupino was also gendered masculine (and for some, "antifeminist") because of the types of television programmes she directed. Applauded as television's most successful woman, Lupino was depicted by *The New York Times* as being "renowned for her ability to spill blood with the best of them".[34] Like some journalists, Lupino found her direction of action programmes to be ironic: "Who, me? I thought. Here I'd always done women's stories and now I couldn't get a woman's story to direct."[35] Lupino notes her frustration at being typecast as an action director, a somewhat totalizing categorization which worked against the possibility of her directing other kinds of programmes: "I did so many Westerns and action shows I was looked upon as a director who could not direct a *man and a woman* story. I could do a lot of soul searching and conjecturing on *that* state of affairs, wonder out loud why the male producers around town did not think a woman knew about love."[36] While Lupino indicates her awareness that there is no direct or natural correlation between gender and practice, those in the industry who commented on her work seemed to find it bewildering that her "different" sex did not lead to television productions which were also "different". Thus, even when some producers felt she could handle a "woman's story", there appears to be some ambiguity as to the kind of perspective Lupino could offer. For example, producer Norman MacDonnell theorized: "You use Ida when you have a story about a woman with some dimension, and you really want it hard-hitting".[37]

Despite Lupino's being gendered masculine as a director of typically male genres, there were just as many comments in the media (if not more) that she still had a "feminine touch", comments which demonstrate an attempt to offset the threat of a woman performing a "man's job". For example, Peter Bart of *The New York Times* notes: "Though she spends her life at a man's calling, she is unstintingly feminine in bearing and manner. 'I'm not the kind of woman who can bark orders,' she observed the other day, her fingers cradling a vodka martini."[38] In one *TV Guide* article, the writer focuses almost exclusively on the "new lingo" Lupino had brought to directing, a language which made obsolete "every Western studio cliché used in Hollywood since William S. Hart first rode the celluloid range".[39] Over-emphasizing her British accent ("Dahling"), the writer never mentions Lupino's ability or skill in directing actors and crew, focusing instead on this "different" (feminine) language. In the first of many misogynistic interpretations of Lupino's speech, the writer, for instance, translates her rather straightforward direction, "Cut. Printsville. How does it look?" as "End of scene. Print it. How does *my face* look?".[40]

In another article, entitled "Mother Lupino", the director's approach is represented as "rul[ing] more by sex appeal than by fiat".[41] Like the *TV Guide* piece, this article also focuses on the "feminine" nature of Lupino's speech, again emphasizing her use of "darling" and "sweetheart" when addressing actors and crew. *TV Guide* returned to its focus on the novelty of Lupino's language in an article by Dwight Whitney entitled "'Follow Mother, Here We Go, Kiddies!'" (the title taken from one of Lupino's directorial cues). Dubbing Lupino "the first and maybe the last of the lady TV directors", Whitney highlights her use of "darling", "baby", "sweetie", "love", "sweetheart" and "kiddies". To illustrate how she does everything "the instinctively feminine way", he quotes Lupino as affirming, "I don't believe in wearing the pants ... . You don't tell a man, actors, crews. You suggest to them."[42]

This "feminine" mode of "suggestion" on the set was profoundly (if not problematically) emphasized in Lupino's article for *Action* magazine in 1967. Provocatively titled, "Me, Mother Directress", the article notes her distaste for "bossy" women who assert their power and control over men by "barking orders":

> I would never shout orders to anyone. I hate women who order men around—professionally or personally ... . I've seen bossy women push their men around and I have no respect for the gal who does the shoving or the man who lets himself get pushed around ... . [On the set] I say, "Darlings, mother has a problem. I'd love to do this. Can you do it? It sounds kooky but I want to do it. Now, can you do it for me?" And they do it—they just do it.[43]

In an interview ten years later, Lupino stressed this point again, asking her interviewer, "You'd want to help me, wouldn't you?".[44] Lupino's question here points to a lack of awareness that her "damsel in distress" routine might not be the only alternative to being aggressive on the set.

In addition to this emphasis on Lupino's "feminine" power of suggestion is the unrelenting focus on her physical appearance on the set while directing, undoubtedly an extension of her career in acting where she was trained to be a glamorous spectacle. From the 1956 review of her television directing debut which dubbed her "the purtiest [sic] director of the year", to Whitney's article in 1966 where he finds "Mother all aplomb, which is not easy for a girl with the dust of Iverson's [Ranch] sifting down over her", articles focused not on her skill as a director but on the spectacle of her female body and its "feminine" accoutrements.[45] For example, in Humphrey's article on Lupino as a "stander", the writer spends considerable space focusing on Lupino's exotic directorial fashions:

She used to wear "dainty flats," as she calls them, to match her silk one-piece mechanic's suits, but now she's shod in tennis shoes. "The boys on the set advised the tennis shoes," reports Ida. "They said they realized that from the ankles down I was not going to look sexy, but I would feel better at the end of the day." On outdoor location work Ida wears kookie hats with wild feathers, kerchiefs and other bric-a-brac ("It gives the boys a kick"), and in cold weather she adds a "mad" sweater.[46]

Similarly, *TV Guide* notes that, rather than puttees and a riding crop, "Miss Lupino wore velvet pants [and] brandished a lipstick".[47]

Apparently, the media were not alone in their interest in her appearance. Relating a story of being on a studio backlot preparing for an episode of *The Virginian*, Lupino describes the horror she felt when a flock of tourists came upon her: "There I was on the set, dripping wet in the killing heat, wearing no makeup, looking like a witch searching for an old house to haunt ... ".[48] Luckily, she found a studio policeman who would let her know when the tourists were coming so that she could hide her unglamorous appearance from the public.

In addition to the written discourse on Lupino's television work, it would appear that certain photographs primarily depicted her not as a director but as an exotic spectacle "hamming" it up for the photographer. For example, in an anthology on *Gilligan's Island* Lupino is photographed in the arms of The Skipper and Gilligan as she is about to be tossed into the "lagoon".[49] In another photo for an article on five directors who came to television from acting careers, Lupino (the only woman) is centred high upon a ladder, balancing precariously above the four men who surround her. In addition to her spectacularization in these photographs, the placement of Lupino's body in relation to the men metaphorically emphasizes the tenuous position she was made to occupy in this male-dominated industry.[50] As these photographs attest, Lupino's role as director seemed overshadowed by her persona as an actress and Hollywood celebrity.

Among other discursive negotiations of Lupino's threat to the masculine sphere of television production were the numerous attempts to discover and rationalize her reasons for choosing this occupation over others, especially acting. While many journalists argued that she could have made more money as an actress, no one seemed to believe that she could have any ambitions other than earning a huge income. When Humphrey points out to her that she was making less money directing than she did acting, Lupino replies, "Of course, darling, but that just proves how dedicated I am to my work, you see".[51] Lupino's "sexy little laugh that lets you know absolutely nothing" seems to take Humphrey off guard. Could she be serious? Does she actually *enjoy* directing?

Lupino herself added to the confusion about her choice of careers by implying at various times that she considered directing television nothing but a job to pay the bills: "So I take the [directing] job, what else? My old boy and I have gotta eat, don't we?" When asked why she chooses directing over writing short stories, which she would prefer, "Mother furrows her brow. 'Who would pay for this?' she says, with a wave toward the swimming pool".[52]

The contradictions which surround Lupino's decision to direct television (as well as her representation as a woman director) are best considered historically in relation to the tensions arising from the increase in the numbers of white, middle-class women working outside the home during the 1950s and 1960s. As many scholars have noted, a postwar emphasis on the updated ideal of the nuclear family, the new model of suburban living, and the glorification of the housewife/mother figure led to considerable debate over the "proper place" of women in US society.[53] While the media, advertisers and real estate agents focused on the leisure allegedly inherent in the suburban lifestyle, many women felt frustrated by their containment and sacrifice as mothers and housewives.[54] In addition, the blissful life upon which the suburban dream was based proved quite expensive to maintain, and those women pursuing the suburban fantasy became entwined in an unforeseen paradox: while the media glorified the suburban housewife ideal, many women were forced to work outside the home in order to maintain the middle-class standard of living to which their families aspired.

While Ida Lupino was anything but a middle-class suburban housewife, those who believe that a Hollywood actress-cum-television director would be spared this paradox deny the extent and power of patriarchal ideology. The contradictions which reveal themselves in media representations of Lupino as a television director point to the considerable tensions surrounding the ideology of gender and labour during the postwar years. It should come as no surprise, therefore, that the nickname bestowed upon Lupino by her production crews – "Mother" – itself worked to contain her in the dominant role for women at the time. Indeed, Lupino herself seemed somewhat aware that, while this nickname was meant as a term of endearment on the set, as a mother (and as a wife) she had quite different obligations which, at times, seriously conflicted with her career as a director. As she indicated in 1967: "I've had some offers to direct out of the country... . But I have my old boy and my daughter and I love them and life is too short for me to leave them and go flipping off for five or six or seven months. I just won't go."[55] By 1977, however, Lupino seemed much more aware of the disparities in parenting generated and maintained by patriarchal ideology: "That's where being a man [director] makes a great deal of difference. I don't suppose the men particularly care about leaving their wives and children. During the vacation period the wife can always fly over and be with him. It's difficult for a wife to say to her husband, come sit on the set and watch."[56] For an anomaly such as Lupino, whose idiosyncratic career peaked just prior to the birth of the women's movement, perhaps retirement from directing was the only possible recourse.

Notes

[1] Ida Lupino, "Me, Mother Directress", *Action* 2: 3 (1967): 14. This article was later reprinted in Richard Koszarski's anthology, *Hollywood Directors 1941-1976* (New York: Oxford University Press, 1977).

[2] "A Fourth for TV: Ida Lupino Joins Trio of Stars in Film Series", *TV Guide* 3 December 1955: 16. Lupino has been fond of this phrase, which appears in several stories in the popular press over the next two decades.

[3] As told in Lupino: 15.

[4] Ibid.

[5] Dwight Whitney, "'Follow Mother, Here We Go, Kiddies!'", *TV Guide* 8 October 1966: 15.

[6] Lupino: 15.

[7] Whitney: 18.

[8] As Horace Newcomb and Robert S Alley indicate in their text, *The Producer's Medium: Conversations with Creators of American TV*, television production is primarily the result of the "self-conscious, creative producer": "The producer, involved with the project from beginning to end, sees to it that continuity is maintained, that peace is kept among other members of the team, and, most importantly, that the series concept remains secure". (New York: Oxford University Press, 1983): xii-xiii.

[9] Perhaps the only series that Lupino genuinely shaped as director is *Thriller*, a mystery anthology hosted by Boris Karloff, for whom she directed at least ten episodes in its first two seasons. Unfortunately, none of these episodes is currently archived for public viewing or available for video rental. Her directorial debut in television, the *Screen Directors Playhouse* presentation of "No. 5 Checked Out", adapted from her own story, is probably the only episode of her television career to which one might apply an auteurist reading, as the series was designed as a showcase for theatrical film talent. Other anthology programmes which may bear more of Lupino's mark are *General Electric Theater*, *Kraft Suspense Theater* and Rod Serling's *The Twilight Zone*, although as the latter itself suggests, these programmes had already been well-defined by their producers by the time Lupino took the reins as director.

[10] It should be noted that Lupino acted in many other directors' segments of virtually all the series on which she directed.

[11] See Jack Edmund Nolan, "Ida Lupino: Director", *Film Fan Monthly* 89 (1968): 10.

[12] "A Fourth for TV": 17.

[13] Lupino, quoted in an unpublished NBC New York Biography dated 27 October 1970, transcribed from the clipping files at the University of Southern California Cinema and Television Archives.

[14] Lupino, quoted in an unpublished CBS-TV Hollywood Biography dated 22 March 1956, transcribed from the clipping files at the University of Southern California Cinema and Television Archives.

[15] Lupino, quoted in a UPI syndicated column dated 1966 (source unspecified), transcribed from the clipping files at the Margaret Herrick Library of the Academy of Motion Picture Arts and Sciences in Beverly Hills, CA.

[16] Lupino, quoted in Whitney: 18.

[17] Indeed, the first woman to have considerable power in the US media arrived long before Lupino's directorial debut in television. Frieda Hennock became the first female commissioner of the Federal Communications Commission (FCC) in 1948, at the early days of television history. It would take thirty years until a woman, Jane Cahill Pfeiffer, would become chair of one of the networks.

[18] Lupino, quoted in *The Hollywood Reporter®* 16 November 1972: n.p. In another interview Lupino noted: "I never thought of myself as a *crusader*, you know". Quoted in Ginger Varney, "Ida Lupino, Director", *LA Weekly* 12-18 November 1982: 10.

[19] While other women had worked in television production before her, they were usually confined to occupations that were conventionally coded as "feminine" (e.g. hair styling, make-up, costume design), and therefore were not seen to be a threat to the predominantly male work force. Even women actors were considered non-threatening since they could be easily categorized and contained as visual spectacles.

[20] This is not to say that Lupino was never involved in television as a producer. With her third husband, Howard Duff, she formed Bridget Productions (named after their daughter), which produced the *Mr Adams and Eve* series, in which Duff and Lupino acted. In the mid-1960s she formed Stanley Productions with her then-husband, Howard Duff. The third partner in the company was either Fred Hamilton (as Lupino indicated in an interview with Richard Gehman and Michael McFadden in 1963) or her second husband, Collier Young (as she stated in an interview with Humphrey in 1966). See Richard Gehman and Michael McFadden's article, "The Golden Sex: They Use Beauty, Brains to Produce TV", *Los Angeles Herald-Examiner* 14 May 1963:

B1, B8; and Hal Humphrey's, "Ida Does It All in World of Films", *The Los Angeles Times* 19 May 1966: Sec. 5: 20.

[21] Thus, it is somewhat disturbing to note how little research has been done on women television directors. For example, Betsy Covington Smith's text on women in television does not discuss one woman television director, although most other occupations in television production are represented. See *Breakthrough: Women in Television* (New York: Walker and Company, 1981).

[22] This was not necessarily true for women of colour and working-class women, who for years had worked outside the home to support both their families and the ideal of the "non-working" middle-class housewife.

[23] This is true of most *Variety* reviews of episodes directed by Lupino.

[24] Gehman and McFadden: B1.

[25] Ibid.

[26] Ibid.

[27] Ibid: B8.

[28] In a *TV Guide* article on Lupino's direction of one episode of *The Virginian*, one of her crew members remarked, "She directs like a man", a comment which writer Dwight Whitney assumes can only be favourable. See Whitney: 16.

[29] Hal Humphrey, "In the Directing Business Ida Classes Herself a [sic] a 'Stander'", *Mirror News* 6 December 1960: n.p.

[30] Jack Edmund Nolan, "Ida Lupino", *Films in Review* 16: 1 (1965): 62. See also Jerry Vermilye, *Ida Lupino: A Pyramid Illustrated History of the Movies* (New York: Pyramid Publications, 1977): 125.

[31] Whitney: 15.

[32] Surely the fact that there is little written about the physical weariness of male directors on the set has less to do with their not experiencing fatigue than with an erasure of bodily pain and suffering in the discourse about men's labour.

[33] Lupino, quoted in Debra Weiner, "Interview with Ida Lupino", in Karyn Kay and Gerald Peary (eds), *Women and the Cinema: A Critical Anthology* (New York: E P Dutton, 1977): 170.

[34] Peter Bart, "Lupino, the Dynamo", *The New York Times* 7 March 1965: Sec. 2: 7.

[35] Lupino, quoted in Weiner: 177. Although Lupino was nicknamed "the female Hitch", no one has noted the irony that when a male director such as Brian De Palma is compared to Hitchcock, he is never dubbed a "male Hitch".

[36] Lupino: 15. Lupino later fails to notice the irony in her own statement that she cannot envision a woman directing *The Wild Bunch*. *The Hollywood Reporter®* 16 November 1972: n.p.

[37] MacDonnell, quoted in Whitney: 16.

[38] Bart: 7.

[39] "Director Ida Lupino Creates a New Lingo", *TV Guide* 24 January 1959: 29.

[40] Ibid (emphasis added).

[41] "Mother Lupino", *Time* 8 February 1963: 46.

[42] Lupino, quoted in Whitney: 16.

[43] Lupino: 14.

[44] Lupino, quoted in Weiner: 177.

[45] *Daily Variety* 20 January 1956: n.p., and Whitney: 15.

[46] Humphrey (1960): n.p.

[47] "Director Ida Lupino Creates a New Lingo": 29. The article also contains a photograph of Lupino applying lipstick.

[48] Lupino: 14.

[49] Sherwood Schwartz, *Inside Gilligan's Island: From Creation to Syndication* (London: McFarland, 1988): 275.

[50] "They Work Both Sides of the Camera", *TV Guide* 14 July 1962: 19.

[51] Lupino, quoted in Humphrey (1960): n.p.

[52] Whitney: 16, 18.

[53] See, for example, Lynn Spigel, *Make Room for TV: Television and the Family Ideal in Postwar America* (Chicago: University of Chicago Press, 1992).

[54] Elaine Tyler May, *Homeward Bound: American Families in the Cold War Era* (New York: Basic Books, 1988).

[55] Lupino: 15.

[56] Lupino, quoted in Weiner: 178.

Films directed, scripted and produced by Ida Lupino

Annette Kuhn

Information is presented in the following format:

year · title
       alternative title

country of production   running time
production information (producer, writer, cast, crew, etc.)
summary
viewing availability
unlisted credits, with sources

The following abbreviations have been used:

art dir	art director	*mus dir*	musical director
ass dir	assistant director	*phot*	director of
ass prod	associate producer		photography
dir	director	*prod*	producer
ed	film editor	*prod comp*	production company
mins	minutes	*prod des*	production design
mus	music	*sc*	script

1946 · Young Widow

USA 100 mins
dir Edwin L Marin
prod Hunt Stromberg
prod comp Special Pictures
sc Richard Macaulay and
Margaret Buell Wilder
phot Lee Garmass

cast Jane Russell (Joan
Kenwood), Louis Hayward (Jim
Cameron), Faith Domergue
(Gerry Taylor), Penny Singleton
(Peg Martin), Kent Taylor (Peter
Waring).

Sentimental drama of a war widow who is persuaded to marry someone
else.

Co-producer (BFI); co-producer, uncredited (FD).

1948 · The Judge
The Gamblers

USA 69 mins
dir Elmer Clifton
prod Anson Bond
prod comp Emerald/Film
Classics
sc Samuel Newman, Elmer
Clifton and Anson Bond
original story Julius Long
phot Tom Holland
ed Fred Maguire

choral effects Gene Manhan
cast Milburn Stone (Martin
Strang), Katherine deMille
(Lucille Strang), Paul Guilfoyle
(William Jackson), Stanley
Waxman (Dr James Anderson),
Norman Budd (James Tilton),
Jonathan Hale (the judge).

Melodrama involving the wrongdoings of a criminal lawyer and the fatal
price he finally pays through trying to blackmail one of his guilty clients.

Co-producer (BFI); made by Lupino's production company (FD).

1949 · Not Wanted

USA 94 mins
dir Elmer Clifton
prod **Ida Lupino** and Anson
Bond
prod comp Emerald/Film
Classics
sc Paul Jarrico and **Ida Lupino**
original story Paul Jarrico and
Malvin Wald
phot Henry Freulich
ed William Ziegler

mus Leith Stevens
art dir Charles D Hall
cast Sally Forrest (Sally Kelton),
Keefe Brasselle (Drew Baxter),
Leo Penn (Steve Ryan), Dorothy
Adams (Mrs Kelton), Wheaton
Chambers (Mr Kelton), Rita
Lupino (Joan), Audrey Farr
(Nancy), Carole Donne (Jane),
Ruth Clifford (Mrs Stone).

Summary: see pages 13-14.

Available for viewing at Library of Congress.

In a number of interviews Lupino has stated that when Elmer Clifton
was taken ill three days into shooting, she took over directing the film
but declined to take screen credit.

1950 · The Vicious Years
       The Gangster We Made

USA   80 mins
dir Robert Florey
prod Anson Bond
prod comp Emerald/Film Classics
sc N Richard Nash
phot Henry Freulich
ed Fred Allen
mus Arthur Lange

art dir Charles B Hall
cast Tommy Cooke (Mario), Gar Moore (Luca Rossi), Sybil Merritt (Dina), Eduard Franz (Emilio), Marjorie Eaton (Zia Lolo), Anthony Ross (Spezia), Myron Welton (Tino).

An orphan boy living on his wits blackmails a murderer to bring him up. Affection grows on both sides, and he becomes more stable.

Made by Lupino's production company (FD, FII).

1950 · Never Fear
       The Young Lovers

USA   81 mins
dir **Ida Lupino**
prod Collier Young
prod comp The Filmakers
sc **Ida Lupino** and Collier Young
phot Archie Stout
ed William Ziegler, Harvey Manger
mus Leith Stevens
art dir McClure Capps

prod des Van Nest Polglase
songs John Franco, William Earley
cast Sally Forrest (Carol Williams), Keefe Brasselle (Guy Richards), Hugh O'Brian (Len Randall), Eve Miller (Phyllis Townsend), Larry Dobkin (Dr Middleton), Rita Lupino (Josie).

Summary: see page 40.

Available for viewing at Museum of Modern Art.
Co-producer (BFI).

1950 · Outrage

USA   75 mins
dir **Ida Lupino**
prod Collier Young
prod comp The Filmakers

sc Collier Young, Malvin Wald and **Ida Lupino**
phot Archie Stout

ed Harvey Manger
mus dir Constantin Bakaleinikoff
prod des Harry Horner
cast Mala Powers (Ann Walton), Tod Andrews (Ferguson), Robert Clarke (Jim Owens), Raymond Bond (Mr Walton), Lilian Hamilton (Mrs Walton), Rita Lupino (Stella Carter), Jerry Paris (Frank Marini), Hal March (Sgt Hendrix), Kenneth Patterson (Mr Harrison).

Summary: see pages 57-58.

Available for viewing at National Film and Television Archive. Co-producer (BFI, IDFF).

1951 · Hard, Fast and Beautiful

USA 78 mins
dir **Ida Lupino**
prod Collier Young
prod comp The Filmakers
sc Martha Wilkerson
original novel John R Tunis
phot Archie Stout
ed William Ziegler
mus Roy Webb
mus dir Constantin Bakaleinikoff
art dir Albert S D'Agostino and Jack Okey
cast Claire Trevor (Milly Farley), Sally Forrest (Florence Farley), Carleton G Young (Fletcher Locke), Robert Clarke (Gordon McKay), Kenneth Patterson (Will Farley), Marcella Cisney (Miss Martin), Arthur Little, Jr (commentator), Joseph Kearns (J R Carpenter).

Summary: see pages 73-74.

Available for viewing at National Film and Television Archive. Co-producer (BFI, IDFF).

1951 · On the Loose

USA 74 mins
dir Charles Lederer
prod Collier Young
prod comp The Filmakers
sc Dale Eunson and Katherine Albert
original story Malvin Wald and Collier Young
phot Archie Stout
ed Desmond Marquette
mus Leigh Harline
mus dir Constantin Bakaleinikoff
art dir Albert S D'Agostino
cast Joan Evans (Jill Bradley),

Melvyn Douglas (Frank Bradley), Lynn Bari (Alice Bradley), Robert Arthur (Larry Lindsay), Hugh O'Brian (Dr Phillips), Constance Hilton (Susan Tanner), Michael Kuhn (Bob Vance).

Unhappy home life in the United States and its effects on a teenager.

Made by Lupino's production company (FD); producer (SS).

1952 · Beware, My Lovely

USA 77 mins
dir Harry Horner
prod Collier Young
prod comp The Filmakers
sc, original play Mel Dinelli
phot George E Diskant
ed Paul Weatherwax
mus Leith Stevens
art dir Albert S D'Agostino and

Alfred Herman
cast **Ida Lupino** (Mrs Gordon), Robert Ryan (Howard), Taylor Holmes (Mr Armstrong), Barbara Whiting (Ruth Williams), James Willmas (Mr Stevens), O Z Whitehead (Mr Franks), Dee Pollack (grocery boy).

An itinerant handyman flees from what looks like a murder and is hired by a war widow for a house-cleaning job.

Co-producer (BFI); producer (SS).

1953 · The Hitch-Hiker

USA 64 mins
dir **Ida Lupino**
prod Collier Young
prod comp The Filmakers
ass prod Christian Nyby
sc Collier Young and **Ida Lupino**
phot Nicholas Musuraca
ed Douglas Stewart
mus Leith Stevens
mus dir Constantin Bakaleinikoff
art dir Albert S D'Agostino and

Walter Keller
cast Edmond O'Brien (Roy Collins), Frank Lovejoy (Gilbert Bowen), William Talman (Emmett Myers), Jose Torvay (Captain Alvarado), Sam Mayes (himself), Wendel Niles (himself), Jean Del Val (Inspector General), Clark Howat (Government agent), Natividad Vacio (Jose).

Summary: see page 90.

Available for viewing at Library of Congress and National Film and Television Archive.
Co-producer (BFI, IDFF).

1953 · The Bigamist

USA 83 mins
dir **Ida Lupino**
prod Collier Young
prod comp The Filmakers
sc Collier Young
original story Larry Marcus and Lou Schor
phot George Diskant
ed Stanford Tischler
mus Leith Stevens

art dir James Sullivan
cast Edmond O'Brien (Harry Graham), Joan Fontaine (Eve Graham), **Ida Lupino** (Phyllis Martin), Edmund Gwenn (Mr Jordan), Jane Darwell (Mrs Connelley), Kenneth Tobey (Tom Morgan), John Maxwell (judge).

Summary: see pages 103-105.

Available for viewing at National Film and Television Archive.
Co-producer (IDFF); co-producer, script (BFI).

1954 · Private Hell 36

USA 80 mins
dir Don Siegel
prod Collier Young
prod comp The Filmakers
sc Collier Young and **Ida Lupino**
phot Burnett Guffey
ed Stanford Tischler

mus Leith Stevens
art dir Walter Keller
cast **Ida Lupino** (Lilli Marlowe), Steve Cochran (Cal Brunner), Howard Duff (Jack Farnham), Dean Jagger (Captain Michaels), Dorothy Malone (Francey).

Study of a dishonest detective who forces his colleague to share some of the money they have recovered from a robbery.

Available for viewing at National Film and Television Archive.
Co-producer (BFI).

1955 · Mad at the World

USA   63 mins
dir Harry Essex
prod Collier Young
prod comp The Filmakers
sc Harry Essex
phot William Snyder
ed Stanford Tischler
mus Leith Stevens
art dir Walter Keller

cast Frank Lovejoy (Tom Lynn),
Keefe Brasselle (Sam Bennett),
Cathy O'Donnell (Anne Bennett),
Karen Sharpe (Tess), Stanley
Clements (Pete), Paul Bryar
(Matt), Paul Dubov (Jamie),
James Delgado (Marty).

Young thugs kill a baby whose father then sets out to get them. He is
dissuaded by a detective from killing the boy who was responsible.

Co-producer (BFI).

1966 · The Trouble With Angels

USA   111 mins
dir **Ida Lupino**
prod William Frye
prod comp William Frye
Productions/Columbia Pictures
Corporation
sc Blanche Hanalis
original novel Jane Trahey
phot Lionel Lindon
ed Robert C Jones
mus Jerry Goldsmith
art dir John Beckman
cast Rosalind Russell (Mother
Superior), Hayley Mills (Mary
Clancy), June Harding (Rachel
Devery), Marge Redmond (Sister
Liguori), Binnie Barnes (Sister
Celestine), Gypsy Rose Lee (Mrs
Phipps), Barbara Hunter (Marvel
Ann), Camilla Sparv (Sister
Constance), Mary Wickes (Sister
Clarissa), Dolores Sutton (Sister
Rose Marie), Marjorie Eaton
(Sister Ursula), Barbara Bell
Wright (Sister Margaret), Judith
Lowry (Sister Prudence), Vicky
Albright (Charlotte), Jim Hutton
(Mr Petrie), Jim Boles (Mr
Gottschalk).

Summary: see pages 118-119.

Available for viewing at Library of Congress and National Film and
Television Archive.
Co-producer (IDFF).

Sources

BFI   British Film Institute Library and Information Service
       microfiche: "Ida Lupino"

FD   *Film Dope* 37 (June 1987)

FII   *Film Index International* (BFI CD-ROM)

IDFF *International Dictionary of Films and Filmmakers*,
       volume 3 (Chicago and London: St James Press, 1991)

SS   Patricia Erens, *Sexual Stratagems: the World of Women
       in Film* (New York: Horizon Press, 1979): 298.

Television programmes and series episodes directed by Ida Lupino

Mary Celeste Kearney and James M Moran

Information is presented in the following format:

season
title of programme
genre/network/executive producer/broadcast day and time/season
broadcast date   title of episode
production information (producer, writer, cast, crew, etc.)
summary (unless indicated otherwise, all summaries are from *TV Guide*)
review information
viewing/rental availability

The following abbreviations have been used:

art dir	art director	*prod*	producer
ass dir	assistant director	*prod ass*	assistant to producer
ass ed	assistant film editor	*prod coord*	production
ass prod	assistant producer		coordinator
assoc prod	associate producer	*prod man*	production manager
dir	director	*prod mix*	production mixer
ed	film editor	*prod sup*	production supervisor
ed sup	editing supervisor	*sc*	script
hair	hair stylist	*sc sup*	script supervisor
mus	music	*sd*	sound
mus coord	music coordinator	*sd ed*	sound editor
mus ed	music editor	*sd eng*	sound engineer
mus sup	music supervisor	*set dec*	set decorator
phot	director of	*set dir*	set director
	photography	*sp*	sponsor
phot effects	photographic effects	*story ed*	story editor

Only valid sources have been consulted in the compilation of this list. Wherever possible, the replication of errors and hearsay has been avoided and incomplete indexes have been supplemented by primary research. Unfortunately, Lupino seems to have kept no personal records documenting her career. In addition, archival files tend to focus upon Lupino's personal life and her career as an actress; and the number of extant episodes available for public viewing are limited and scattered between locations across the United States. For these reasons, certain entries are fuller than others. This document therefore claims only to be the most comprehensive listing of Lupino's television work to date based upon serviceable resources.

1955-56

Screen Directors Playhouse
dramatic anthology/NBC/Hal Roach/Wednesday 8-8.30 pm/1st season
18 January   "No. 5 Checked Out"

sc Willard Wiener
story **Ida Lupino**
cast Teresa Wright (Mary), Peter Lorre (Willie), William Talman (Barney), Ralph Moody (Jarvis).
prod sup Sidney Van Keuren
phot Lester H White, Paul Ivano
prod coord William M Sterling
ass dir Arthur Lueker
ed Bruce Schoengarth

art dir McClure Capps
set dir Rudy Butler
phot effects Jack R Glass
sd Jack Goodrich and Joel Moss
makeup Jack P Pierce
hair Carmen Dirigo
story ed James J Geller
casting Ruth Burch
sp Eastman Kodak Company

A young woman, although deaf, is left alone to look after the resort cabins owned by her father. Two dangerous bank robbers then move in, using the secluded spot as a temporary hideout.

Reviewed in *Daily Variety* 20 January 1956: n.p.
Available for viewing at UCLA Film and Television Archive.

1956-57

On Trial
law drama/NBC/Joseph Cotten/Friday 9-9.30 pm/1st season
23 November   "Trial of Mary Surratt"

cast Joseph Cotten, Ray Collins, Frank Milan, Virginia Gregg, Harry Tyler.

An ex-cavalry officer of the US Army returns to his law practice after the assassination of Abraham Lincoln. He is convinced of Mary Surratt's guilt in the conspiracy, but friends persuade him to talk to Mary and possibly defend her.

Available for viewing at Library of Congress.

1958-59

Mr Adams and Eve
sitcom/CBS/Howard Duff/Tuesday 8-8.30 pm/summer episode
8 July   "The Teenage Idol"

regular cast Howard Duff (Howard Adams), **Ida Lupino** (Eve
Adams), Hayden Rorke (Steve), Olive Carey (Elsie), Alan Reed (J B
Hafter).
guest cast Darrell Howe (Swivelhips), Patrick Wayne (Walter).

[Pilot episode for possible new series entitled *The Teenage Idol*.] "The
misadventures of Swivelhips Jackson, a rock and roll singer who
becomes America's newest teenage sensation.   The pilot episode,
broadcast as a segment of "Mr Adams and Eve," relates Howard's efforts
to help his housekeepers's [sic] nephew Walter impress a girl who has
eyes only for Swivelhips."[1]

1959-60

The Donna Reed Show
sitcom/ABC/Tony Owen/Thursday 8-8.30 pm/2nd season
10 December   "A Difference of Opinion"

sc Nate Monaster
regular cast Donna Reed (Donna Stone), Carl Betz (Dr Alex Stone),
Shelley Fabares (Mary Stone), Paul Petersen (Jeff Stone), Patty
Petersen (Trisha Stone).
guest cast Chet Stratton (Harry Baker), Ann Rutherford (Phyllis
Baker), Hal Smith (Rod), Holly Harris (Elsie), Renny McEvoy (Fred),
Alice Foote (Joan).

"Donna and Alex try to hide their arguments from the children when
they learn that they become embarrassed by the manner in which their
friends' parents fight."[2]

Have Gun, Will Travel
western/CBS/Sam Rolfe/Saturday 9.30-10 pm/3rd season/no. 3
12 September "First, Catch a Tiger"

regular cast Richard Boone (Paladin), Kam Tong (Hey Boy), Lisa Lu (Hey Girl).
guest cast Harry Bartell (Mordain), John Anderson (Dunne), Don Megowan (Huston), King Calder (Droggan), Pamela Lincoln (Mary).

Stopping at a public house along the trail, Paladin encounters the bitter father of a desperado he recently sent to the gallows. Paladin is forced to a showdown.

Reviewed in *Variety* 216: 3 (16 September 1959): 27.

9 April   "Lady with a Gun"

guest cast Jack Weston (Rudy Rossback), Paula Raymond (Miss MacIntosh), Jean Eager (Katie), Ron Soble (gunslinger).

The staid atmosphere of the Carleton Hotel lobby is ruffled when a guest ducks for cover. His reason: a gun-wielding young lady.

11 June   "The Trial"

guest cast Robert F Simon (Morgan Gibbs), Bud Slater (David Gibbs), Raymond Hatton (bounty hunter), Harry Antrim (merchant), Tom Jackson (Doc Richardson), James Bell (Charlie), Hal Smith (desk clerk), John Thye (trailhand), Bill Hunt (freighter), Rick Silver (Frank), Angela Stevens (woman).

Morgan Gibbs has a job for Paladin. His son David ran away after killing a woman, and Gibbs wants the boy brought back alive.

1960-61

Hong Kong
Asian adventure/ABC/William Self/Wednesday 7.30-8.30 pm/only season
28 September "Clear for Action" [debut episode]

prod Herbert Hirschman
sc Robert Buckner
regular cast Rod Taylor (Glenn Evans), Lloyd Bochner (Neil

Campbell), Jack Kruschen (Tully), Harold Fong (Fong), Gerald Jann (Ying), Mai Tai Sing (Ching Mei).
guest cast France Nuyen (Happy Cheung), Burt Brinckerhoff (Johnny McGuire), Frank Maxwell (Commander Harris), Noel Drayton (Governor), Robert Burton (Admiral), Leonard Strong (intelligence officer).

Evans (an American newsman stationed in Hong Kong) insists on showing his old friend Johnny McGuire around town.

Reviewed in *Variety* 220: 6 (5 October 1960): 29.
Available for viewing at Library of Congress.

23 November   "The Turncoat"

guest cast Christopher Dark (Harry Keefer), James Yagi (Li Sung), Lisa Lu (Mai Loo), Val Avery (Michael Fortune), Peter Chong (Tong Kai).

During the Korean War Harry Keefer was captured by the Communists and chose to remain with them. Now he is disillusioned and seeks political asylum in Hong Kong – with Evans's help.

Available for viewing at Library of Congress.

Alfred Hitchcock Presents
mystery/NBC/Alfred Hitchcock/Tuesday 8.30-9 pm/6th season
6 December   "Sybilla"

sc Charlotte Armstrong
story Margaret Manners
cast Barbara Bel Geddes (Sybilla), Alexander Scourby (Horace Meade).

"Feeling trapped by his marriage to Sybilla (Barbara Bel Geddes), Horace Meade (Alexander Scourby) fantasizes about killing her and jots down the details of how he would do so in his diary. Later, Sybilla tells him of an idea she has for a book in which a wife, having read her husband's diary, learns that he's planning to kill her and protects herself by sending a copy of the diary to her lawyer with instructions that it be made public should anything happen. Convinced that Sybilla is actually giving him a warning, he realises that he must protect her from harm at all costs. Eventually, she becomes terminally ill, however, and, as she lies dying, he demands the truth from her. But she expires without answering. Subsequently he learns that, although Sybilla had read his diary, she never did send a copy of it to her lawyer, for her goal had not been to save herself, but to save her husband's soul. Tearfully, he realizes just how lonely he'll be without her."[3]

24 January   "A Crime for Mothers"

sc Henry Slesar
cast Claire Trevor (Lottie Mead), Biff Elliott (Phil Ames), Patricia Smith (Jane Birdwell), Robert Samson (Ralph Birdwell), Howard McNear (Mr Maxwell), King Calder (Charlie Vance), Gail Bonney (secretary), Sally Smith (young girl).

"Alcoholic Lottie Mead (Claire Trevor) is determined to regain custody of the daughter she has not seen since surrendering her to the care of a couple named Birdwell. When the Birdwells refuse to cooperate, Lottie, whose only aim is money, demands a pay-off. Only then will she stop bothering them. Again, the Birdwells refuse. Lottie meets a detective named Ames (Biff Elliott), and together they devise a scheme to kidnap the girl and demand a $25,000 ransom from the Birdwells for her safe return. Ames brings Lottie to the schoolyard, points her daughter out to her, and, the next day, Lottie carries out the bogus kidnapping. Ames arrives with news that she had kidnapped the wrong girl and now faces a real kidnapping charge. He will help her, however, by returning the girl unharmed – provided Lottie promises to stop harassing the Birdwells. It seems Ames is really a friend of the couple. And the kidnap victim is his own daughter."[4]

Thriller
mystery/NBC/Hubbell Robinson/Monday 9-10 pm/1st season
14 March   "Trio for Terror" (3 one-act dramas, each 18 minutes)

Act I – "The Extra Passenger"
sc Barré Lyndon
short story Stephen Grendon
cast Richard Lupino (Simon), Terence De Marney (uncle Julian), Iris Bristol (Katie), Gil Stuart (train guard), Nelson Welch (doctor).

Simon tells his girl Katie he will soon inherit his wealthy uncle's estate.

Act II – "A Terribly Strange Bed"
sc Barré Lyndon
short story Wilkie Collins
cast Reginald Owen (Hussar), Robin Hughes (Collins), Peter Brocco (Major Domo), Jacqueline Squire (old woman), Reginald Plato (croupier).

An old woman approaches a pair of adventuresome guardsmen who show a fondness for gambling.

Act III – "The Medusa"
sc Barré Lyndon
short story Nelson Bond
cast John Abbott (Kriss Milo), Michael Pate (Shanner), Noel Drayton (superintendent), Richard Peel (inspector).

Police trail a desperate strangler named Shanner.

9 May   "Mr George"

sc Donald Sanford
short story Stephen Grendon
cast Gina Gillespie (Priscilla), Virginia Gregg (Edna), Howard Freeman (Jared), Lillian Bronson (Adelaide), Joan Tompkins (Laura), John Qualen, Ruth Parrot.

With the death of her parents, young Priscilla has inherited a large estate. The child's guardians, Edna, Jared and Adelaide, aware that the property could be theirs if Priscilla were out of the way, decide to protect the girl from the anxieties of adulthood – by killing her now.

The Rifleman
western/ABC/Jules Levy, Arthur Gardner, Arnold Laven/Tuesday
8-8.30 pm/3rd season
21 March   "Assault"

sc Jay Simms
regular cast Chuck Connors (Lucas McCain), Johnny Crawford (Mark McCain), Paul Fix (Marshall Micah Torrance), Joan Taylor (Miss Milly Scott), Patricia Blair (Lou Mallory), Bill Quinn (Sweeney, the bartender), Hope Summers (Hattie Denton).

guest cast Bob Sweeney (Speed Sullivan), Danny Richards Jr (Swifty Sullivan), Linda Lawson (Vashti Croxton), King Calder (King Croxton), Med Florey (Thes Croxton).

Speed Sullivan, a hot-shot salesman, needs all his persuasive powers to convince King Croxton that he is not the bounder who gave Croxton's daughter, Vashti, a black eye.

1961-62

Thriller
crime-horror/NBC/Hubbell Robinson/Monday 10-11 pm/2nd season
18 September "What Beckoning Ghost?"

prod William Frye
sc Donald Sanford, from Harold Lawler's magazine story and (uncredited) Pierre Boileau and Thomas Narcejac's novel, "Les Diaboliques"

cast Judith Evelyn (Mildred Beaumont), Tom Helmore (Eric Beaumont), Adele Mara (Lydia Beaumont), Frank Wilcox (detective).

Mildred Beaumont returns home to convalesce after a siege in the hospital with a heart ailment. Her husband Eric and sister Lydia do everything to make her comfortable, but Mildred begins to have strange visions of a casket and a funeral wreath – and imagines that she is hearing the ominous sounds of a dirge.

Reviewed in *Variety* 234: 4 (20 September 1961): 35.

25 September "Guillotine"

sc Charles Beaumont
story Cornell Woolrich
cast Robert Middleton (DeParis), Alejandro Rey (Robert Lamont), Danielle de Metz (Babette Lamont), Gregory Morton (prison director), Marcel Hillaire, Gaylord Cavallaro, Peter Brocco, Louise Mercier, Janine Grandel, Peter Camlin, Vance Howard, Jacques Villon, Ted Roter, Guy de Vestel, David R Cross, Charles La Torre.

Robert Lamont has been sentenced to death, and his last chance hangs on the unwritten law that a convict is pardoned if the executioner dies on the eve of the execution.

6 November   "The Last of the Sommervilles"

sc **Ida Lupino** and Richard Lupino
cast Boris Karloff (Dr Farnham), Phyllis Thaxter (Ursula Sommerville), Martita Hunt (Celia Sommerville), Peter Walker (Rutherford Sommerville), Chet Stratton (Mr Parchester).

Rutherford Sommerville, last male member of the family, returns to his ancestral home with a plan to put the touch on his rich and eccentric Aunt Celia. Then, a thousand dollars richer, he will continue on his way to Paris. But there have been some changes around the house since the last time Rutherford dropped in – his distant cousin Ursula has been living there for ten years now, and seems to be solidly on the inside track with Aunt Celia.

27 November   "The Closed Cabinet"

sc, short story Kay Leonard and Jess Carneol
cast Olive Sturgess (Evie Bishop), David Frankham (Alan Mervyn), Peter Forster (George Mervyn), Jennifer Raine (Lucy Mervyn), Isobel Elsom (Mrs Purdy), Patricia Manning, Kendrick Huxham, Molly Glessing, Myra Carter.

American Evie Bishop is travelling across England to visit her cousin Lucy. On the train, Evie tells a woman passenger about cousin Lucy, Lucy's husband George and their family mansion Mervyn Castle. But the woman knows all about Mervyn Castle – and the curse that was placed on it.

4 December   "Dialogs with Death" (two dramas, each 27 minutes)

Act I – "Friend of the Dead"
sc, short story Robert Arthur
cast Boris Karloff (Pop Jenkins), Ed Nelson (Tom Ellinson), George Kane (Harry Jervis), Ben Hammer (Dan Gordon).

Morgue attendant Pop Jenkins claims he can talk with his charges.

Act II – "Welcome Home"
cast Boris Karloff (Colonel Jackson), Estelle Winwood (Emily Jackson), Ed Nelson (Daniel Lejan).

Escaped convict Daniel Lejan and his wife Nell are met by Dan's aunt Emily and his uncle Colonel Jackson – who seem surprised that Daniel is alive.

15 January   "La Strega"

sc Alan Caillou
cast Ursula Andress (Luana), Alejandro Rey (Tonio Bellini), Jeanette Nolan (La Strega), Frank de Kova (Lieutenant Vincoli), Ramon Novarro (Maestro Giuliano), Ernest Sarracino (Padre Lupari).

Artist Tonio Bellini comes upon a shocking scene in his village: townspeople have seized a girl named Luana, the daughter of a woman they believe to be a witch, and are trying to drown her. Tonio intervenes, even though the villagers warn him that Luana is under her mother's evil spell.

19 March   "The Bride Who Died Twice"

sc Robert Hardy Andrews
cast Mala Powers (Consuela), Eduardo Ciannelli (General de la Verra), Joe de Santis (Colonel Sangriento), Robert Colbert (Captain Fernandez), Carl Don (Sergeant Vibora), Alex Montoya, Ramon Novarro, Peter Brocco, Marya Stevens, Pepe Hern, Robert Contreras, Frank Corsaro, Albert Monte, Natividad Vacio.

General de la Verra may be the official ruler of his Latin American country, but blackmail has made Colonel Sangriento the power behind the throne.

16 April   "The Lethal Ladies" (two dramas, each 27 minutes)

Act I – "Murder on the Rocks"
sc Boris Sobelman
story Joseph Payne Crennan
cast Rosemary Murphy (Lavinia Sills), Howard Morris (Myron Sills), Pamela Curran (Gloria), Marjorie Bennett (Mercedes), Ralph Moody, Ralph Carson, Henry Brandt.

Myron Sills likes the manner in which he is supported by his rich wife – but he does not like her.

Act II – "Goodbye, Dr Bliss"
sc Boris Sobelman
story Joseph Payne Crennan
cast Howard Morris (Dr Wilfred Bliss), Rosemary Murphy (Alice Quimby), Jackie Russell (Martha Foster), Henry Brandt (Mr Sutter), Pamela Curran, Ralph Moody, Marjorie Bennett, Ralph Carson.

Spinster Alice Quimby aspires to be the head of the college library.

General Electric Theater
dramatic anthology/CBS/Stanley Rubin & Norman Felton/Sunday 9-9.30 pm/10th season
11 March   "A Very Special Girl"

cast Barbara Rush (Alice Lockman), Miriam Hopkins (Mrs Cynthia Lockman), Edward Binns (Harry Wilson), Jane Withers (Betty Hamilton), Gary Vinson (Doug Wilson), Quinn O'Hara (Beverly Maxwell).

Successful, attractive society-reporter Alice Lockman would not mind being married. But the available eligible bachelors really do not measure up to Alice's standards – or her mother's either.

Have Gun, Will Travel
western/CBS/Frank Pierson/Saturday 9.30-10 pm/4th season
17 March   "The Gold Bar"

cast Jena Engstrom (Maya), Jeanette Nolan (Alice), Richard Shannon (Morgan), Perry Cook (Briggs), Mary Gregory (Mrs Briggs), William Stevens (the Reverend Bigley).

Paladin is approached by a girl named Maya who wants him to locate her mother. Maya, who has been attending school in the East, says she became alarmed when her tuition was cut off – just after her mother's letters suddenly changed in tone.

1962-63

Sam Benedict
law drama/NBC/William Froug/Saturday 7.30-8.30 pm/only season
1 December   "Everybody's Playing Polo"

regular cast Edmond O'Brien (Sam Benedict), Richard Rust (Hank Tabor), Joan Tompkins (Trudy Wagner).
guest cast Burgess Meredith (Cyrus Carter), Joby Baker (Nick), Milton Selzer (Dr Michaels), Yvonne Craig (Angela Larkin), Irene Dailey (Amelia Carter).

Sam has his hands full representing eccentric millionaire Cyrus Carter, who enjoys making speeches from park benches while draped in a toga.

Available for viewing at Library of Congress.

2 February   "Sugar and Spice and Everything"

guest cast Arthur O'Connell (Noah Jackson), Yvonne Craig (Amy Vickers), Robert Emhardt (judge), Gail Kobe (Beth Kendall), Paul Birch (Captain Boyd), William Schallert.

When Sam is called in to handle the defence of dancer Amy Vickers, charged with murder, he is busy with another trial – so he sends Hank to fill in for him.

Available for viewing at Library of Congress.

The Untouchables
crime drama/ABC/Leonard Freeman/Tuesday 9.30-10.30 pm/4th season
4 December   "A Fist of Five"

prod Alvin Cooperman
sc Herman Groves
regular cast Robert Stack (Eliot Ness), Jerry Paris (Agent Martin Flaherty), Abel Fernandez (Agent William Youngfellow), Nick Georgiade (Agent Enrico Rossi), Anthony George (Agent Cam Allison), Paul Picerni (Agent Lee Hobson), Steve London (Agent Rossman), Bruce Gordon (Frank Nitti).
guest cast Lee Marvin (Mike Brannon), James Caan (Keir Brannon),

Roy Thinnes (Denny Brannon), Mark Allen (Clarence Brannon), Whitney Armstrong (Sean Brannon), Mary Adams (Kate Brannon), Frank de Kova (Tony Lamberto), Phyllis Coates (Angela Carney Lamberto), Marianna Hill (Laurie Reagan), Tom Brown (Captain Bellows).

ass prod Del Reisman
phot Charles Straumer
art dir Rolland M Brooks and Howard Hollander
mus Wilbur Hatch
ed Ben H Ray
ass dir Ted Schilz
set dec Harry Gordon
sd eng S G Haughton
prod sup James A Paisley
prod man Marvin Stuart
ed sup Bill Heath
sd ed Ross Taylor

mus ed Robert Raff
mus coord Julian Davidson
research Kellem de Forest
property master Allan Levine
costumes Frank Delmar
casting Stalmaster-Lister Company
makeup Kiva Hoffman
hair Jean Udko
phot effects Howard Anderson Company
sd Glen Glenn Sound Company

"Police officer Mike Brannon has spent his entire career on the up and up, trying to put elusive racketeers behind bars. Yet all he gets for his efforts is dismissal from the force by a captain on the syndicate's payroll. Thinking that crime just might pay after all, Brannon convinces his brothers to forge an illegal get-rich-quick scheme. Things are looking up for the five Brannon brothers – that is, until the mob starts playing hardball. Mike Brannon begins to make rookie mistakes, such as kidnapping a kingpin. As the mob rushes to retaliate, Eliot Ness heads to the scene of one of the bloodiest shootouts in Chicago history."[5]

Available on video from:
Columbia House Video Library
1400 N Fruitridge Avenue
Terre Haute, IN 47811

Available for viewing at UCLA Film and Television Archive and Library of Congress.

5 March   "The Man in the Cooler"

prod Alvin Cooperman
sc John D F Black
guest cast J D Cannon (Al Remp), Peter Whitney (Fat Augie), Salome Jens (Marcy Remp), Eddie Firestone (Bitsy Whyller), Steve Gravers

(Harry Tazik), I Stanford Jolley (Pete Laffey), Paul Marin (Sam Deroy), Johnny Pop (watchman).

assoc prod Del Reisman
phot Charles Straumer
art dir Rolland M Brooks and Frank T Smith
mus Wilbur Hatch
ed Alex Hubert
ass dir Russ Haverik
set dec Harry Gordon
sd eng S G Haughton
prod sup James A Paisley
prod man Marvin Stuart
ed sup Bill Heath
sd ed Ross Taylor
mus ed Robert Raff

mus coord Julian Davidson
research Kellem de Forest
property master Allan Levine
costumes Frank Delmar
casting Stalmaster-Lister Company
makeup Kiva Hoffman
hair Jane Chabra
phot effects Howard Anderson Company
sd Glen Glenn Sound Company
sp Goodyear, Anacin, Ban Roll-on, Rolaids

Convicted bootlegger Al Remp is promised a shortened jail sentence by Eliot Ness if he helps put away Fat Augie, one of Chicago's main bootleggers and Remp's former boss. After Remp regains employment with Augie, he decides – unknown to his wife, Marcy, and Ness – that it is more profitable to work in the bootlegging business than to act as a stool pigeon. Caught between the crossfire of the federal agents and Augie's hit men, Remp is killed and Ness is able to destroy Augie's illegitimate bootlegging trade.

Available for viewing at UCLA Film and Television Archive and Library of Congress.

7 May   "The Torpedo"

prod Alan Armer
sc Ed Adamson
guest cast Charles McGraw (Holly Kester), John Anderson (Vic Kurtz), John Milford (Burt Engle), James Griffith (Monk Lyselle), George Keymas (Carl Danzig), Jason Wingreen (Frank), David Manley (Charlie), Anthony Barr (Phil), Gail Kobe (Rita).

assoc prod Del Reisman
phot Charles Straumer
art dir Rolland M Brooks and Howard Hollander
mus Wilbur Hatch
ed Ben H Ray

ass dir Bud Grace
set dec Harry Gordon
sd eng Joseph G Sorokin
prod sup James A Paisley
prod man Marvin Stuart
ed sup Bill Heath

sd ed Ross Taylor
mus ed Robert Raff
mus coord Julian Davidson
research Kellem de Forest
property master Don D Smith
costumes Frank Delmar
casting Stalmaster-Lister
Company

makeup Louis J Haszillo
hair Jane Chabra
phot effects Howard Anderson
Company
sd Glen Glenn Sound Company
sp Scotch tape, Gillette razors,
Anacin

Despite a pact between bootleggers Vic Kurtz and Monk Lyselle, which has put a rest to the in-fighting between Chicago mobsters, trucks carrying bootlegged alcohol begin to be hit again. Although Eliot Ness and his Untouchables are responsible, Kurtz thinks that Lyselle is behind this interference and begins to wage war on Lyselle's illegitimate trade. Kurtz's right-hand man, Holly Kester ("The Torpedo"), has grown old during the peace between the mobsters and no longer has the nerve to defend Kurtz by attacking Lyselle's operation. Caught between Kurtz's demands for a ruthless "enforcer" and Ness who wants to put the bootleggers behind bars, in the end Holly is forced to rat on his boss in order to protect himself and get out of the mob. (MCK)

Available for viewing at UCLA Film and Television Archive and Library of Congress.

1963-64

The Fugitive
adventure/ABC/Quinn Martin/Tuesday 10-11 pm/1st season
19 November   "Fatso"

sc Robert Pirosh
regular cast David Janssen (Dr Richard Kimble), Barry Morse (Lt. Philip Gerard), Jacqueline Scott (Donna Taft), Bill Raisch (Fred Johnson, the One-Armed Man).
guest cast Jack Weston (Davey), Burt Brinckerhoff (Frank), Paul Langton (sheriff), Vaughan Taylor (Crowley), Henry Beckman (Brown), Paul Birch (Cpt Carpenter), Garry Walberg (mechanic).
assoc prod Arthur Weiss
prod man Fred Ahern
phot Fred Mandl
mus Peter Rugulo
prod ass John Conwell

art dir Serge Krizman
ed Walter Hannemann
ass dir Lloyd Allen
2nd ass dir Read Killgore
property master Don Smith

chief electrician James Potevin	*hair* Lynn Burke
2nd cameraman J S August	*ass ed* John Shouse
special photo effects Howard Anderson Company	*sc sup* Duane Toler
	sd Goldwyn Studio
mus sup Ken Wilhoit	*prod mix* John Kean
set dec Sandy Grace	*sd ed* Chuck Overhulser
makeup artist Walter Schenck	*re-recording* Clem Portman
costume supervisor Elmer Ellsworth	*sp* Viceroy cigarettes, Remington shavers

"In a small town jail cell for a traffic violation, Kimble befriends his cellmate Davey Lambert (Jack Weston), a troubled overweight man who is being cheated out of his inheritance and birthright by his mean younger brother. Realizing that Gerard will soon be arriving, Kimble is frantic about finding a way out of jail. With Davey's help, he is not only able to escape, but to hide on Davey's family farm. There, Kimble risks capture to help gentle soul Davey assert his rights and reconcile with his family. In an exciting conclusion, Kimble is able to elude Gerard and continue his search for The One-Armed Man."[6]

Available on video from:
NuVentures Video
PO Box 661880
Los Angeles, CA 90066

Available for viewing at Library of Congress.

3 December "The Glass Tightrope"

sc Robert C Dennis
guest cast Leslie Nielsen (Rowland), Diana Van Der Vlis (Ginny), Edward Binns (Angstrom), Jay Adler (Tibbets).

Kimble is walking a tightrope – if he helps clear an accused murderer, he will endanger his own freedom.

Available for viewing at Library of Congress.

14 January "The Garden House"

sc Sheldon Stark

174

guest cast Robert Webber (Harlan Guthrie), Peggy McCay (Ann Guthrie), Pippa Scott (Carol).

Working on a Long Island estate, Kimble notices that his employer is paying more attention to his wife's sister than to his wife.

Available for viewing at Library of Congress.

Mr Novak
high school drama/NBC/E Jack Neuman/Tuesday 7.30-8.30 pm/1st season
3 December   "Love in the Wrong Season"

sc Richard DePoy
regular cast James Franciscus (John Novak), Dean Jagger (Albert Vane), Jeanne Bal (Jean Pagano), Burgess Meredith (Martin Woodridge), Jim Hendricks (Larry Thor), Marion Ross (Nurse Bromfield).
guest cast Patricia Crowley (Ariel Wilder), Tommy Kirk (Tod Seaton), June Vincent.

Novak, who is dating a teacher, has some competition from one of his students.

Available for viewing at Library of Congress.

24 March   "Day in the Year"

sc Sidney Marshall
guest cast Malachi Throne (Medford), Patricia Hyland (Martha), Richard Eyer (Jeff).

A girl in Novak's home room collapses from an overdose of narcotics.

Available for viewing at Library of Congress.

Breaking Point
medical drama/ABC/George Lefferts/Monday 10-11 pm/only season
23 December   "Heart of Marble, Body of Stone"

sc Steven Gethers

regular cast Paul Richards (Dr McKinley Thompson), Eduard Franz (Dr Edward Raymer).
guest cast Burgess Meredith (Walter Osborne), Gena Rowlands (Shelley Osborne Peters), John Milford (Carl Peters).

An attractive model turns up at the hospital in a sorry state – drunk, injured, and convinced she is about to give birth.

Script available at USC Cinema-Television Library.

Dr Kildare
medical drama/NBC/Norman Felton/Thursday 8.30-9.30 pm/3rd season/no. 19
13 February   "To Walk in Grace"

sc Joy Dexter
regular cast Richard Chamberlain (Dr James Kildare), Raymond Massey (Dr Leonard Gillespie), Eddie Ryder (Dr Simon Agurski), Jud Taylor (Dr Thomas Gerson), Joan Patrick (Susan Deigh), Lee Kurty (nurse Zoe Lawton).
guest cast Gena Rowlands (Helen Scott), Joan Tompkins (Mrs Hutchinson).

Gillespie assigns Kildare to help a novelist do medical research for her next book, unaware that Kildare thinks the woman's writing is dreadful.

Kraft Suspense Theater
mystery/NBC/Frank P Rosenberg/Thursday 10-11 pm/1st season
12 March   "The Threatening Eye"
cast Pat O'Brien (Lieutenant John Curwood), Annie Fargé (Yvette Duval), Jack Klugman (Steve Zaro), Phyllis Thaxter (Mildred), Coleen Gray (Dorothy Nehf).

A beautiful young office worker unaccountably tries to attract the attention of an unlikely candidate for romance: a plain, introverted man who is already married.

The Twilight Zone
mystery-sci-fi/CBS/Rod Serling/Friday 9.30-10 pm/4th season
20 March   "The Masks"

prod Bert Granet
sc Rod Serling
cast Robert Keith (Jason Foster), Milton Selzer (Wilfred Harper), Alan Sues (Wilfred Harper Jr), Virginia Gregg (Emily Harper), Brooke Hayward (Paula Harper), Willis Bouchey (Dr Samuel Thorne).
phot George T Clemens
prod man Ralph W Nelson

art dir George W Davis and Walter Holscher
ed Richard Heermance
set dec Henry Grace and Robert R Benton
casting Patricia Rose
makeup William Tuttle
ass dir Charles Bonniwell Jr
sd Franklin Milton and Philip N Mitchell
sp Pall Mall cigarettes

"Knowing he is about to die, [Jason] Foster [Robert Keith] summons his heirs – with whom he shares no affection – to his mansion for a bizarre Mardi Gras ritual. A Cajun has fashioned grotesque masks for him that reflect the true inner natures of his family... Foster demands that they wear the masks until midnight; as for him, *he* will wear a death's-head. They refuse – until he informs them that they'll be disinherited unless they comply. Their greed overcomes their disgust; they all don the masks. As the hours slowly tick by, Foster's kin beg to be allowed to discard the masks, but Foster is steadfast in his determination. As midnight tolls, Foster dies. Overjoyed to be rid of him and to have gained his wealth, his family throw off their disguises – and are horrified to see that their faces have taken on the hideous physical characteristics of the masks."[7]

Available on video from:
CBS Video Library
51 West 52nd Street
New York, NY 10019

1964-65

Gilligan's Island
sitcom/CBS/Sherwood Schwartz/Saturday 8.30-9 pm/1st season/no. 18
17 October   "Goodnight, Sweet Skipper"

sc Dick Conway and Roland MacLane
regular cast Bob Denver (Gilligan), Alan Hale Jr (The Skipper), Jim Backus (Thurston Howell III), Natalie Schafer (Mrs "Lovey" Howell III), Tina Louise (Ginger Grant), Dawn Wells (Mary Ann Summers), Russell Johnson (the Professor).

"A round-the-world lady flyer is passing over 'Gilligan's Island.' The Skipper once turned a radio into a transmitter when he was in the Navy, but he's forgotten how. The Professor hypnotizes the Skipper in the hope he'll recall the procedure. The rest of the Castaways pretend they are shipmates of the Skipper in order to recreate the original background. The Skipper manages to make the transmitter and the Castaways are sure they're going to contact the flyer and are all ready to be rescued. At the last moment, however, Gilligan smashes the transmitter."[8]

Available for viewing at Library of Congress.

24 October   "Wrong Way Feldman"

sc Fred Freeman and Lawrence J Cohen
guest star Hans Conreid (Wrongway Feldman).

"The Castaways discover an ancient plane on the other side of the island. Then they discover the pilot, Wrongway Feldman. Wrongway still has fuel, but he can't fly the plane to get help because he's lost his nerve. He teaches Gilligan how to fly the plane, but then he realizes he'd be endangering Gilligan's life, and he himself flies back to civilization. Unfortunately, Wrongway's calculations about the island are so wrong the authorities have no idea where the Castaways are."[9]

Available on video from:
Columbia House Video Library
1400 N Fruitridge Avenue
Terre Haute, IN 47811

Available for viewing at Library of Congress.

The Rogues
comedy-drama/NBC/Collier Young/Sunday 10-11 pm/only season
20 December "Hugger-Mugger by the Sea"

sc Stephen Lord
story Stephen Lord and Stephen Kandel
regular cast Gig Young (Tony Fleming), David Niven (Alec Fleming), Charles Boyer (Marcel St Clair), Robert Coote (Timmy St Clair), Gladys Cooper (Margaret St Clair), John Williams (Inspector Briscoe).

guest cast Ricardo Montalban (Marius Koenig), Kamala Devi (Giana Lupescu), Marie Windsor (Gloria Treat), Raquel Welch (Miss France).

Marius Koenig's murderous hatred for a rival shipping magnate is a weakness Tony hopes to cash in on – to the tune of $200 000.

7 February   "Bow to a Master"

sc William Bast and Stephen Kandel
guest cast Zachary Scott (Le Chat), Laura Devon (Barbara Cayasta), Christopher Dark (Ali), James Griffith.

It is beginning to look as if there is no honour left among thieves: Le Chat, a cultured con man, and his attractive assistant Barbara have made off with a diamond necklace the Rogues lifted from a swindling jeweller.

Bewitched
sitcom/ABC/Harry Ackerman/Thursday 9-9.30 pm/1st season/no. 2
14 January   "'A' is for Aardvark"

regular cast Elizabeth Montgomery (Samantha Stephens), Dick York (Darrin Stephens), Agnes Moorehead (Endora).

Samantha tires of catering to her bedridden spouse, and so decides to make things easy by endowing him with magical powers.

Available for viewing at Library of Congress.

Mr Novak
high school drama/NBC/E Jack Neuman/Tuesday 7.30-8.30 pm/2nd season
2 March   "May Day, May Day..."

sc John D F Black
guest cast Irene Tredow (Mrs Ring), Marjorie Corley (Miss Dorsey), Vince Howard (Butler), Marian Collier (Miss Scott), André Philippe (Johns).

It is teacher evaluation time at Jefferson High, but English instructor Bud Walker is not worried; he is convinced that he will be fired.

Available for viewing at Library of Congress.

1965-66

Bob Hope Presents the Chrysler Theater
dramatic anthology/NBC/Stephen Cannell/Wednesday 9-10 pm/3rd
season/this pilot episode was broadcast as part of the Chrysler
Theater
11 May   "Holloway's Daughters"

cast Robert Young (Nick Holloway), David Wayne (George
Holloway), Marion Moses (Martha Holloway), Brooke Bundy
(Fleming Holloway), Barbara Hershey (Casey Holloway), Ellen Corby
(Miss Purdy), Meg Wyllie (Mrs Ransworth), Bruce Gordon (Hartford).

"When he retires, Nick Holloway, private investigator and owner of the
Holloway Detective Agency, turns over the business to his son, George.
George, who dislikes the way his father ran the company (by instinct),
changes it to a by-the-books operation. The change not only angers
Nick, who decides to remain active and run the company as he feels it
should, but his two beautiful granddaughters, Fleming and Casey,
amateur sleuths who side with their grandfather. The would-be (but
unsold) series was to focus on the investigations of Nick and his
granddaughters as they strive to solve crimes. The pilot episode relates
the Holloways' efforts to solve a jewel theft."[10]

1966-67

The Virginian
western/NBC/Richard Irving and Norman MacDonnell/Wednesday
7.30-9 pm/5th season/no. 10
9 November   "Deadeye Dick"

prod Frank Price
regular cast Lee J Cobb (Judge Henry Garth), James Drury (The
Virginian), Doug McClure (Trampas).
guest cast Alice Rawlings (Marjorie Hammond) David Macklin (Bob
Foley), William Schallert (Harry Foley), June Vincent (Lucille
Hammond), Patricia Donahue (Livvy Underhill).

Young Easterner Marjorie Hammond is not paying much attention to the dude who's wooing her. The pretty 16-year-old, whose image of the West comes from a romantic dime novel, is set on lassoing the Virginian, her dream hero come to life.

1967-68

Daniel Boone
western/NBC/Aaron Rosenberg/Thursday 7.30-8.30 pm/4th season
19 October   "The King's Shilling"

regular cast Fess Parker (Daniel Boone), Ed Ames (Mingo), Patricia Blair (Rebecca Boone), Darby Hinton (Israel Boone), Dal McKennon (Cincinnatus).
guest cast Mort Mills (Andrew Hubbard), Jeff Pomerantz (Davey Hubbard), Robie Porter (Tom Chapin), Barbara Hershey (Dinah Hubbard), Peter Bromilow (Colonel Holland), John Orchard (British sergeant).

As unrest boils in the Colonies, Daniel moves to prevent two executions that could trigger open warfare. The prisoners are revolutionary zealot Davey Hubbard, who is a captive of the British, and Redcoat Tom Chapin, held as a hostage by Davey's father.

Available for viewing at Library of Congress.

Dundee and the Culhane
western/CBS/Sam H Rolfe/Wednesday 10-11 pm/only season
22 November "Thy Brother's Keeper Brief"

regular cast John Mills (Dundee), Sean Garrison (Culhane).
guest cast William Windom (Robert Campbell), Mitch Vogel (Jeffrey Bennett), Dallas McKennon (Al), Dave Perna (Garth), Billy Beck (Dick), Harry Holcombe (judge), Ben Dobbins (Simpson), Buff Brady (Pinky), Patrick O'Moore (clerk).

The death of a gold miner leads to acute discomfort for Dundee who is been named legal guardian of the miner's young son. When the boy is kidnapped, the erudite attorney is forced into the unfamiliar role of gun-toting cowboy.

Available for viewing at Library of Congress.

1968-69

The Ghost and Mrs Muir
sitcom/NBC/David Gerber/Saturday 8.30-9 pm/1st season
14 December   "Madeira, My Dear?"

sc Nate Monaster
regular cast Hope Lange (Mrs Carolyn Muir), Edward Mulhare
(Captain Daniel Gregg), Reta Shaw (Martha Grant), Kellie Flanagan
(Candy Muir), Harlan Carraher (Jonathan Muir), Charles Nelson Reilly
(Claymore Gregg).
guest cast Kathleen Hughes (Mrs Coburn), James McCallion (Abner),
Linda Sue Risk (Linda).

The Captain tries to get Mrs Muir to become romantically interested in
him.

Addendum

Although the details of Lupino's contribution as director for these series
could not be verified via available archival material on television
programming, we nevertheless believe that the sources reporting this
information are valid.

1958-64   *77 Sunset Strip*
detective drama/ABC/William T Orr/ABC/Friday evenings
unknown episode(s)
[cited in Terrace, Lupino, and *TV Guide*, and by the Museum of
Television and Radio]

1959-61   *Manhunt*
police drama/Screen Gems/78 syndicated episodes
unknown episode(s)
[cited in Weiner]

1960   *Tate*
western/NBC/Alvin Cooperman/Wednesday 9.30-10 pm/summer
replacement for second half of *The Perry Como Show*

unknown episode(s)
[cited in Lupino, *TV Guide*, and by the Museum of Television and Radio]

1961   *The Dick Powell Show*
dramatic anthology/NBC/Dick Powell/Tuesday 9-10 pm
unknown episode(s)
[cited in Heck-Rabi]

1961   *Zane Grey Theater*
western anthology/CBS-Dick Powell/Thursday 8.30-9 pm/5th season
unknown episode(s)
[cited by the Museum of Television and Radio]

1965-66   *Honey West*
sitcom/ABC/Friday 9-9.30 pm
unknown episode(s)
[cited in Nolan, 1968]

1965-67   *Please Don't Eat the Daisies*
sitcom/NBC/Paul West/Saturday 8-8.30 pm
unknown episode(s)
[cited in Terrace]

1966   *The Big Valley*
western/ABC/Lou Morheim/Wednesday 9-10 pm
unknown episode(s)
[cited in Terrace, Heck-Rabi, and by the Museum of Television and Radio]

1969   *The Bill Cosby Show*
sitcom/NBC/William H Cosby Jr/Sunday 8.30-9 pm
unknown episode(s)
[cited in Vermilye, and by the Museum of Television and Radio]

Notes

[1] Vincent Terrace, *Encyclopedia of Television Series, Pilots, and Specials: The Index: Who's Who in Television, 1937-1984* (New York: New York Zoetrope, 1986): 425.

[2] Joel Eisner and David Krinsky, *Television Comedy Series: An Episode Guide to 153 TV Sitcoms in Syndication* (Jefferson, NC: McFarland and Company, 1984): 224.

[3] John McCarty and Brian Kelleher, *Alfred Hitchcock Presents: An Illustrated Guide to the Ten-Year Television Career of the Master of Suspense* (New York: St Martin's Press, 1985): 196-197.

[4] Ibid: 200.

[5] Columbia House Video Library (videocassette jacket summary).

[6] NuVentures Video (videocassette jacket summary).

[7] Marc Scott Zicree, *The Twilight Zone Companion*, second edition (Los Angeles: Silman-James Press, 1989): 377.

[8] Sherwood Schwartz, *Inside Gilligan's Island: From Creation to Syndication* (London: McFarland, 1988): 274-275.

[9] Ibid: 275.

[10] Terrace: 204.

Sources

Anon. "Director Ida Lupino Creates a New Lingo", *TV Guide* 24 January 1959: 28-29.

———. "Mother Lupino". *Time* 8 February 1963: 46.

———. "They Work Both Sides of the Camera", *TV Guide* 14 July 1962: 18-20.

Bart, Peter. "Lupino, the Dynamo", *The New York Times* 7 March 1965: Sec. 2: 7.

Brooks, Tim and Earl Marsh. *The Complete Directory to Prime Time Network TV Shows, 1946–Present*, fourth edition (New York: Ballantine, 1992).

Brown, Les. *Encyclopedia of Television*, third edition (Detroit: Gale Research, 1992).

Eisner, Joel and David Krinsky. *Television Comedy Series: An Episode Guide to 153 TV Sitcoms in Syndication* (Jefferson, NC: McFarland and Company, 1984).

Gehman, Richard and Michael McFadden. "The Golden Sex: They Use Beauty, Brains to Produce TV", *Los Angeles Herald-Examiner* 14 May 1963: B1, B8.

Gianakos, Larry James. *Television Drama Series Programming: A Comprehensive Chronicle* (Metuchen, NJ: Scarecrow Press, 1978).

Heck-Rabi, Louise. "Ida Lupino: Daring the Family Tradition" in *Women Filmmakers: a Critical Reception* (Metuchen, NJ: Scarecrow Press, 1984): 223-251.

Humphrey, Hal. "Ida Does It All in World of Films", *The Los Angeles Times* 19 May 1966: Sec. 5: 20.

——————. "In the Directing Business Ida Classes Herself a [sic] a 'Stander'", *Mirror News* 6 December 1960: n.p.

Inman, David. *The TV Encyclopedia* (New York: Perigee Books, 1991).

Lentz, Harris M., III. *Science Fiction, Horror and Fantasy Film and Television Credits*. 3 volumes (London: McFarland and Co, 1983-1989).

Lupino, Ida. "Me, Mother Directress", *Action* 2: 3 (1967): 14-15.

McCarty, John and Brian Kelleher. *Alfred Hitchcock Presents: An Illustrated Guide to the Ten-Year Television Career of the Master of Suspense* (New York: St Martin's Press, 1985).

McNeil, Alex. *Total Television: A Comprehensive Guide to Programming from 1948 to the Present* (New York: Penguin Books, 1991).

Montgomery, Sarah. *Women and Television Bibliography* (London: BFI Education, 1984).

Nolan, Jack Edmund. "Ida Lupino", *Films in Review* 16: 1 (1965): 61-62.

——————. "Ida Lupino: Director", *Film Fan Monthly* 89 (1968): 8-11, 23.

Perry, Jeb H. *Screen Gems: A History of Columbia Pictures Television from Cohn to Coke, 1948-1983* (Metuchen, NJ: Scarecrow Press, 1991).

——————. *Universal Television: The Studio and Its Programs, 1950-1980* (Metuchen, NJ: Scarecrow Press, 1983).

Pilato, Herbie J. *The* Bewitched *Book: The Cosmic Companion to TV's Most Magical Supernatural Situation Comedy* (New York: Delta, 1992).

Rouse, Sarah and Katharine Loughney. *Three Decades of Television: A Catalog of Television Programming Acquired by the Library of Congress 1949-1979* (Washington, DC: Library of Congress, 1989).

Royce, Brenda Scott. *Donna Reed: A Bio-Bibliography* (New York: Greenwood Press, 1990).

Schwartz, Sherwood. *Inside* Gilligan's Island: *From Creation to Syndication* (London: McFarland, 1988).

Terrace, Vincent. *Encyclopedia of Television Series, Pilots, and Specials: The Index: Who's Who in Television, 1937-1984* (New York: New York Zoetrope, 1986).

Vermilye, Jerry. "Television: The Director's Chair", *Ida Lupino: A Pyramid Illustrated History of the Movies* (New York: Pyramid Publications, 1977): 121-140.

Weiner, Debra. "Interview with Ida Lupino", in Karyn Kay and Gerald Peary (eds), *Women and the Cinema: A Critical Anthology* (New York: E P Dutton, 1977): 169-178.

Whitney, Dwight. "'Follow Mother, Here We Go, Kiddies!'", *TV Guide* 8 October 1966: 14-18.

Wood, C. "TV Personalities Biographical Sketchbook", *TV Personalities* (1957): 16.

Zicree, Marc Scott. *The Twilight Zone Companion*, second edition (Los Angeles: Silman-James Press, 1989).

Archives and other research resources

Academy of Motion Picture Arts
and Sciences (AMPAS)
The Margaret Herrick Library
333 South La Cienaga Boulevard
Beverly Hills, CA 90211, USA
tel   +1 310 247 3020

Academy of Television Arts and
Sciences (ATAS)
The Landmark Building
5200 Lankershim Blvd., Suite 340
North Hollywood, CA 91606, USA
tel   +1 310 247 3000
fax +1 310 859 9619

British Film Institute (BFI)
Library and Information Service
21 Stephen Street
London W1P 1PL, England
tel   +44 171 255 1444
fax +44 171 436 0165

Eddie Brandt's Saturday Matinee
6310 Colfax Avenue
North Hollywood, CA 91606, USA
tel   +1 818 506 4242/7722

Library of Congress
Motion Picture, Broadcasting and
Recorded Sound Division
Motion Picture and Television
Reading Room
Madison Building 336
Washington, DC 20540-4800, USA
tel   +1 202 707 8572
fax +1 202 707 2371

Museum of Modern Art (MOMA)
Film Study Center
11 West 53rd Street

New York
NY 10019-5486, USA
tel   +1 212 708 9400
fax +1 212 708 9889

Museum of Television and Radio
25 West 52nd Street
New York, NY 10019, USA
tel   +1 212 621 6600
fax +1 212 621 6700

National Film & Television Archive
(NFTVA)
21 Stephen Street
London W1P 1PL, England
tel   +44 171 255 1444
fax +44 171 580 7503

UCLA Film & Television Archive
160 Powell Library
405 Higard Avenue
Los Angeles, CA 90024-1517, USA
tel   +1 310 206 5388
fax +1 310 206 5392

University of Southern California,
Cinema-Television Library
Doheny Library – Second Floor
University Park
Los Angeles, CA 90089, USA
tel   +1 213 740 3994
fax +1 213 747 3301

Wisconsin Center for Film and
Theater Research
6040 Vilas Communication Hall
University of Wisconsin-Madison
Madison, WI 53706, USA
tel   +1 608 262 9706

Ida Lupino: bibliography

Annette Kuhn

This listing excludes reviews of individual films and television programmes, and brief biofilmographies in reference books and elsewhere.

Acker, Ally. *Reel Women: Pioneers of the Cinema, 1896 to the Present.* New York: Continuum, 1991: 74-78.
- Extended biofilmography.

Anon. "A Fourth for TV: Ida Lupino Joins Trio of Stars in Film Series", *TV Guide* 3 December 1955: 16-17.

———. "A New Twist", *TV Guide* 13 July 1957: 28-29.

———. "As Film Star, Director, Composer, Ida Lupino Excels in Entertainment", *Boxoffice* 29 September 1975: SE14, SE16.

———. "Catching Up With Ida Lupino", *Modern Screen* 66: 11 (November 1972): 68.

———. "Director Ida Lupino Creates a New Lingo", *TV Guide* 24 January 1959: 28-29.

———. "Ida Lupino", *Film Dope* 37 (June 1987): 5-8.
- Biofilmography, including listing of films and television programmes acted in and directed and films produced, with an extract from Sue Cameron's *The Hollywood Reporter*® interview.

———. "Ida Lupino and the Lion", *TV Guide* 11 January 1958: 12-13.

———. "Mother Lupino", *Time* 8 February 1963: 46.
- Lupino directs an episode of *The Untouchables*, ruling "more by sex appeal than by fiat".

———. "Rencontre avec Ida Lupino", *Cahiers du Cinéma* 178 (May 1966): 10-11.

- Interview following release of *The Trouble With Angels*.

—————. "They Work Both Sides of the Camera", *TV Guide* 14 July 1962: 18-20.

Bart, Peter. "Lupino, the Dynamo", *The New York Times* 7 March 1965: Sec. 2: 7.

Braucourt, Guy. "*Avant de t'aimer*; *Faire face*: l'apprentissage de la vie", *Cinéma 70* 151 (1970): 138-140.
- Review article on *Not Wanted* and *Never Fear*.

Cameron, Sue. "Coast to Coast", *The Hollywood Reporter®* 223: 45 (16 November 1972): 10.
- Report of an interview with Lupino in which she describes the pressures on a woman director.

Colton, Helen. "Ida Lupino, Filmland's Lady of Distinction", *The New York Times* 30 April 1950: X5.
- On Lupino's forays into independent production, and her "independence of mind".

Dozoretz, Wendy. "The Mother's Lost Voice in *Hard, Fast and Beautiful*", *Wide Angle* 6: 3 (1984): 50-57.
- Psychoanalytic reading of *Hard, Fast and Beautiful*, emphasizing the mother-daughter relationship.

Ellis, Robert. "Ida Lupino Brings New Hope to Hollywood", *Negro Digest* August 1950: 47-49.
- Lupino plans to "integrate Negro actors in all our productions".

Eyquem, Olivier. "Biofilmographie d'Ida Lupino", *Cahiers de la Cinémathèque* 28 (1979): 121-130.
- Filmography includes films in which Lupino acted, as well as those she directed.

—————————. "Une femme en transit: les débuts d'Ida Lupino à la Warner", *Positif* 301 (March 1986): 23-25.
- Overview of Lupino's early acting career.

Fuller, Graham. "Ida Lupino", *Interview* 20: 10 (October 1990): 118-121.
- Very brief interview, lavishly illustrated.

Galligan, David. "Ida Lupino", *Interview* 6: 2 (February 1976): 10-12.

- Brief interview, emphasizing Lupino's acting career.

Gehman, Richard and Michael McFadden. "The Golden Sex: They Use Beauty, Brains to Produce TV", *Los Angeles Herald-Examiner* 14 May 1963: B1, B8.

Heck-Rabi, Louise. "Ida Lupino: Daring the Family Tradition", in *Women Filmmakers: a Critical Reception*. Metuchen, NJ: Scarecrow Press, 1984: 223-251.
- Essay, with listing of films and television programmes directed by Lupino.

Hill, Gladwin. "Hollywood's Beautiful Bulldozer", *Collier's* 12 May 1951: 18-19, 76-78.
- "She acts, writes, directs, produces—no film job is too big for Ida Lupino".

Hinxman, Margaret. "She's Demure, But She's Dynamite", *Picturegoer* 27 December 1952: 8-9.
- Lupino, interviewed during a visit to UK, is compared with Stanley Kramer ("master-minding, 'message' pushing").

Humphrey, Hal. "Ida Does It All in World of Films", *The Los Angeles Times* 19 May 1966: Sec. 5: 20.

——————. "In the Directing Business Ida Classes Herself a [sic] a 'Stander'", *Mirror News* 6 December 1960: n.p.

Interim, Louella. "Ida Lupino derrière la caméra: une femme dangereuse", *Cahiers du Cinéma* 347 (May 1983): vi-vii.
- Reappraisal of Lupino's work in light of a screening of six of her films at the Sceaux Film Festival.

Johnson, B. "Mr Duff and Ida", *TV Guide* 1 June 1957: 17-19.

Keats, P. "Ida Takes Over in No-Woman's Land", *Silver Screen* June 1950: 36.

Kelly, Bill. "Ida Lupino: gem of the Emerald Isle", *Hollywood Studio Magazine* 16: 3 (February 1983): 26-27.
- Incoherently reported interview.

Koszarski, Richard (ed). *Hollywood Directors 1941-1976*. New York: Oxford University Press, 1977: 371-377.

- Reprint of "Me, Mother Directress", with brief introduction.

Kowalski, Rosemary. "Imitator: Ida Lupino", in *A Vision of One's Own: Four Women Film Directors*. PhD dissertation. Ann Arbor: University of Michigan-Ann Arbor, 1980: 52-136.

Legrand, Gérard. "La corde sensible", *Positif* 125 (March 1971): 74-77.
- On *Not Wanted* and *Never Fear*.

Lockhart, Freda Bruce. "Girl of Two Worlds", *Film Weekly* 15 May 1937: 13, 26.
- Lupino's adoption of Hollywood, and her "ingrained" acting skills.

Lupino, Ida. "I Cannot Be Good", *Silver Screen* June 1949: 42.

——————. "Me, Mother Directress", *Action* 2: 3 (1967): 14-15.
- Lupino talks about directing. (Reprinted in Koszarski, *Hollywood Directors 1941-1976*, and translated in *Positif*.)

——————. "Moi, la mère metteur en scène", *Positif* 301 (March 1986): 14-16.
- Translation of "Me, Mother Directress".

——————. "My Fight For Life", *Photoplay* February 1946: 58.

——————. "My Secret Dream", *Photoplay* October 1943: 54.

——————. "New Faces in New Places: They Are Needed Behind the Camera, Too", *Films in Review* 1: 9 (1950): 17-19.
- Lupino writes about finding new production and acting talent for her film company.

——————. "The Trouble with Men is Women", *Silver Screen* April 1947: 36.

——————. "Who Says Men Are People?", *Silver Screen* June 1948: 44.

Lupino, Stanley. "Ida's Adventures in Hollywood", *Film Weekly* 5 September 1936: 8-9.
- Account of Lupino's move to Hollywood, written by her father.

——————. "My $120 a Week Daughter", *Film Weekly* 24 November 1933: 7.
- On how Ida was trained for the stage from early childhood.

Minoff, P. "Non-private lives?", *Cue* 26: 3 (19 January 1957): 12.

Mooring, W H. "Hollywood Once-Over", *Picturegoer* 19 July 1941: 9.
- On Lupino's acting career to date, with account of the hiatus after leaving Paramount.

——————————. "Ida Lupino Changes Over", *Picturegoer* 16 July 1949: 9.
- On Lupino's career and recent move from acting to independent production.

Nacache, Jacqueline. "Sur six films d'Ida Lupino", *Cinéma* 298 (October 1983): 6-10.
- Well-informed critical discussion of all Lupino's films, except *The Trouble With Angels*, following screenings at the Sceaux Film Festival.

Nolan, Jack Edmund. "Ida Lupino", *Films in Review* 16: 1 (1965): 61-62.
- Letter, with short listing of television programmes directed by Lupino.

——————————. "Ida Lupino: Director", *Film Fan Monthly* 89 (1968): 8-11, 23.
- Includes listing of credits (film and television directing; acting).

Parker, Francine. "Discovering Ida Lupino", *Action* 8: 4 (1973): 19-23.
- Overview of Lupino's career, emphasizing the Emerald/The Filmakers films.

Parish, James Robert and Don E Stanke. *The Forties Gals*. Westport, CT: Arlington House, 1980: 131-193.
- Account of Lupino's career, with list of films in which she acted.

Rickey, Carrie. "Lupino Noir", *Village Voice* 29 October-4 November 1980: 43-45.
- Overview of Lupino's filmmaking career.

Scheib, Ronnie. "Ida Lupino: Auteuress", *Film Comment* 16: 1 (1980): 54-64.
- Auteurist reading of films directed by Lupino.

Siclier, Jacques. "Le cinéma féminin d'Ida Lupino", *Cahiers de la Cinémathèque* 28 (1979): 119-120.
- As part of a special issue on film melodrama, *Not Wanted*, *Never Fear* and *The Bigamist* are discussed as women's films.

St John, A R. "Story of Ida Lupino", *Cosmopolitan* January 1943: n.p.

Stewart, Lucy. *Ida Lupino as Film Director, 1949-1953: an 'Auteur' Approach*. New York: Arno Press, 1980.
- Reprint of PhD dissertation (University of Michigan-Ann Arbor, 1979), with in-depth studies of *Outrage, Hard, Fast and Beautiful, The Hitch-Hiker* and *The Bigamist*.

Thibaud, Cécile. "Un pathétique en creux: Ida Lupino cinéaste", *Positif* 301 (March 1986): 17-22.
- In-depth reading of the six films Lupino directed between 1949 and 1953.

Varney, Ginger. "Ida Lupino, Director", *LA Weekly* 12-18 November 1982: 10.

Vermilye, Jerry. *Ida Lupino: A Pyramid Illustrated History of the Movies*. New York: Pyramid Publications, 1977.
- Detailed descriptive account of Lupino's career as performer, filmmaker and television director, with listings of films she acted in and directed.

—————————. "Ida Lupino is a Knowledgeable Trouper Who Hasn't Been Fully Appreciated", *Films in Review* 10: 5 (May 1959): 266-283.
- Overview of Lupino's acting and directing career, with filmography.

Weiner, Debra. "Interview with Ida Lupino", in Karyn Kay and Gerald Peary (eds), *Women and the Cinema: A Critical Anthology*. New York: E P Dutton, 1977: 169-178.
- Lupino interviewed from a feminist standpoint.

White, Patricia. "Ida in Wonderland", *Village Voice* 5 February 1991: 64.
- Career overview written to coincide with Lupino retrospective at the Museum of Modern Art, New York.

Whitney, Dwight. "'Follow Mother, Here We Go, Kiddies!'", *TV Guide* 8 October 1966: 14-18.

Wood, C. "TV Personalities Biographical Sketchbook", *TV Personalities* (1957): 16.

Index

Notes on contributors

Pam Cook lectures in film at the University of East Anglia. She has written widely on feminism and cinema, and is co-author and editor of *The Cinema Book*. Her forthcoming study of costume and national identity in British cinema is to be published by the British Film Institute.

Mary Beth Haralovich teaches film and television history at the University of Arizona in Tucson. Recent publications include "Too Much Guilt Is Never Enough for Working Mothers: Joan Crawford, *Mildred Pierce* and *Mommie Dearest*", in *The Velvet Light Trap*, and "Black and White in Living Color: *I Spy* at the Confluence of Civil Rights and the Cold War", in a forthcoming anthology edited by Lynn Spigel and Michael Curtin.

Janet R Jakobsen teaches women's studies and religious studies at the University of Arizona in Tucson. Her recent publications include "Agency and Alliance in US Public Discourses about Sexuality", in *Hypatia: a Journal of Feminist Philosophy*, and "Beyond the Legal Limit: US Women's Movements for Reproductive Rights and Freedoms", in *Journal of Feminist Studies in Religion*.

Mary Celeste Kearney is a doctoral candidate in the Film, Literature and Culture programme within the Division of Critical Studies at the University of Southern California School of Cinema-Television. She is currently working on feminist theory, teenage girl culture, music television and popular music.

Annette Kuhn teaches film and television studies at the University of Glasgow, and has written widely on cultural theory, feminism and cinema, and film history. Her publications include *The Power of the Image: Essays on Representation and Sexuality* and *Cinema, Censorship and Sexuality, 1909 to 1925* and, as editor, *The Women's Companion to International Film*.

Mandy Merck teaches media studies at the University of Sussex. She is the author of *Perversions: Deviant Readings*, was editor of *Screen* and of the C4 television series, *Out On Tuesday*, and script advisor on the 1994 BBC documentary, *Martina: Farewell to a Champion*.

James M Moran is a doctoral candidate in the Division of Critical Studies at the University of Southern California School of Cinema-Television. He has published on independent videographers, wedding video and Universal Studios theme park.

Lauren Rabinovitz is professor of American studies and of film studies at the University of Iowa. She is the author of *Points of Resistance: Women, Power & Politics in the New York Avant-garde Cinema, 1943-71*, and co-editor of *Seeing Through the Media: the Persian Gulf War*.

Ronnie Scheib is a writer and critic based in New York, and is currently writing for cartoon characters.

Ellen Seiter is professor of telecommunications and of film studies at Indiana University. She is the author of *Sold Separately: Children and Parents in Consumer Culture*, as well as of articles on feminist criticism for *Screen*, *Cultural Studies* and *Journal of Film and Video*.

Diane Waldman teaches media studies and women's studies courses and is director of the Cultural and Critical Studies programme at the University of Denver. She has published essays on feminist film theory and criticism, and on film and social history in journals such as *Wide Angle*, *Cinema Journal* and *Camera Obscura*.

Susan White teaches film and comparative literature at the University of Arizona in Tucson. She is the author of *The Cinema of Max Ophuls: Magisterial Vision and the Figure of Woman*.

ISBN 0-313-29732-0

90000>

EAN

9 780313 297328

HARDCOVER BAR CODE

2817